The Real Frankenstein

The Real Frankenstein

How Tragedy and Science Shaped Mary Shelley's Classic Novel

Laura Silverman

WHITE OWL
AN IMPRINT OF PEN & SWORD BOOKS LTD.
YORKSHIRE – PHILADELPHIA

First published in Great Britain in 2026 by
White Owl
An imprint of Pen & Sword Books Limited
Yorkshire – Philadelphia

ISBN 978 1 03612 663 6

A CIP catalogue record for this book is available from the British Library.

Typeset by Mac Style
Printed in the UK by CPI Group (UK) Ltd, Croydon, CR0 4YY.

MIX
Paper | Supporting responsible forestry
FSC® C013604

The Publisher's authorised representative in the EU for product safety is Authorised Rep Compliance Ltd., Ground Floor, 71 Lower Baggot Street, Dublin D02 P593, Ireland.
www.arccompliance.com

For a complete list of Pen & Sword titles please contact

PEN & SWORD BOOKS LIMITED
47 Church Street, Barnsley, South Yorkshire, S70 2AS, England
E-mail: enquiries@pen-and-sword.co.uk
Website: www.pen-and-sword.co.uk
or
PEN AND SWORD BOOKS
1950 Lawrence Road, Havertown, PA 19083, USA
E-mail: uspen-and-sword@casematepublishers.com
Website: www.penandswordbooks.com

Contents

Preface

'Lo and behold! I found myself famous'
Mary Shelley, after watching *Presumption! Or the Fate of Frankenstein* in 1823

A note on names

Writers who marry each other face a problem: who keeps the surname when they both appear in a book? To distinguish between the Shelleys and help us get to know them a little better, this book uses their first names. We can hope they wouldn't mind the assumed familiarity.

Frankenstein should never have made Mary Shelley famous. Like most debuts of the day, it had come out anonymously. But when this slim novel hit the shelves in 1818, it caused such a stir that people couldn't stop talking about it. They took bets on the identity of the writer. Who would propose that a scientist could create life – and a monster at that? Who would have the gall? Who would have the gumption? Even the publishers were in the dark. When Percy Bysshe Shelley, then a minor poet, offered *Frankenstein* to Lackington and Co, a run-of-the-mill publishing house, he said that it had been written by 'a friend'. The novelist Sir Walter Scott wasn't so sure. 'It is said to be written by Mr Percy Bysshe Shelley,' he wrote in his review in *Blackwood's Edinburgh Magazine.* Scott noted that the book had been dedicated to William Godwin, a big Enlightenment philosopher and Percy's father-in-law. The reviewer in *The Scots Magazine* said *Frankenstein* was shaped in the 'Godwinian manner'. We can see today how both authors explore the constraints of society, the dangers of ambition and the collapse of family life. Like *Frankenstein*, Godwin's greatest novel, *Things as They Are; or, The Adventures of Caleb Williams* (1794), also followed two characters in hot pursuit of each other.

But while *Caleb Williams* was a hit, reviews of *Frankenstein* were mixed. 'Many parts of it are strikingly good, and the description of the scenery is excellent,' said the critic in *The Gentleman's Magazine*. The reviewer who had noticed the Godwinian influence was less impressed. The story was a 'caricature'. It bordered on 'impiety'. The piece in *The British Critic: A New Review* was even more damning. 'These volumes have neither principle, object, nor moral,' scorned the writer; 'the horror which abounds in them is too grotesque and bizarre ever to approach near the sublime.' There were three murders and a couple more deaths. The author had a 'diseased and wandering imagination'. Worse, they believed, they were a woman. She had opposed 'the gentleness of her sex'. The only way to get through the book was to 'hurry over the pages in disgust'. What an assignment. 'We shall… dismiss the novel without further comment,' they concluded, slamming the covers shut. *The British Critic* might have wished that to have been the end of it, but it was not to be. Readers agreed that *Frankenstein* was shocking – and they loved it. The critic was right. The author was a woman. It was Percy's wife, Mary Shelley.

The first edition of *Frankenstein* had a print run of just 500. William Godwin, Mary's father, did a few light edits before it came out again in 1823. Mary would revise it and add an introduction for the 1831 edition, the one we tend to read today. The book, which still sells about 40,000 copies a year, has never been out of print and is widely seen as the first science fiction novel. In the early days, anyone who hadn't read it would have seen the play. Richard Brinsley Peake's *Presumption! Or the Fate of Frankenstein,* complete with songs, was staged in 1823 and was as chilling as it was thrilling. The monster was slathered in bright blue make-up. People were warned to keep their wives and daughters away. 'The piece upon the whole has little to recommend it,' a critic in the *Evening Mail* scorned, 'but that, as times go, will be no great obstacle to its success.' They were right. People wanted to see it even more – Mary included. 'Lo and behold,' Mary wrote to her friend Leigh Hunt after going, 'I found myself famous.' Since then, there have been about 100 further stage adaptations and 170 TV dramas and films featuring Victor Frankenstein's monster. If only Mary had been alive to see the creature played by Boris Karloff in James Whale's 1931 film, *Frankenstein*. Never mind blue make-up. The creature now had neck bolts and a rectangular head. Three years later, Whale would bring out a sequel, *The Bride of Frankenstein*, starring the creature's female companion, the one that Victor couldn't bring himself to make.

Mary would write six more novels, before dying of brain cancer in 1851. She would recreate the world of fourteenth-century Italy in *Valperga* (1823) and imagine a dystopian future in *The Last Man* (1826). *Frankenstein* would be the work that people remembered. 'How I, then a young girl, came to think of, and to dilate upon, so very hideous an idea?' Mary asked in her introduction. It sounds like a reasonable question. Mary was just 18 when she started *Frankenstein* and 19 when she finished it. It's no skeleton of a story. It's a page-turner packed with literary allusions and philosophical ideas and pioneering science. But the question also has a very clear answer. When we look at Mary's life and the context of her novel, we will realise not only that Mary could have thought up so 'hideous an idea', but that only she could have done so.

Section I

Love and Loss

'I, the miserable and the abandoned, am an abortion, to be spurned at, and kicked, and trampled on' – the creature in *Frankenstein*

The First Feminist

1797

Mary Shelley's birth reads like Gothic horror. On 30 August 1797, her mother had gone into labour. Mary Wollstonecraft's first child, Fanny, had been born three years earlier. The birth had been trouble-free. This one should have been no different. It was early afternoon. She expected to be up for dinner the next day. William Godwin, her husband, had wanted a male doctor to supervise. The risk of death in childbirth was high. Wollstonecraft refused. A standard midwife – a woman – would be fine. She smiled (we can imagine) and turned to him. Soon they would welcome their first child together into the world: baby William. They would be a family. The couple were chatting at the top of their home in the Polygon, a new development in Somers Town in London, just north of St Paul's. Number 29, a four-storey townhouse, was one of a semi-circle of buildings. It was spacious and elegant. In the parlour, Godwin, a novelist and thinker, entertained his celebrity friends – scientists, politicians and poets. From the balcony, you could smell the crisp night air and gaze out across the wild heaths of Hampstead and Highgate.

After nine hours of contractions, Wollstonecraft gave birth. It was 11.20pm. Baby William was a girl. No one minded. Godwin popped his head round the door just before midnight. How happy he was. The joy would not last. A couple of hours later, the midwife told Godwin all was not well. The placenta had not come away. His wife was losing blood. Her life was in the balance. Godwin heard her cry out in pain. Leaping into a carriage, he raced across London to Westminster Hospital to get help and returned with Dr Louis Poignand. He wished his wife had agreed to a man from the start. Dr Poignand removed the placenta. Wollstonecraft improved a little. Then she was sick and began to shake. As days rolled into nights, she got worse. Godwin sent for doctor after doctor. One banned Wollstonecraft from feeding her baby so that she wouldn't poison her. Wollstonecraft's milk was drained by puppies. Godwin sat by his wife's bed, his head in his hands. If only he believed in God so that he could pray for her recovery. She was everything to him. His love could not save her. On 10 September, Mary Wollstonecraft died of septicaemia. Her daughter, Mary Shelley, was 11 days old.

Godwin was heartbroken. They had only been married for five months. He buried his wife at St Pancras Old Church. He would bring Fanny and Mary to the cemetery many times over the coming years. Mary would learn to read by tracing her fingers along the engraved letters on the memorial stone and would find that she shared her mother's initials. Mary and Percy Shelley stopped by the grave in 1814, soon after they first met. It would be here that they would declare their love for each other and Mary's fate would be sealed.

* * *

Mary Wollstonecraft had spent her life arguing that women should have similar rights to men. The way she died was a reminder that men and women were innately different. Women gave birth. Wollstonecraft's feminist leanings may well have resulted from her poor experiences of men growing up. She was born in 1759 in Spitalfields in east London. Her father, Edward, was a silk weaver. He could have been rich, but he preferred to drink and gamble. He also liked women. Wollstonecraft's mother, Elizabeth, was little comfort to her daughter. She was indolent and self-absorbed, and preferred Wollstonecraft's older brother, Ned. Wollstonecraft was the second eldest of seven children. She would be frequently overlooked. Yet she refused to stay in the background. Even as a child, she was principled, protective and possibly a little fierce. She worried about what her father might do to her mother after a night out.

To stop anything bad happening, Wollstonecraft curled up outside her mother's room so that he couldn't barge in.

When Wollstonecraft was 4, her father moved the family to Essex. Edward tried farming but struggled to stop drinking. Wollstonecraft took solace in the countryside. By the time she was 10, the family had moved to Beverley in Yorkshire. Wollstonecraft befriended a girl called Jane Arden. Jane's father John, a lecturer and philosopher, would become a mentor. But it would have been unwise for Wollstonecraft to feel settled. When she was 16, Edward dragged the family back to London. Separated from the Ardens, Wollstonecraft bonded with a neighbour, Reverend Clare. He introduced her to Fanny Blood, who would become her closest friend. She would even name her first child after her.

At 19, Wollstonecraft left home and became a ladies' companion in Bath. She had wanted independence but found society life superficial. She was almost relieved when she was called home. Her mother was gravely ill. Elizabeth died in 1782. Edward soon remarried. Marriage held little appeal for Wollstonecraft. She had seen the unhappiness it had caused her parents and now her sister, Eliza. It was bad enough, she might have thought, that Eliza had postnatal depression; now she had to endure a violent husband. Wollstonecraft helped her leave the relationship. Girl power is nothing new. It just took a different form back then. In 1784, Wollstonecraft would set up not a band but a girls' school with Eliza, their sister Everina and Fanny Blood. If only men hadn't got in the way. In January 1785, Fanny left London to marry a man in Lisbon. She would soon become pregnant and call on Wollstonecraft for support. Wollstonecraft sailed for Portugal. Fanny died in premature labour. Wollstonecraft was by her side.

Without Wollstonecraft, the school floundered and then closed. Wollstonecraft reluctantly became a governess to the daughters of Viscount and Lady Kingsborough in Cork in Ireland. She wished she didn't have to serve other people, but she needed the money. On the side, she wrote, channelling her experiences into *Thoughts on the Education of Daughters* (1787). Girls were currently taught to value their looks and excel in trivial accomplishments like sewing and singing. They should be taught to form independent judgments, she argued.

Frustrated with her governess role, Wollstonecraft returned to London. The following year, she brought out another book. *Original Stories from Real Life* was a series of fictional tales for children. They are narrated by a governess called Mrs Mason, who wants her two charges, Mary and Caroline, to become rational young women. The tales champion empathy and charity, the importance of telling the truth and the advantages of displaying a calm nature. Mary Shelley would go on to read it and understand the value of having someone like Mrs Mason in a child's life as a moral guide. It is a role, she might have thought, that Frankenstein's creature lacks with dire consequences. Mary might also have been influenced by William Blake's illustration of Mrs Mason's *The Story of Crazy Robin*. The tale follows a farmer called Robin who is driven 'crazy' by his efforts first to support his family and then by their deaths. In the end, he lives alone in a cave. Blake's drawing shows Robin, a tall dark character, looming over the corpses of his children. In build, Robin resembles the creature. Both Robin and the creature end up lonely and unhinged, sharing responsibility for a litany of deaths.

The same year that *Original Stories* came out, Wollstonecraft published her first novel, *Mary: A Fiction*. Over the next few years, she translated books from French, German, Italian and Dutch, wrote literary reviews for Joseph Johnson's *Analytical Review* and compiled an anthology of prose and poetry. Her greatest work was still to come. In 1790, she published *A Vindication of the Rights of Men* as a quick response to Edmund Burke's *Reflections on the Revolution in France* (1790). The Anglo-Irish philosopher had railed against the ideas of the French revolution. He argued that inherited rights and traditions should be upheld. Wollstonecraft disagreed. The days of hierarchy and arbitrary power were over, she said. Society needed a shake-up. It should be remade on the principles of liberty and reason.

In November 1791, Joseph Johnson invited Wollstonecraft for supper. On Sunday evenings, he would hold popular gatherings for his writer friends. Thomas Paine, a Founding Father and political philosopher, was to be the guest of honour. Wollstonecraft looked forward to it. The invitation showed she was part of the London literary scene. But the evening turned out to be highly unpleasant. On every topic from Voltaire to religion (these dinners were not light affairs), she clashed with a man called William Godwin. What a nightmare he was. She hoped their paths would never cross again. Men were taking Wollstonecraft from her work. It was time for her to knuckle down. She focused on writing *A Vindication of the Rights of Woman* (1792). In Wollstonecraft's proto-feminist work, she argued that women have the same capacity for reason as men. If they were educated properly, they could contribute significantly to society. The work would make her name as a radical thinker.

Some people were outraged. Thomas Taylor, a translator, responded with his satire, *A Vindication of the Rights of Brutes* (1792), arguing that if women had rights, animals and minerals had them, too. Others protested that Wollstonecraft was corrupting their daughters. Wollstonecraft would certainly influence her own. Mary Shelley would later champion her mother's work. Wollstonecraft, however, was more daring. She had argued in *Rights of Woman* that girls should be taught about anatomy and medicine. Embracing her own interest in science, she would go on to review William Smellie's *The Philosophy of Natural History (1790)*. Mary was interested in science, too. It would be a major thread of *Frankenstein*. She would also read Smellie's book. Yet in her 1831 preface to *Frankenstein*, she insists she was a 'nearly silent listener' when Byron and Shelley were chatting about the principle of life. Was she really 'nearly silent' or did she just want to fit gender stereotypes to help her work sell?

Wollstonecraft would never have wanted to be perceived this way. She was much more vocal in her views and her desires. At the time, Wollstonecraft was madly in love with a painter called Henry Fuseli. She suggested she move in with him. Unfortunately, his wife didn't think it was such a great idea and made it difficult for her husband to see Wollstonecraft anymore. Wollstonecraft looked for an escape. She would go to Paris to witness the French Revolution. At the end of 1792, she sailed for France. She was excited by the ideas of liberty, equality and fraternity. When she arrived, Louis XVI was on trial for high treason.

Wollstonecraft got stuck into political debates with anyone who would have them. She also met Gilbert Imlay, an American businessman, and they began an affair. Their child, Françoise Imlay, known as Fanny, would be born in May 1794. Three months later, Imlay went to England. Wollstonecraft thought he was going there on business and would soon be back. He wasn't. He eventually asked her to join him, but by the time she did, he had a new lover. Wollstonecraft was distraught. In May 1795, she tried to take her life by overdosing on laudanum. Guilty and ashamed, Imlay saved her. Wollstonecraft hoped she could save their relationship by going to Scandinavia for him to conduct a business deal. When she returned home four months later, she discovered that Imlay was moving in with a new mistress. In October, she tried again to take her life. This time, she jumped off Putney Bridge. The universe had other plans for her. Wollstonecraft was rescued.

Wollstonecraft distracted herself by turning to work. She would write about her Scandinavia trip. *Letters Written During a Short Residence in Sweden, Norway, and Denmark* (1796) was part-travelogue, part-memoir and part-philosophical treatise. It would become Wollstonecraft's bestselling book in her lifetime. In *Letters*, Wollstonecraft sees herself as itinerant, miserable, despairing and lost. Mary would read it in the summer of 1814 when she was in France with Percy. Mary was in the honeymoon phase of her relationship, but her happiness wouldn't last. Over the next few years, she would be able to empathize a lot more with her mother.

For Wollstonecraft, things were finally looking up. High on literary success, she visited the home of Mary Hays, a friend and fellow feminist. Hays had another person over: William Godwin. This time, Wollstonecraft and Godwin got on considerably better. They soon started having tea together, meeting each other's friends and popping over to each other's homes for supper. Wollstonecraft also sent Godwin the last volume of Jean-Jacques Rousseau's *Julie: or the New Heloise* (1761) about a passionate love affair. In *A Vindication of the Rights of Woman*, Wollstonecraft had criticized women who gave themselves up to men for love. In practice, she had struggled. How hurt she had been by Imlay's rejection. But Godwin was different. Wollstonecraft had fallen for him. Neither Godwin nor

Wollstonecraft had been great advocates for marriage, but now she was changing her mind. Wollstonecraft was pregnant. She had already had one child out of wedlock with a man who would go on to leave her. Marriage would mean that the new child would be born into a more secure home.

Wollstonecraft and Godwin married on 29 March 1797 at St Pancras Old Church. They kept their own rooms for work and wrote frequently to each other, referring to their unborn baby as 'William'. William would turn out to be Mary. How did Mary feel about initially being thought of as a boy? Was it significant that she would call her own child William? When she killed off a boy called William in *Frankenstein*, was she killing off a version of herself? How she might have liked to discuss this with her mother. She couldn't, of course. Her mother would soon be dead.

In October 1797, the month after Wollstonecraft died, the *Gentleman's Magazine* ran an obituary praising her lively conversation, her manners and her intellect. Godwin had more to say. Early the following year, he brought out *Memoirs of the Author of A Vindication of the Rights of Woman*, a biography of his late wife. He meant well. But for many, his candour painted Wollstonecraft in a poor light. His account contained Wollstonecraft's difficult relationship with her drunken father, her love affair with Gilbert Imlay, their illegitimate child Fanny, her suicide attempts and their own relationship. It was salacious. That year, under the heading 'Prostitution', *The Anti-Jacobin Review and Magazine* wrote: 'See Mary Wollstonecraft'. Her reputation was blackened. It would be 200 years before it was reclaimed by second-wave feminists.

At the time, Godwin was too immersed in his grief to fight back. The only thing he could control was how his late wife was seen at home. He still adored her. He hung a portrait of Wollstonecraft painted by John Opie above the fireplace in his study and vowed to tell Mary all about her as soon as she was old enough to understand. He would also take her to her mother's grave. Godwin turned out to be a highly capable solo parent. He quickly found a nanny for the children and put himself in charge of their education. But it would never be enough. Mary would become obsessed with the mother she never knew, an obsession driven in part perhaps by all the ways Godwin tried to honour her – from the portrait to the references he would make to her work in conversation. Godwin would go on to marry again, largely to bring a maternal figure into Mary's life, but it would only make her feel more alone. No one could compete with her mother, certainly not the idealized version she would create in her mind. As she grew up, Mary couldn't help but feel abandoned by her, even if she hadn't chosen to die. The facts were clear: her mother created her; her mother left her.

When she wrote *Frankenstein*, Mary identified with the creature. Victor Frankenstein brings him to life and then immediately leaves him. Horrified at the sight of 'the wretch', he scurries out of the room. 'You, my creator, detest and spurn me, thy creature,' the wretch says later. He feels lonely, hurt, rejected, worthless. 'I, the miserable and the abandoned, am an abortion, to be spurned at, and kicked, and trampled on.' The details of the creature's life echo Mary's, too. Was it just coincidence that they were both born at the top of a house? Would it be too much of a stretch to say that their lives had both come out of death? For Mary, this was the death of her mother; for the creature, it was the death of all the people and animals he was made of. What should we make of the fact that both their lives lead to the death of others? Wollstonecraft had died giving birth to Mary. Victor survived the creature's birth but dies running away from him – and after the creature has killed his brother, his best friend and his wife. In *Frankenstein*, Mary's fears take shape. Could a child who grows up without a parent turn out to be a murderer? Had she killed her own mother?

Mary's anxieties played on her mind so much that she may have even written her mother's pregnancy into *Frankenstein*. The framing narrative comprises Walton's letters to his sister, Margaret Saville. They are dated from December to September. Margaret Saville shares Mary's initials after she got married. Mary had been born at the end of August. December to September was the rough period she would have been in her mother's womb. Shaped by her mother's ideas, Mary was determined to be the sort of woman her mother would admire. She would use reason and be independent rather than trade on any talent for sewing or singing. She might even continue her mother's legacy. Her worry? She might not be as brilliant. For an absent mother, Wollstonecraft is remarkably present in Mary's writing and thoughts. Mary didn't just grow up without a mother, she might have said; she grew up with a dead mother. When Percy Shelley drowns in 1822 off the coast of Tuscany, Mary asks her father and stepmother for comfort. They send one of her mother's rings and a lock of hair once belonging to Fanny Blood, her mother's closest friend. Mary Wollstonecraft couldn't be there to console her daughter, but it is the best anyone can do.

A Serious Man

1797–1800

Mary Wollstonecraft was buried in the cemetery of St Pancras Old Church in September 1797. She had got married there just five months earlier. William Godwin was too grief-stricken to go to the funeral. He hung John Opie's portrait of his late wife above the fireplace in his study and made notes for a work to preserve her memory. *Memoirs of the Author of A Vindication of the Rights of Woman* would come out the following year. More immediately, he had to take care of Mary, their newborn, and 3-year-old Fanny, Wollstonecraft's daughter by the American businessman Gilbert Imlay. Godwin and Wollstonecraft had talked a lot about parenting. 'Mama' and 'Papa' hoped their first child together would be interested in science and philosophy, eloquent and inquisitive, kind and happy. They would give them a rounded and rigorous education. Godwin had been so excited by the idea of being a father. But the idea of being a single parent bewildered him. 'I am the most unfit person for this office,' he wrote soon after his wife died. 'She [Mary Wollstonecraft] was the best qualified in the world.'

* * *

Godwin's own upbringing had been austere. He had been born on 3 March 1756 in Wisbech in Cambridgeshire and was the seventh of thirteen children. His father, John, was a dissenting minister. Unfortunately, he often also dissented with his congregation, moving the family around frequently when Godwin was young to escape quarrels with them. The family would eventually settle in Guestwick in Norfolk. Godwin's parents were big on the Calvinist doctrines of predestination and original sin. For light relief, his aunt read him *The Pilgrim's Progress*, and he composed sermons, which he delivered from his highchair in the kitchen on Sunday afternoons wearing a wig. Few mothers would have more recourse than Anne Godwin to call their child 'Little Solomon'. At least no babies were cut in half. While they admired their son's early interest in morality, neither parent was keen for their son to join the church. Godwin had other ideas. He believed it was his vocation.

After a spell at the village school, Godwin went to study at a dissenting seminary under Samuel Newton. A stern man whom Godwin would later liken to Nero, Newton preached the devil and threatened his pupils with the rod. Godwin stuck at it for three years, before dropping out. The only upside to the seminary had been access to Newton's library. Godwin had enjoyed throwing himself into novels by Samuel Richardson and Henry Fielding, as well as works on ancient history. Maybe, he thought, he would become a bookseller. Several months later, however, he returned to the seminary, believing the ministry was his calling after all. He graduated to a dissenting academy to train to become a minister and was encouraged to join debates and think independently. Godwin learned about John Locke and was taken with his idea that man has fundamental rights to life, liberty and property. He also learned about Jean-Jacques Rousseau and agreed with him that man is born free but has his freedom curbed by society. His tutors were adamant that man's character could be formed by education and was not predetermined from birth. Godwin agreed. He studied history, too, learning about periods when England had experienced radical shake-ups from the Reformation to the Glorious Revolution of 1688. Such inspirational times! But he couldn't learn forever. Eventually, he had to start work. In 1779, Godwin began his ministry in Suffolk. Yet his training at the dissenting academy had changed him. Godwin had been encouraged to question everything. God was not immune. Godwin had lost his faith.

In 1783, now in his early thirties, Godwin moved to London. He needed to make a living and decided to start a school. He rented a building in Surrey and advertised it in a pamphlet. His teachers, he said, would not impose any views on the pupils. Instead, they would give them books and engage them in conversation. They would stimulate their imaginations and develop their critical faculties. Godwin had worked out all the big ideas. Unfortunately, he had not worked out the little ones like the school fees or the meals or the term dates – or at least he forgot to mention any of these trivialities in his advert. He got very little response. There was only one career Godwin was really suited to and that was writing. Even back then, writing didn't always pay and he spent at least one night in jail because he was in debt. But on he went. In 1783, Godwin brought out his first work, *The History of the Life of William Pitt, Earl of Chatham*. He also started writing for the *English Review*. Over the next couple of years, he wrote three novels, two political pamphlets, a collection of sermons and several entries on British and foreign history for the *New Annual Register*. He was prolific and good, gaining credibility in the literary circles of London. One Sunday in November 1791, Godwin was invited to a dinner held by the publisher Joseph Johnson in honour of Thomas Paine, the Founding Father and political philosopher. Godwin was keen to meet Paine, but the evening did not go well. Godwin encountered a woman there called Mary Wollstonecraft. She spent the whole time arguing with him about the French Enlightenment philosopher Voltaire and religion. Poor Thomas Paine could hardly get a word in. Godwin was all for independent thinking, but he hoped their paths would never cross again.

Godwin did, however, have some opinions of his own that he wanted to share. Edmund Burke's *Reflections on the Revolution in France* had been published in 1790. Godwin had been inspired. He wanted to write his own treatise on political principles. *An Enquiry Concerning Political Justice* would come out in 1793. Godwin argued that people should be encouraged to think for themselves and act on their own judgments. It would make for a better society. Government, laws, organised religion and marriage had no place in his new world order. The revolutionaries in France had the right idea. A hit, *Political Justice* sold more than 4,000 copies. It championed philosophical anarchy and made Godwin a hero of the left. Percy Shelley would come across the work almost twenty years later and become a fan. The following year, Godwin explored some of his ideas in *Political Justice* in *Things as They Are, or The Adventures of Caleb Williams*, which would become his most successful novel. The story traces a young servant called Caleb Williams, who discovers a dark secret about his master, Mr Falkland. Falkland then pursues him. Elements of the plot and the idea of a codependent relationship would influence *Frankenstein*.

Godwin was now at the height of his fame, mixing with everyone from the playwright Thomas Holcroft and political reformer John Thelwell to the early Romantics, Samuel Taylor Coleridge and William Wordsworth. At the start of 1796, he was invited to tea at the home of feminist writer Mary Hays. He was not the only guest. Hays had another writer over: Mary Wollstonecraft. How things had changed since Godwin had first met her. Godwin had published *Political Justice*. Wollstonecraft had published *A Vindication of the Rights of Woman*. Wollstonecraft seemed different. Perhaps it was because of the time she had spent in revolutionary France. Perhaps it was because she had been bruised from her doomed affair with the American businessman Gilbert Imlay. Perhaps it was because she was now a mother. Her daughter Fanny was 2. It didn't really matter. Godwin wasn't looking for romance. He was still hung up on a woman called Maria Reveley. Maria had studied painting in Rome under Angelica Kauffman. Unfortunately, she was also married. Yet he couldn't get Mary Wollstonecraft out of his head. Maybe he had misjudged her. She wasn't the loudmouth he remembered. She was clever and attractive. Soon afterwards, Godwin would read her most recent work, *Letters Written During a Short Residence in Sweden, Norway, and Denmark*, and be impressed. They would have tea together. They would meet each other's friends. They would pop round to each other's homes for supper. Things would get serious.

In early 1797, Wollstonecraft became pregnant with Godwin's child. Godwin had never intended to marry; he believed marriage was at best a form of ownership and at worst a form of slavery. But he also wanted the best for his future son or daughter and knew that society was likely to shun a child born out of wedlock. Putting his ideals aside, Godwin married Wollstonecraft in March 1797 at St Pancras Old Church and they moved in together. They lived at 29 The Polygon in Somers Town. They looked forward to the arrival of their baby. For months, the couple were happy, until Wollstonecraft went into labour that September. Wollstonecraft would have but days with her daughter Mary.

After his wife's death, Godwin was distraught. His publisher, Joseph Johnson, suggested printing Wollstonecraft's most recent writings, including her novel-in-progress *Maria, or the Wrongs of Woman*, a few of her letters and an essay by Godwin about her life. Godwin got down to work. He re-read everything Wollstonecraft had ever written, dated and numbered the 160 letters they had sent each other, asked her friends and family for stories about her and pulled together his own journal notes of their conversations. The essay Holcroft had commissioned became a full-length work. *Memoirs of the Author of a Vindication of the Rights of Woman* came out in 1798 and was rich in gossipy details, especially when it came to Wollstonecraft's love life. Johnson warned Godwin about being so open, but Godwin saw no reason to hide any of Wollstonecraft's traits or experiences: they made her who she was, the woman he had loved. Readers were not quite so understanding. The memoirs didn't just destroy Wollstonecraft's reputation; they trampled over Godwin's. People were not just shocked at the details of Wollstonecraft's life; they were outraged at Godwin for revealing them. Godwin was caricatured as arrogant and heartless. His professional life as well as his personal life started falling apart. He had come so far, Godwin might have thought, only for his happiness to be snatched away. What he needed was a reason to go on living. He had one, of course: his wife's children. Godwin adopted Fanny and hired Louisa Jones as a nanny. For the first three years, Fanny and Mary were happy. But Louisa had her own life to lead and in 1800, she ran off with a man. Godwin did his best without her, but he worried about the children. He was concerned about their education. When he was away, he wrote home asking how they were getting on with their spelling and their geography. He also wanted to give them a mother. Godwin proposed to a couple of women but was turned down.

Godwin's efforts to make sure Mary felt loved might lead us to question whether Wollstonecraft's absence affected her as much as we have imagined. Mary might have grown up without a mother, but she did have a father who cared. Yet Godwin had little chance of competing with his wife. Mary might have felt she had developed a bond with her mother in the womb, even if she couldn't remember it. They were also connected by a more uncomfortable truth: Mary's life had led to her mother's death. Finally, Godwin was at a disadvantage because he was a man. He was expected to be stoic and independent. Society would have thought Wollstonecraft, as a woman, would be naturally kind and gentle and have an instinct to nurture. Mary may well have felt she was lacking someone like this in her life. It is this that comes out in *Frankenstein*.

The world of *Frankenstein* is an inversion of the natural order. It is a dystopian world without mothers and strong women to check male ambition and provide empathy and understanding. The trouble starts at conception. Exploiting the masculine trait of ambition, Victor creates life – and worse, he does so alone. In bypassing the need for a woman to create life, he takes away one of women's key roles in society. He compounds his faults by abandoning the creature, removing any chance that he could be a sort of omni-parent, playing the role of mother and father by nurturing the creature (a feminine trait) and offering him a role model in leadership (a masculine one). It doesn't help that the creature is hideous with his yellow skin, watery eyes and straight black lips, but Victor feels no instant parental bond, no spark of unconditional love. He fails to realize how important it is that the creature is cared for, whatever he looks like. When Victor considers becoming a parent again, he has a panic attack. 'Every thought that was devoted to it was an extreme anguish,' he says, 'and every word that I spoke in allusion to it caused my lips to quiver, and my heart to palpitate.'

Victor also fails to appreciate how valuable it would be for the creature to have a companion, focusing instead on his own concerns. The female creature might have wants that can't be controlled, he thinks. She might be 'ten thousand times' more evil than the creature and 'delight' in killing. She might be so ugly that the creature won't want her. She might mate with men, maybe against their will. Or she might stick with the creature and they will produce a generation of monsters. Any of these scenarios would be a disaster. After submitting to the creature (a feminine trait) by agreeing to his request, Victor exercises control (a masculine trait) by taking back his promise. His actions hint at rape. 'Trembling with passion, [I] tore to pieces the thing on which I was engaged,' he says. The following morning, 'the remains of the half-finished creature… lay scattered on the floor'. It is a disturbing image. 'I almost felt as if I had mangled the living flesh of a human being,' says Victor. What a violent place the world would be without women.

As a woman, perhaps with a little of her mother's proto-feminist spirit, Mary can't let Victor, a man, succeed. Victor has gone against nature in creating life. Now, nature (depicted in the novel as female) will take revenge, destroying his mental and physical health. 'Every night I was oppressed by a slow fever, and I became nervous to a most painful degree,' he says after making the creature. Making the creature's mate, he falls ill again. '[M]y spirits became unequal; I grew restless and nervous.' He will die of mental and physical exhaustion at just 25. A world that excludes women – especially from the act of conception and in the formative stages of a child's life – is a dangerous one, suggests Mary. Let us hope Godwin finds her a new mother soon.

A Second Mamma

1801–1811

In 1801, a new family moved into 27 The Polygon, next door to the Godwins. Mary Jane Clairmont had two children: Charles, nearly 6, and Jane, 4. A curvaceous woman with green-tinted glasses, she was blunt and fiercely intelligent. She was 'clever [and] bustling', said one of Godwin's friends. She was a 'second-rate woman', said another. Mary Jane brings momentum and liveliness to our story. 'Is it possible that I behold the immortal Godwin?', she would call from her balcony, whenever she saw her neighbour leaving his house. 'You great being, how I adore you!' she liked to cry, pacing her lawn, whenever she saw 'the immortal Godwin' in the garden. Mary Jane knew what she wanted in life – and, at that very moment, it was him. Her blatant flattery, if not blatantly bizarre behaviour, worked. Singletons, take note. Godwin met Mary Jane in early May. On 21 December that year, barely six months later, they got married. Now Mary and Fanny would feel secure and settled, thought Godwin. Let us raise a toast to happy families!

* * *

Mary Jane Clairmont's life before Godwin is hazy. She was born sometime in 1768, in Exeter, probably to Peter de Vial, a merchant, and his wife, Mary Tremlett. The family name, Vial, might come from Geneva. Mary Jane spoke several European languages. She said she had travelled a lot on the Continent. By her late twenties, Mary was living in Bristol, then a lively port city, where she had her son, Charles. Children born out of wedlock faced stigma, as did their mother, so Mary Jane passed herself off as the widow of Karl Abram Marc Gaulis, a merchant she had met in Cadiz, Spain. Karl had used the anglicized version of his name, Charles, after moving to England. There is no proof that they got married. Four years later, Mary Jane was living in Brislington, a village close by, where she had her daughter, Clara Mary Jane (known as Jane as a child and Claire after she left home). Jane's father was probably a landowner called John Lethbridge, from Somerset. Mary Jane asked for financial support from him for their daughter through her lawyers. After a couple of spells in debtors' prison in Somerset, Mary Jane turned up in Somers Town. Mary Jane and Godwin married possibly because she was pregnant again. Their child, William, would be born the following June. He didn't survive, but, by that time, the Godwin-Clairmont union was complete: their households were one.

* * *

Mary Shelley now belonged to a blended family. Another son, another William, would be born in March 1803. No two children would have the same parents. The quiet Godwin household was no more. Mary Jane was loud, garrulous and prone to losing her temper. She banned mentions of Wollstonecraft and ordered Fanny and Mary to address her as their mother. Mary Jane hired new staff and expected all the children, Mary included, to help with household chores. Godwin made sure he did his bit by seeing to his children's education. He read to them all and employed tutors to teach them geography, maths and chemistry. He wouldn't have said this out loud, but Mary was still his favourite. He was amused that she would sometimes write sermons to be read out by her half-brother William from a homemade pulpit. It reminded him of his own hobby as a boy. Influenced by her father, Mary's speeches sometimes had a political spin. One week she wrote about 'The Influence of Governments on the Character of the People'.

It wasn't all work. Mary Jane took the children to plays and exhibitions and taught the girls to sew and embroider. Godwin took them to JMW Turner's studio in Harley Street so that they could appreciate the value of creativity and imagination. He also encouraged the children to talk to his guests. What an illustrious collection of people they were! Many of them were keen to meet Mary, the child of the author of *Political Justice* and *Rights of Woman*. Mary shook hands with Humphry Davy, the most famous chemist of the day, and Aaron Burr, one of the Founding Fathers. Samuel Taylor Coleridge, the Romantic poet, had known her since she was 2. It was an encounter with Coleridge, Mary might have thought, that showed how little her stepmother understood her. When Mary was 8, she had wanted to stay up to listen to him recite a poem after dinner. Mary Jane had told her it was late and she must go to bed. Mary thought it unfair and hid behind the sofa in the parlour so that she could hear it. It was *The Rime of the Ancient Mariner*, which she loved. When Mary Jane found out, she wanted to punish her. For once, Godwin intervened. Mary wished her father would speak up for her more. He usually refused to take sides, locking himself in his study. It left Mary feeling alone and vulnerable.

Mary probably couldn't have appreciated it at the time, but her stepmother was entrepreneurial. It was her idea, back in 1803, for Godwin to start a children's publisher, cashing in on the growing interest in children's education. To sell their work, she suggested they open a children's bookshop. The shop just off Oxford Street was funded by a loan from Thomas Wedgwood, son of Josiah, the founder of the pottery dynasty and a friend of Godwin's. In many ways, Mary Jane thought, Godwin was immensely well-suited to this line of business. With her encouragement, he wrote children's books under pseudonyms. They did well. He also had an eye for a bestseller. In 1807, he published *Tales from Shakespeare*, retelling Shakespearean plays for a young audience. The book has never been out of print. Mary Jane had a talent for publishing, too. She translated French and Swiss fairytales and would become the most eminent female publisher in London of her day. Her translation of the Swiss Family Robinson would still be in print more than 200 years later. They had several publishing sensations on their hands. But Mary Jane failed to see that, in another way, Godwin was immensely ill-suited to any line of business. He was hopeless with money. Neither of them saw for months that their shop manager Thomas Hodgkins had been stealing from them. They ended up firing him and re-registering the firm in Mary Jane's name. Godwin's reputation was still suffering from the memoir he had brought out about his late wife. It was 1807. They could have been ruined. Alert to flaws in her stepmother, Mary may well have blamed Mary Jane for the family's financial difficulties. While she was growing up, they always seemed to be short of money.

Towards the end of that year, just before Mary turned 10, the family moved to 41 Skinner Street in Holborn. The five-storey building was in the heart of town and had enough room for their bookshop on the ground floor. One room on the first floor was also perfect for Godwin's soirées. But for Mary, it was another story. Skinner Street took her further away from where her mother used to live. The building was also unpainted and unsightly, and the location would have been a hard sell even for the most dogged of estate agents. Smithfield slaughterhouses were nearby. Every night, you could hear the cries of animals meeting their maker. Fresh carcasses of cows, sheep and pigs hung outside butcher shops, puddles of blood forming on the ground. The smell was putrid. Newgate Prison and the gallows at Tyburn were close by, too. On execution days, you could hear the ringing of the bells of a local church. Crowds gathered gleefully to watch the hangings. Godwin's children might have had famous parents, but at least they wouldn't lead sheltered lives.

When Mary was 13, she developed a skin condition on her arms – psoriasis, maybe, or eczema. Doctors recommended salt bathing and sea air. Godwin and Mary Jane decided she should spend a few months in Ramsgate in Kent. Mary Jane helped her settle in and wrote to her while she was away. Godwin did not. His only communication with her was through his wife's letters. Perhaps he hoped that Mary Jane would provide the emotional support. If only Mary and her stepmother had enjoyed that sort of relationship. Mary was not having a good time of it. First, she had lost her mother. Now, her father thought she would be okay if he left her in the hands of Mary Jane Clairmont. Mary had always seen Mary Jane as a poor substitute for her mother. She had never understood how her father could have a new wife without betraying the love he had for Mary Wollstonecraft, a woman he once idolized and who had brought Mary into the world. Godwin also wanted Mary to think of Mary Jane as a 'second mamma'. The idea was ridiculous. Unlike her mother who had pioneered new ground with her politics and her writing, Mary Jane was so dull and conventional. She could never live up to her mother's reputation.

Perhaps Mary also couldn't help fearing that Godwin's need for someone else meant she wasn't enough for him. Why did he want anyone else? And now that he had found someone, where did Mary fit in? Once she had been doted on as the baby of the family; now she was the middle child. She and Fanny no longer had their father's undivided attention. Godwin had Mary Jane and her children to think about. She wasn't sure that Mary Jane even liked her. Why did she not get French lessons like Jane? Mary struggled to find her place. Fanny was too timid to be much comfort. Jane was more like a frenemy than someone you could trust. Jane could be fun, but she was also competitive. There was also no way they could be sisters: they looked so different. Mary had pale skin, grey-green eyes and strawberry-blonde hair. Jane had a darker complexion, brown eyes and chocolate curls. How alone Mary felt, an outsider even in her own family.

Mary would come to loathe Mary Jane Clairmont, referring to her as 'a woman I shudder to think of' in her diary in 1814. 'I detest Mrs G she plagues my father out of his life,' she wrote to Percy, soon after they eloped together. She felt 'disgust' and 'bitterness' when she thought of her. Mary blamed her stepmother for Godwin's attempt to separate her from Percy when they first got together and ignoring her after she disobeyed him. Several accounts back up Mary's opinion. They describe Mary Jane as common and artificial, a gossip and a liar. This unfortunate legacy was not all Mary Jane's fault. She suffered from a broader smear on the Godwin family by nineteenth-century biographers keen to paint Percy in a good light. Whatever the truth, Mary really didn't like her.

Mary Jane might not inspire a specific character in *Frankenstein* – the creature does not have a female guardian with green-tinted glasses and a love of tittle-tattle – but Mary Jane's influence can still be felt among its pages. Mary Jane, as we have seen, exacerbated Mary's greatest wound: her perceived abandonment by her mother. She made Mary feel her mother's absence more keenly. This is partly because Mary saw them as very different sorts of people. In Mary's mind, Wollstonecraft had been a celebrated intellectual with charming manners. Mary Jane, on the other hand, was looked down on by some of her father's friends, was a housewife (as well as a publisher) and lacked any sort of grace. It didn't help that Godwin thought Mary Jane was a good maternal substitute. Casting them in the same role highlighted their contrasting traits. Mary Jane may have also made Mary feel more distant from her father. How could he think that she would get on with her and that she was the right person to look after his family? Was Godwin really a good father? Perhaps he didn't understand his daughter after all. It made Mary feel lonely and misunderstood, emotions that, as we have seen, are echoed by the creature.

Mary Jane might have also influenced how Mary felt about herself and her relationships, ideas she would also explore in her novel. At home, Mary could be stroppy. We know from Godwin that she could be 'imperious'. We also know that she ignored Mary Jane when she felt like it. She had a tendency to sulk. This might have been because she felt abandoned and unloved. It was mostly Mary Jane's fault, she might have told us. Maybe this was what happened to someone if they didn't have loving, understanding parents. Maybe they became not just stroppy but unkind. In *Frankenstein*, Mary airs her deepest fears – that a child like herself could become cruel. Mary wasn't inherently bad, just like the creature tells us he wasn't inherently evil. Mary just acted badly sometimes and felt she was on the verge of acting in worse ways. She 'detested' Mary Jane. Did she sometimes worry, in an extreme circumstance, that she could kill her? If she identified with the creature, this would be within her reach. 'I was benevolent and good,' the creature says, 'misery made a fiend.' Mary knew how he felt.

After six months in Kent, Mary returned to London, but she wouldn't be there for long. Mary kept arguing with her stepmother. Godwin knew Mary had many good qualities – she was clever, determined and conscientious. Yet he felt she could be arrogant and stubborn, too. Teenagers, he might have sighed. All he wanted was a family. This one was becoming unbearable.

The Meaning of Home

1812–1814

On 7 June 1812, a couple of months before her fifteenth birthday, Mary Shelley sailed north on the *Osnaburgh* for Dundee, leaving her family behind. William Godwin had waved her off in London, accompanied by Fanny and Jane. Mary would be staying with Godwin's friend William Baxter. Godwin had met Baxter, a linen manufacturer and fan of *Enquiry Concerning Political Justice*, a few years earlier through a mutual friend. They had similar outlooks, believing the church should be separate from state politics. They also both valued education for girls as well as boys. Godwin had made it clear in a letter to Baxter that he wanted Mary to be brought up 'like a philosopher'. He hoped she would be conscientious. 'She has occasionally great perseverance, but occasionally, too, she shows great need to be roused,' he wrote. In Scotland, formal education for girls stopped when they were 14 – but not at the Baxter household, where the girls had private tutors. Baxter also encouraged them to borrow books from his home library, where they would find works by Shakespeare, Milton and William Godwin.

Baxter had agreed to host Mary at his home in Scotland for six months in return for Godwin entertaining his daughters occasionally at Skinner Street. Godwin would miss Mary, but he had good reasons for sending her away. Mary's skin was still bad. Her doctor had prescribed more poultices and sea bathing, adding that a sea voyage might help. Another break from the family, reasoned Godwin, might benefit them all. Like many homes with teenagers, the Godwin household was a hotbed of tension. Godwin's wife and daughter clashed at every opportunity. Mary Jane was prone to flying off the handle at the best of times. When she did try to be kind to Mary, Mary returned her efforts with an icy silence. They all needed some space. For now, Godwin's thoughts were on Mary's journey. He must warn Baxter that she might look more 'dead than alive' when she arrived. The journey would take almost a week and Mary may well be seasick.

For many people in England in the early nineteenth century, much of Scotland seemed like a faraway land. They could imagine Edinburgh, which was the seat of a great university and once home to Enlightenment thinkers David Hume and Adam Smith, but further north, it was said, was another place entirely. The countryside was wild, inhospitable and, for those who didn't get hot under the collar at the thought of Hume, exciting. Godwin and Mary might well have heard about the Highlands, just north of where she was going, from William Wordsworth and Samuel Taylor Coleridge, Godwin's friends. They had ventured there several years earlier, trekking across wide expanses of heath and chancing upon military garrisons. It was a place that could inspire the imagination and stir the heart. Godwin could picture Mary's amazement at the dramatic landscape – the gorges and the waterfalls. He also thought she might admire the people. There was something about Scotland that cultivated independent thought and a spirit of rebellion. It hadn't been that long since the Jacobite Uprisings, when Scottish rebels had tried to overthrow the House of Hanover and restore the House of Stuart to the British throne. The Jacobites had been defeated in 1746, but a sense of unrest lingered in Scotland and Parliament knew it. To show their dominance, they had made it illegal for civilian men and boys to wear Highland dress, waiting until 1782 before lifting the ban. It was no coincidence that Mary returned to England wearing a dress made of tartan, a fabric that showed her own independence. Scotland, the home of Flora Macdonald, who had helped Bonnie Prince Charlie escape Scotland after the Battle of Culloden, was a land of heroes and heroines. Like the Jacobites, Mary also saw herself as a freedom fighter. Her enemy was not England, but Mary Jane.

Mary would live with William Baxter and his four daughters on Broughty Ferry Road, a wealthy area on the north bank of the Firth of Tay, near the North Sea. Although she was an outsider at the Baxters' home, she never felt like one. The family took her to Edinburgh and Perth, cities that would both appear in *Frankenstein*. They also went through the Grampians to Inverness. Mary got on particularly well with Baxter's daughter Isabella, who was a couple of years older than her. Like Mary, Isabella was intelligent, imaginative and into big ideas. Isabella was especially interested in the French Revolution and hoped to follow the example of women such as Charlotte Corday, who had assassinated a Jacobin leader, and Madame Roland, a Parisian writer and acquaintance of Mary's mother. Isabella wanted to fight oppression. The girls formed an emotional bond, too. Isabella's mother had also died. For the first time, Mary felt seen. The two girls shared a room and imagined a future in which they would lead extraordinary lives. Surrounded by people who understood her, Mary's skin cleared up. She was brighter and stronger. The Baxters offered Mary a new understanding of what family life could be like. They were her De Laceys – the family the creature observes, learns from and hopes will accept him in *Frankenstein*. Mary was only meant to stay with the Baxters for six months and returned home, as agreed, in November. It wasn't long, however, before Mary and her stepmother were at each other's throats again. Godwin agreed that Mary could go back to Scotland for the winter.

Scotland was important to Mary because it is where she became a writer. By the time she composed the introduction to the 1831 edition of *Frankenstein*, she had romanticized her teenage trip. 'The blank and dreary northern shores of the Tay' where she had lived had become 'the eyry of freedom'. She remembered it as 'the pleasant region where unheeded I could commune with the creatures of my fancy'. But why was it here that Mary started writing? Was it because she now had enough words in her vocabulary? Was it because she was bored? Was it because she had time? Was it because she didn't feel the burden of living with one writer who was alive, William Godwin, and one who was dead, her mother? Perhaps there was something about being away from home, away from the place she associated with feelings of loss and longing and guilt and anger and frustration about not fitting in that shifted something inside her, that freed her. Finally, she had the energy and headspace to think about something else, to let 'the airy flights of [her] imagination' soar free.

Then there was Scotland itself. The Baxters' imposing house, which locals called 'The Cottage' as an in-joke looked out across the harbour. As an international port, Dundee was lively and cosmopolitan. It was a hub for trade. Ships brought flax from places in the Baltic and Russia, including Archangel, the port in *Frankenstein* where Captain Walton posts his second letter, and sailed away to Quebec, New York and Jamaica laden with linen sheets, bags, sailcloth and rope. In the spring, gangs of tall ships left the dock destined for the Arctic. The sailors were hunting whales. Sometimes, they brought back dead ones tied to the hull of their boat, along with bodies of polar bears. They might have harpooned the odd seal, too. Returning fleets smelled of fish, sweat and adventure. The story of the *Rodney*, a whaling ship that had become trapped in pack ice and lost in 1810, just before Mary arrived, may well have been doing the rounds while she was there, making anyone who dared go seem especially foolhardy or courageous. Other sailors sought out undiscovered lands as much as whale oil and seal tusks. The previous century had seen lots of new pins impaled in the world map. Australia had only been discovered by Europeans about forty years earlier when Captain Cook claimed it for the British crown. There had been pioneering trips around that time to the South Pacific and Alaska. Some explorers had sought out the North Pole. No one had yet found it. Some thought it was a frozen island surrounded by sea; others, an expanse of sea walled in by ice. Getting there was fraught with danger. The elusive Northwest Passage, a sea route across the Arctic, connecting the Atlantic and Pacific Oceans, was also on people's lists. Its discovery, they knew, could really benefit trade. Some doubted whether it even existed.

The elevator pitch for *Frankenstein* would focus on a scientist who brings a creature to life. It need not mention ships or whaling or the North Pole or the Northwest Passage. And yet, when Mary expanded her original ghost story in 1816, she made a point of adding a framing narrative with a strong maritime-exploration theme. We hear Victor's story from Captain Walton, who is writing home to his sister as Victor recovers on his ship. Captain Walton is an Arctic explorer. On a previous expedition he had been whaling. Now he is looking for the Northwest Passage, which he hopes will bestow an 'inestimable benefit' on mankind, and the North Pole, which will help him understand the 'wondrous power which attracts the needle' or why compasses point in the same direction. He is excited. In Walton's first letter home to his sister, he imagines the North Pole 'as the region of beauty and delight'. It appears otherworldly. 'There snow and frost are banished,' he says, 'and, sailing over a calm sea, we may be wafted to a land surpassing in wonders and in beauty every region hitherto undiscovered on the habitable globe.' While others might see it as 'the seat of frost and desolation', Walton is psyched to reach 'those icy climes'.

Walton is both a mirror of Victor and a foil for him. At first, Walton is driven by a similar drive as he seeks to 'accomplish some great purpose'. He becomes so fixated on his quest that he endangers the lives of his crew. But in the end, Victor's story teaches Walton (and the reader) that a desire to become great and achieve extraordinary things can go too far. 'Seek happiness in tranquillity, and avoid ambition,' cautions Victor, 'even if it be only the apparently innocent one of distinguishing yourself in science and discoveries.' Walton listens and turns back, saving his life and those of his men. By highlighting the dangers, Mary undermines the macho claims of explorers of the time. Man cannot conquer nature. Walton's story, wrapped around Victor's, underlines the danger of Promethean ambition. You don't have to succumb to it, Mary suggests. It is not the only way.

Victor, however, cannot turn back. He is so exhausted from chasing and being chased by the creature that he dies on Walton's ship. The inhospitable landscape comprising 'mountainous ices of the ocean' isn't just part of Walton's journey; it is part of the culmination of Victor's. His 'misery' – a mix of regret at carrying out his experiment, guilt at what the creature has done and pain at losing people he loved – is reflected in the terrifying landscape. 'Immense and rugged mountains of ice often barred up my passage,' Victor says of his journey, 'and I often heard the thunder of the ground sea, which threatened my destruction.' For Victor, destruction is the only outcome.

Mary might have used the framing narrative to write herself into the story. As we have seen, she called Walton's sister Margaret Saville Walton, giving her character initials that would match her own after she married Percy. When Mary came to write this part of *Frankenstein*, she would seek out books about 'old voyages' for background. She might also have read about planned journeys to the North Pole in the press. She might have drawn on her experiences in Dundee, too. She was at a different stage of her life now: no longer a teenager at the mercy of her parents, no longer having to escape her family by living with another one on the Scottish coast. But her time in Scotland hadn't been that long ago: it would have been fresh enough to draw on. Mary finally returned to Skinner Street in March 1814. She was more confident. She had more energy. She had at least one tartan dress. She missed Isabella, but she wouldn't be alone for long. Soon she would meet a particularly important man in her life.

The Great Escape

1814

In May 1814, Percy Shelley dropped into 41 Skinner Street to see William Godwin. They had struck up a friendship a couple of years earlier after Percy had written to him out of the blue. Percy was a huge fan of *Enquiry Concerning Political Justice*. He had daydreamed about one day meeting its author, although – as he later admitted – he had thought he was dead. How delighted he was to find out Godwin was alive. Percy's first letter was gushing. Godwin was 'a luminary too dazzling for the darkness which surrounds him'. Percy would later give Godwin a potted autobiography. To anchor him in society, he would tell him that his father was 'a man of fortune in Sussex'. In a longer version, he might add that this man was Sir Timothy Shelley, a baronet and MP. In an even longer version, he might tell Godwin that he was born on 4 August 1792, grew up at Field Place near Horsham and was the eldest of six children. Not that Godwin needed to know all that straight away.

For now, Percy stuck to the essentials: as a boy, he said, he enjoyed reading and studying. His favourite subject had been chemistry. He had also written two novels before he was 17: *St Irvine* and *Zastrozzi* (he was actually 17 and 18 at the time). Guessing correctly that Godwin was interested in education, he told him about his time at Eton, where he was, unfortunately, thrown out twice, and Oxford, where, he had to admit, he 'could not descend to common life' and was sent down, the Oxonian term for expelled. He had published a pamphlet that questioned, if not rejected, the existence of God. In *The Necessity of Atheism* (1811), Percy argued that there was little empirical evidence for religion and promoted a worldview based on reason and science. That had to be right, Percy might later say to Godwin. Wouldn't he agree? Godwin may have been particularly keen to correspond with Percy after Percy had given details of the 'fortune' he had mentioned at the start. Percy was heir to an estate of £6,000 a year. At some point, Godwin hinted he could do with a little money. Percy said he was happy to oblige. Over the next few months, Percy invited Godwin and his family to a farmhouse in Nantgwyllt, south Wales, where he was staying with his wife Harriet Westbrook, and later to a cottage in Lynmouth, Devon. Godwin declined both offers, although he would return the invitations by having Percy and Harriet over to his house. They would soon become frequent visitors. Godwin found Harriet delightful, even if she wasn't intellectual like his friends.

So it was nothing out of the ordinary for Mary to one day find Percy Shelley in the front room. She thought she had met him before, just briefly in November 1812, when she was home the first time from Scotland. She had only been back a couple of months from her second and final stay up there and was wearing a tartan dress. Godwin was out. Percy was with his friend Thomas Jefferson Hogg. The door was ajar. Mary and Percy spotted each other through the gap. Percy had been longing to meet Mary properly. She was, after all, the daughter of Godwin, Percy's hero, and his brilliant first wife, Mary Wollstonecraft – the writer who was actually dead. When Percy saw her, he was instantly enchanted. How beautiful she was with her pale skin and her reddish-gold hair. Mary was instantly attracted to Percy, too. She liked his wild curly brown hair and his large blue eyes. He was charming.

As they got to know each other, they found they had lots in common. For a start, they had both clashed with a parent. Mary had a difficult relationship with her stepmother, Mary Jane. Percy had a difficult relationship with his father, who had threatened to cut him off from his inheritance after his behaviour at Oxford. It would be a shame, Percy might have thought, if that happened, but a man must have principles. Like Mary, Percy was strong-willed and a freethinker. Mary had just spent nearly two years in a country that glorified rebellion. A couple of years before, Percy had gone to Dublin and distributed his own political pamphlets supporting Irish independence and calling for Catholic emancipation.

When it came to Percy's personal life, his free-thinking approach might have occasionally gone a little far. It was perturbing, some might have said, that he was going after Mary when he was married. He also had a child, Ianthe. Another was on the way. But if Mary heard this alarm bell, Percy was quick to silence it. His relationship with Harriet, he might tell her, was over. He left his wife six months ago. And anyway, Mary must understand that no one should feel tied to anyone for the rest of their life. It was absurd to promise that you would love the same person forever. Percy thought you should go wherever your passion took you. 'Love', he had written in his notes to his poem *Queen Mab*, 'is free'. There was nothing for Mary to worry about.

Mary and Percy saw each other frequently over the coming months. Percy now had an extra reason to dine with Godwin and would find further reasons to pop into the family bookshop. Mary and Percy went on dates, usually chaperoned by Jane (needs must). One of their favourite spots was St Pancras Old Churchyard, where Mary's mother was buried. Her graveside was the perfect spot for reading aloud from her books and discussing big questions such as whether there was life after death. It was here that Mary and Percy declared their love for each other. William Godwin might have been glad at first that his daughter was taking an interest in his guests. She had matured from her earlier years when she would spend days locked in petty battles with Mary Jane. He soon realized his mistake. Mary and Percy weren't just interested in each other's ideas. They were interested in each other. In early July, Mary and Percy told Godwin they wanted to be together for good.

Godwin panicked. Percy was 21. Mary was just 16. Perhaps he wasn't ready to let her go. It didn't help that Percy was married with a child and another on the way. If the news got out that Mary had started a relationship with a married man, there would be a terrible scandal. Godwin tried to separate the young lovers, telling Percy he was no longer welcome at Skinner Street and forbidding Mary from writing or speaking to him. He urged Percy to get back with Harriet. Mary and Percy, however, wouldn't give up that easily and sent letters to each other full of longing. Jane found she could be useful as their go-between. Percy sent Mary a couple of books she might enjoy, too. One was *A Refutation of Deism*, which he had published anonymously earlier that year. This copy had Mary's name on its binding. The other was his poem *Queen Mab*. It was originally dedicated to Harriet. Now he dedicated it to her.

But the printed word had its limitations. One afternoon at the end of July when Godwin was out, Percy rushed into the house and galloped up the stairs to find Mary. Mary Jane found him brandishing a pistol and thrusting a bottle of laudanum at her stepdaughter. If they can't be together in this life, he said, at least they can be together in death. What a scene. It was too much, even for Mary, who liked the idea of epic romances and agreed with Percy – in theory. All she could do now was to promise herself to him. Eventually, Percy went home. A week later, Percy, in despair, swallowed a large dose of laudanum. His landlord told Godwin and Mary Jane, who visited him, perhaps because they were caring people, perhaps out of guilt. Maybe Percy really did believe he couldn't live without Mary. Mary Jane looked after Percy until he felt better, but she wouldn't change her mind. Mary Jane and Godwin agreed that the ban on Mary and Percy seeing each other must remain. They had to stay apart.

On 28 July 1814, in the dead of night, Percy waited outside Skinner Street in a carriage. At 4am, Mary threw some clothes into a bag and crept into Godwin's study to leave a note. She then tiptoed out the house. Jane was in convoy. They both wore black silk gowns. The three headed to Dover, where they climbed into a fisherman's boat bound for Calais. What an adventure. But they were not safe. Mary Jane was in pursuit, catching up with them in France, where she tried to convince Jane, now calling herself Claire, to come home. Percy persuaded her to stay. Mary Jane, angry and upset, blamed Mary for leading her daughter astray. She always knew Mary was trouble. Mary's punishment was yet to come. Over the summer, the three travelled across France and Switzerland by carriage, by donkey and on foot. Mary and Percy read *Letters Written in Sweden, Norway and Denmark* by Mary Wollstonecraft, as well as her novel, *Mary, a Fiction*. They also wrote a joint journal that they would publish with some letters from a trip two years later as a travelogue, *History of a Six*

Weeks' Tour. Six weeks, it turned out, was all they could afford. They had to return home. The cheapest route was by boat along the Rhine. A stop near Darmstadt in Germany might have inspired Mary when she started to write her novel. She might have been intrigued about the alchemist who once lived in the castle in the distance, Burg Frankenstein.

But writing a novel seemed a long way off for Mary right now. First, she had to adjust to being back home. The first hurdle had come when Percy revealed he couldn't afford their return passage. He promised he would pay when they docked. In England, he tried to get money out of his account, only to find that Harriet had emptied it. Mary tried to borrow money from childhood friends, but they refused. Percy resorted to a loan. It wasn't the money, though, that bothered Mary. She was used to her parents scrabbling around for cash. It was the reaction from people she thought cared about her. Her friends weren't the only ones to shun her. It seemed as if everyone was now ignoring her, including her father.

In the initial days after Mary eloped, Godwin believed it wouldn't last. He anticipated her imminent return, expecting her to seek forgiveness and support. Yet Mary had stayed away for six weeks. When she did return that September, she and Percy were still an item. Now their relationship really would bring them into disgrace. It wasn't just Mary's reputation that was at stake; it was also that of her family. Once Godwin might not have minded what other people thought – he had been perfectly willing to publish *Political Justice*, which was seen as a radical work, as well as the shockingly candid memoir about his first wife. Now he saw things differently. He was older and more settled, and knew that you could never really shake off a scandal. Mixed in with his concerns, Godwin may have also felt disappointed in Mary for choosing Percy over him. Perhaps he felt betrayed by her when she eloped and helpless that he hadn't been able to make her see sense. Perhaps Godwin was lonely without her but had no idea how to express it. We should allow the possibility that Godwin was looking out for Mary's wellbeing, too. Was his daughter really happy with Percy? Did she understand the consequences of giving her life to another person? What would happen if she got pregnant? If Percy could leave his wife after just three years, Godwin might have thought, what would stop him leaving Mary? Perhaps he disapproved of Percy for the way he had treated his wife. Once Godwin would have agreed with Percy's doctrine of free love – it was an idea Percy had got from Godwin in *Political Justice* – but he had since softened his stance. He now believed that society would benefit from holding on to institutions like marriage until there had been more discussion about it. Marriage wasn't always restrictive and confining, not if it were based on mutual affection and respect. He had seen that himself. Percy's disregard for marriage showed a lack of maturity and a worrying lack of respect for relationships that could backfire on his daughter.

Whether or not a scandal was justified, Godwin quickly suffered the consequences. Mary's decision to elope made people think badly of him. He was cancelled. People blamed him for Percy's decision to abandon his wife and accused him of being complicit in the elopement. Some believed he had sold Mary to Percy. Godwin was said to have received £800. It was outrageous to suppose that a daughter could be bought, he might have thought, even if he would have liked the money. Now he needed to decide what to do. Godwin might have been comfortable sparking a philosophical or political argument, but when he came to human conflict, he was avoidant. He had no idea how to handle emotions. Instead of confronting Mary and giving them a chance to sort out their differences, he blocked her out of his life entirely. Mary Jane was quickly on board. When Mary arrived on the doorstep of Skinner Street, she was turned away. When Godwin saw Mary in the street, he ignored her. When Mary's siblings asked if they could see her, they were given a firm no. Mary wrote to Godwin to explain her reasons for staying with Percy and eloping. She tried to make amends. But Godwin refused to back down. He found Mary's letter cold and insensitive. He wouldn't discuss it. In January 1816, nearly a year and a half after Mary had left home, she had a son. She named him William after her father. Still, he wouldn't break his silence.

When Mary got together with Percy, she felt she had finally found someone who understood her, who accepted her, who wanted her, who would care for her. For so long, she had felt that she didn't fit in with her own family. She missed the mother she never knew. She thought her stepmother preferred her siblings. She felt her father, who had once doted on her as the child of his first great love, had grown distant. For a brief time, her despair and loneliness lifted. Then, within weeks, Godwin had tried to split them up. She had no choice, she might have thought, but to elope with Percy. She would do whatever it took to have a chance at happiness. Now she was beginning to realize that the happiness she had found with Percy came at a price. The price was losing her father.

If Mary felt she had been abandoned by one parent, she now felt she had been rejected by the other. Worse, she had been rejected for a reason she didn't fully understand. It made the separation especially painful and destabilizing. When she talked to Percy, she blamed Mary Jane. Her stepmother had influenced her father, said Mary. If it hadn't been for her, they might still be talking. But was this really what Mary believed? Her father had a mind of his own. He wasn't blameless. When Mary started *Frankenstein*, she hadn't spoken to Godwin for two years. The longer they were estranged, the more Mary might have thought about him, wishing he were part of her life. We've seen how Mary might have identified with the creature. Being estranged from her father exacerbated her feelings of loneliness and rejection. She was upset and angry with him. Perhaps, on one level, Mary saw Godwin in the role of Victor. Godwin might not have run from her at birth like Victor ran from the creature, but he had deserted her now. 'He had abandoned me,' the creature cries, 'and, in the bitterness of my heart, I cursed him.' Did Mary also 'curse' Godwin? Like the creature, she at times sounds bitter, resentful and hurt. For much of the novel, Victor tries to ignore the creature and his actions; he wished the creature didn't exist. Godwin might not have wished the same of Mary – he loved her in his own way – but after she returned from eloping with Percy, he also ignored her and showed her a similar disdain. Godwin and Victor also both try to block a romantic relationship – and in one case, succeed. Godwin had tried to stop Mary seeing Percy. Victor started making and then destroyed the creature's female companion. 'Never will I create another like yourself,' Victor tells him. Victor's treatment of the creature has horrific consequences – the creature goes on a murderous rampage. Mary felt the sting of her father pushing her away right from the early days of her relationship with Percy. How much greater that pain would become as the months rolled on. At least she resisted a murderous rampage of her own. Mary had another way to deal with her pain, a law-abiding one: she would write a novel about it.

Starting a Family

1814–1816

Percy and Mary spent much of the autumn of 1814 apart. Percy was in hiding from bailiffs. He feared he would be imprisoned for debt. To stop Percy being caught, they kept their mid-week meet-ups brief. On Sundays, when debtors were spared jail, they could be a little freer. One Sunday, wrote Mary, was 'devoted to Love in idleness'. But snatches of time were not enough. She told Percy she felt like 'a poor widowed deserted thing no one cares for'. The pile-up of adjectives shows her extreme state of mind. She was lonely, horribly so. It didn't help that Percy was writing long letters to her stepsister Claire (once called Jane) and short ones to her. She blamed Claire mostly. Claire had always been manipulative and an attention-seeker. But it would be understandable if she was also a little annoyed with Percy. Like her father, Fanny and so many of her friends, he seemed to be abandoning her, too.

That summer, Mary had become pregnant. She might have felt joy and anxiety at the news in conflicting measure. On the upside, she was building a life with Percy. On the downside, she would have to face childbirth. She had good reason to fear it: her mother had died giving birth to her. Motherhood might have seemed both precious and precarious. She might have feared more than just her own death. Mary was a worrier. She may well have been anxious about her capabilities as a parent. Would she really be able to bring new life into the world? What would she be like as a mother? What if she didn't love her child? Would she abandon or reject them? As the weeks went on, Mary could have done with Percy's support. But Percy had another woman and her child to attend to. That November, Harriet, Percy's wife, had a son. Percy had an heir. He was delighted. Mary less so. It 'ought to be ushered in with [the] ringing of bells,' she scrawled bitterly in her journal, 'for it is the son of his wife'. Percy and Harriet would call their child Charles. Mary was not having much fun carrying Percy's next child. She recorded that on Christmas Day she had 'a very bad side ache'. Over the coming weeks, she would feel frequently unwell.

Early in the new year, Sir Bysshe Shelley, Percy's grandfather, died. It would be Claire who went with Percy to the reading of the will. They stayed overnight at an inn. We don't know what, if anything, happened between them – someone has ripped out pages from Claire and Mary's diaries from the time – but we can imagine what Mary might have been thinking. Were they having an affair? Even if their relationship was platonic, Mary was excluded from it. Percy had betrayed her by prioritizing a relationship with another woman. An affair, whether physical or emotional, might have stung on another level, too. Now Mary knew how her mother felt when her lover, Gilbert Imlay, had left her and pursued other women. An empath, Mary might have felt compounded pain.

Percy had tried to help, she must admit, in his own way. He had been suggesting for months that she sleep with his friend Thomas Jefferson Hogg. Mary liked Hogg and, in January, sent him a lock of her hair, but that was as far as she wanted their relationship to go. She was devoted, hopelessly so, to Percy. How it must have pained Hogg when she told him she loved Percy 'so tenderly & entirely'. How he must have wished he was in Percy's place. '[My] life hangs on the beam of his eye and [my] whole soul is entirely wrapt up in him,' Mary cried. Mary may have been especially hurt by Percy's desertion because it triggered abandonment issues from the death of her mother and rejection trauma from the cold behaviour of her father. Percy was also Mary's first great love. She had thought she had found someone who loved her for who she was. Mary had idealized Percy and had thought the floaty feeling of being in love would last forever. The realization that their relationship had changed was a huge letdown. It couldn't have come at a worse time.

On February 22, Mary gave birth. Mary and Percy called their daughter Clara. Percy recorded the birth in their joint journal. The baby had been eight weeks premature. Mary endured 'very few addit[I]onal pains' during labour, he said, adding that 'All is well'. All might have been well with 'Maie' (Percy's pet name for Mary), but there was another life in the room now. 'The child is not quite seven months,' said Percy. 'The child [is] not expected to live.' The following day, he reported that the child was 'unexpectedly alive' but probably not for long. Over the next week or so, the baby showed 'favourable symptoms'. Then, on March 6, there was heartbreaking news. 'Find my baby dead,' Mary wrote simply in her diary. 'A miserable day.' For comfort, Mary turned to Hogg because he was 'so calm a creature & Shelley is afraid of a fever from the milk'. She was distraught. 'I am no longer a mother now,' she said to him. Mary's entries in her journal over the next few days slip from upsetting to disturbing. 'Still think about my baby,' she wrote plainly, "tis hard indeed for a mother to lose a child.' Clara had lived for just thirteen days.

Mary was haunted by Clara's death. She would have known that lots of children at the time never made it to adulthood: about one in three died before their fifth birthday. But that wouldn't have made it any easier. She had been given so little time with her child – just two days more than her mother had been able to spend with her. Mary may well have felt inadequate. Had she been a better mother, a better person, she might have thought, her child would have lived. It might have seemed particularly cruel that Harriet and Percy now had two children and she had none. As a distraction, Mary turned to books and picked up Ovid's *Metamorphoses*. The epic poem traces the history of the world, starting with its creation or, as Mary might have seen it, its birth. It opens with the lines: '*In nova fert animus mutatas dicera formas / corpora*' or 'I intend to speak of forms changed into new entities.' As the verses go on, the persona speaks of humans turning into animals, plants and inanimate objects, and from one gender or colour to another. Birth, Mary might have thought, was all about change, from a foetus to a baby, from life in the private sphere of the womb to life in the public sphere of society. Birth was the change at the beginning of life. Life, as a state of being, would go on changing until the most dramatic change of all: death. Mary was going through a time of change, too: 'I was a mother and am so no longer,' she had written to Hogg. Now, as she started a new journal, she hoped her life would change again. Her first entry was a poignant one: 'I begin [the journal] with our regeneration.'

Except, as we know from the lasting impact on Mary of her mother's death, Mary found it hard to start completely afresh. How sad she still was after the loss of her child, how desperately she wished Clara was still alive. When she closed her eyes, her emotions may well have mixed with the idea of transformation she had been reading about in *Metamorphosis*. A week after Clara's death, she dreamed that her baby 'came to life again'. It had been 'cold' rather than 'dead', she wrote in her journal. Then she woke up to find her baby was dead after all. In this one episode, Mary's baby had gone, in Mary's mind, from being alive to dead to alive to dead. Mary would have a similar dream 'of the dead being alive' on the anniversary of her child's death, the following year.

She would also weave the idea, deliberately or not, into *Frankenstein*, where the dead – or at least a being made from dead body parts – comes alive in a terrifying form. Mary even tells us in her 1831 preface that her idea for the moment of the being's creation came to her in a dream. She tells us that she pictured Victor, 'the pale student of unhallowed arts', kneeling beside his 'lifeless creation', which then 'stir[s] with an uneasy, half vital motion'. It was not quite the dream she had after her baby had died, but it has odd parallels. It is like a reflection in a distorted hall of mirrors. The dream Mary had after her child's death revealed one of her deepest desires – that her dead baby would come alive. The dream Mary had when she came up with the idea for *Frankenstein* revealed one of her deepest fears – that a creation that is meant to be beautiful would turn out to be a monster. She could have been thinking of the next baby she might have. Or, given that Mary identified with aspects of the creature, she could have been thinking of her own birth as the catastrophe. Was her inner hideousness the reason her mother, her father, Percy and now her newborn child had left her? Giving birth and losing a child might have thrown up so many doubts about herself and so many worries.

For now, however, she had to get on with living after death, coping with the waves of grief anyone would feel. Within weeks, she had a distraction:

she was pregnant again. Percy took out loans to pay off his debts and things started to look up. In May 1815, Claire left for Lynmouth in Devon. At last, Mary and Percy had some time alone. From August that year to May 1816, they lived in a pretty red-brick cottage in Bishopsgate near Windsor. Mary's journal from the time has been lost, but we know that it was here that Percy wrote the poem *Alastor* and Mary would give birth again. On 24 January 1816, Mary and Percy had a son. They called him William or, more affectionately, Willmouse. Some of Mary's possible fears about having a child dissipated. Her baby lived. He was not a monster. She didn't want to kill him. It would be a couple of years before *Frankenstein* came out. Reading the story, we might question whether Mary's fears really disappeared. Victor's young brother is called William. He is also the creature's first victim. Was Mary articulating her infanticidal fears after all? Perhaps she still thought she would be an unfit mother.

A Sublime Landscape

1816

By the spring of 1816, Mary could at least relax about Percy going off with Claire if only because Claire had found someone else. Percy had written a few poems by then, *Alastor* among them. But his best – *Ozymadias* and *To a Skylark* – were yet to come. The poet of the day was Lord Byron, who had reached rock-star status with his first two cantos of *Childe Harold's Pilgrimage*, out a few years earlier. Byron was in London and between lovers. Lady Caroline Lamb, who had once had an affair with him, had called him 'mad, bad and dangerous to know'. He certainly attracted gossip. Many people thought he'd had an affair with his half-sister, Augusta Leigh. He might have had a child with her, too. The litany of sexual scandals continued. That year, his wife, Annabella Millbanke, who had fallen victim to his violent temper, had filed for separation. How tame Percy seemed to Claire now. Byron was a much better catch. She set out to get him. Byron agreed to go on a few dates with her, but something was lost in translation. Byron wanted a fling. Claire wanted a relationship.

It didn't really matter, thought Byron. He would soon be out of the country. Rumours about his love life had been piling up – as had his debts. He would let it all blow over by spending the summer abroad. Geneva would do. He would have to break up with Claire. Never mind. Except Claire did not see it quite like that. He could go on before her if he liked, she said, but she would be close behind. She would persuade Mary and Percy to come, too. Byron left England at the end of April. That May, Mary, Percy, their 6-month-old son, William (he was still alive, despite Mary's fears), and Claire set off to meet him.

Mary and Percy were used to being shunned by society, but their association with Byron took their outsider status to a new level. They arrived in Geneva in time for the season but were excluded from suppers and dances. Newspapers described the group as a 'league of incest'. Their greetings were met with silence and their presence generated gossipy whispers. The atmosphere at their hotel felt so hostile that Percy moved them to a modest chalet. Maison Chapuis was beside Lake Geneva. Byron and his travelling companion and doctor John Polidori rented the Villa Diodati close by. Villa Diodati was a grand stucco house, where John Milton, the Renaissance poet, had stayed. It was a little way up a hill. From the back, you could see the Alps. From the front, Mount Jura and the lake. It even came with its own vineyard. Hotel guests huddled round a telescope on the other side of the lake to spy on the group. One day they spotted sheets of fabric drying on Byron's porch and giggled about them being ladies' petticoats. Sadly, for all concerned, they were boring old bedsheets. Now that Mary could spend time with Percy without the clutter of Claire, she might not have minded about this ostracization as much as she had in London. But the way people were treating them may still have hurt enough to seep into a story she was about to write. 'It is true, we shall be monsters, cut off from all the world,' the creature would later say to Victor in *Frankenstein* when he tries to persuade him to create a female companion, 'but on that account we shall be more attached to one another.' Did Mary think she and Percy, 'cut off from all the world', were also, in some way, 'monsters'? At least they would be 'more attached to one another' than they had been before.

The weather on their trip was terrible. It was, Mary recorded, 'a wet, ungenial summer' with 'incessant rain'. Today, we know the conditions were caused by a volcano. They didn't know that at the time. Mount Tambora on Sumbawa in Indonesia had erupted in April 1815, spewing out lava for a week. The red-hot flow killed all plants, all animals and almost all the people in its wake – more than 10,000 of them. About 100,000 more would die from famine and disease in the coming months. Huge clouds of ash and debris had been blasted into the sky, choking the air, and fine particles of it would stick around for months. The effect, combined with a bout of low solar radiation, made it feel much colder around the world for a good three years. In June 1816, it snowed in New York. In Europe, harvests repeatedly failed. In Switzerland, lakes froze over. People started calling 1816 'the year without a summer'. For days, Mary and Percy could do little but shelter inside. Mary would gaze in wonder out the window. The storms, she wrote to Fanny, were 'grander and more terrific than I have ever seen before'. One night, she said, 'the lake was lit up – the pines on Jura made visible', before 'a pitchy blackness succeeded'. Thunder 'came in frightful bursts over our heads'. A grand and terrific storm, described in a similar way, would later turn up in *Frankenstein*. 'Vivid flashes of lightning dazzled my eyes, illuminating the lake, making it appear like a vast sheet of fire,' Victor says, 'then for an instant everything seemed of a pitchy darkness.'

John Polidori, Byron's doctor, had planned to take notes about Byron while they were away, but he soon developed a crush on Mary and ended up taking notes about her instead. Keen to impress her, he decided to jump off the porch one day so that he could walk her up the rain-splattered path to the villa. Unfortunately, he would soon be the one who needed help to walk. He sprained his ankle in the leap and had to rest on the sofa for several days. The group humoured him by listening to him read out a play he had written about creation and human nature. It might later come to influence one of the group. Polidori also absorbed himself in notes from a lecture he had been to in London by the anatomist William Lawrence. Lawrence was a materialist and believed humans were made purely of bone, muscle and blood. There was no such thing as a soul, he said. He argued that life was not created by God. Polidori may well have been keen to share these ideas with Mary. What did she think? Did she agree?

Mary would begin *Frankenstein* that June. One dark and stormy night the group were sitting by the fire in Byron's drawing room reading ghost stories from *Fantasmagoriana,* a French translation of a German anthology. Byron thought they could do better and challenged them to write their own. Percy started a story based on his childhood but soon gave up. Byron churned out a tale about a vampire, which he would publish as *A Fragment*, alongside his narrative poem *Mazeppa*, the following summer. Polidori topped it by writing a novella he would call *The Vampyre*, which would inspire Bram Stoker's *Dracula* (1897). Mary trumped them all. 'I busied myself to think of a story,' she says in the 1831 preface to *Frankenstein*. 'One which would speak to the mysterious fears of our nature, and awaken thrilling horror.' Inspiration struck a day or so later while she was listening to Byron and Percy talk about scientific theories of spontaneous generation (the idea that living organisms could develop from nonliving matter) and galvanism (electricity produced from chemical action). They were discussing whether a corpse could be brought to life. Later, Mary had a vision of a young scientist doing exactly that and jotted down some ideas. To pass the time, the group continued to read and write. They also recited poems. *Christabel* by Samuel Taylor Coleridge, Mary's father's friend, was on their agenda.

But they couldn't stay inside forever. In July, Mary, Percy and Claire made a week-long visit to the Alps. The destination had become popular with holidaymakers after the Napoleonic Wars had ended the year before. Coleridge had written about it in his poem *Hymn before Sunrise, in the Vale of Chamouni*. The region seemed like another world to Mary and Percy, one that was strange, dangerous and spellbinding. It offered a Romantic vision. It was 'sublime', as Edmund Burke, the philosopher, might have put it, evoking awe and terror in anyone who looked on. In a letter to his friend Thomas Love Peacock, Percy talked of 'intolerably bright' peaks of snow, 'precipices of ice of a dazzling splendour' and a ravine 'so deep that the very roaring of the untameable Arve, which rolled through it, could not be heard above'. Sitting on a rock, Mary and Percy watched ice breaking free from the Mer de Glace, a huge glacier on the northern slopes. Percy recorded how it rushed with 'a loud dull noise' into the vale. The glacier was on the move. The ice turned to powder, which sped and whirled over the rocks like a waterfall. For Mary, it was 'the most desolate place in the world'; one she would later describe as 'a world of ice'. In a similar way to Percy, she saw the summits as 'sharp and naked pinnacles', the lines of the snowy mountains puncturing the clouds 'like things not belonging to this earth'. Mont Blanc seemed like 'a vast animal' with 'frozen blood for ever circulat[ing] through his stony veins'. Together, Mary and Percy hiked through the landscape, writing whenever they could. They captured their thoughts in their joint travelogue, *History of a Six Weeks' Tour*, which combined their 1814 and 1816 trip, and would come out a year later. Percy would be inspired to write the poem *Mont Blanc*: 'Mont Blanc gleams on high: – the power is there.' Mary would channel some of her ideas into *Frankenstein*. Mary also plunges her characters, the creature especially, into the cold. How often we find him on the top of a mountain, in a cave or in the icy Arctic Ocean.

Mary would make the Mer de Glace the backdrop to one of the pivotal scenes in the book. After the creature murders Victor's brother, William, Victor hunts him down. They clash at the glacier. It is the first time Victor and the creature have encountered each other since the 'dreary night of November' when Victor brought the creature to life. The creature tells Victor how he has suffered rejection, blaming Victor for abandoning him and begging him to make him a female companion. Victor's decision will influence the rest of the story. To some, it might seem like a landscape fraught with peril. Yet that isn't the view of Mary's two main characters. The creature is able to cross it with 'superhuman speed' and although Victor describes the ice as 'like the waves of a troubled sea', the view of the glacier doesn't scare him. Instead, it makes him feel 'a sublime ecstasy', an emotion Mary and Percy might have once felt.

Mary, Percy and Claire returned home that September. The trip had been a happy one. When Mary visited the Alps again, she would recall Percy's 'delight… at seeing these wondrous piles of earth's primaeval [sic] matter'. But that wouldn't be for another seven years, after Percy had died. Now, back in England, she was about to lose another person in her life.

An Unfortunate Birth

1816

In September 1816, Mary, Percy and Claire settled in Bath. Claire was pregnant with Byron's child. Mary and Percy had promised they would look after her and keep the news hidden from friends in London. The scandal that Claire was having Byron's illegitimate child was not what they needed right now. Thankfully, their son, William, was thriving. 'We are all now at Bath, well and content,' Percy told Byron in a letter towards the end of the month. 'Claire is writing to you at this instant. Mary is reading over the fire; our cat and kitten are sleeping under the sofa; and little Willy is [*sic*] just gone to sleep.' Little says contentment as much as a sleeping kitten.

But little in life is perfect. Mary and Percy were having to live their life around Claire because Byron refused to support her. Percy still needed money. Mary's father was not speaking to them. There were also murmurs that Fanny, Mary's half-sister, was in low spirits. Fanny was Mary's only connection to the Godwin household. She had been writing to Mary and visiting her, despite Godwin's order that she cut off all contact with her. Godwin and Mary Jane would have been furious with Fanny had they found out, but she needed them. Fanny didn't have many people in her life. Her letters to Mary were becoming increasingly glum. At the end of September, Fanny had revealed that their aunts, Everina and Eliza, had sailed back to Dublin without her. Fanny had been hoping to join them and find work in Ireland as a teacher. Everina and Eliza worried that her association with Mary and Percy would harm their reputation. In another letter, Fanny criticized Percy for not lending Godwin money. Fanny still lived with Godwin. She depended on him. If Godwin was strapped for cash, then that would affect her, even if it was just because he was in a bad mood. Mary's comments in her journal around this time suggest she had little sympathy for Fanny. She described the letter she receives from her in early October as 'stupid'.

* * *

Fanny had never been the sister Mary wanted. She had always been a bit timid. They shared a mother, but not a father. Fanny had been born on 14 May 1794 to Mary Wollstonecraft and Gilbert Imlay, an American businessman. She was illegitimate. She had been a happy toddler. Her parents had lived together on and off before separating, but Wollstonecraft had loved being a mother and Godwin, her mother's next partner, had treated Fanny as his own. When Fanny was three, her mother and Godwin, now her mother's husband, had a daughter, Mary. Her mother soon died of complications from the birth, but Godwin had done his best to care for her. He had adopted Fanny and, when she was old enough to understand, told her about her real parents. But Fanny always felt she came second in Godwin's affections to Mary, his biological daughter. She didn't know for sure, but she had a hunch. She was right. Mary, Godwin had once said, was 'quick' and 'pretty', while Fanny was 'slow' and 'prone to indolence'. Fanny did have positive qualities. She was 'of a quiet, modest, unshowy disposition', while Mary was 'singularly bold [and] somewhat imperious'. But Godwin didn't mind Mary being a little bold. He preferred that to shyness. Comparing them, he had written: 'My own daughter [Mary] is considerably superior in capacity to the one her mother had before [Fanny].' Fanny could never compete with Mary. Mary's father was William Godwin, a great author and thinker. Her father had been Gilbert Imlay, an American gadabout. No wonder she felt inferior.

When Godwin moved in with Mary Jane Clairmont, Fanny had struggled to fit in. As the only child with neither biological parent alive, she had been terrified of being a burden. Fanny was also now the eldest of four children. She carried a burden, too. She may well have felt she had to be responsible and stay out of trouble. Even if she had wanted to pair up with Mary, she couldn't. Jane, her new stepsister, was nearer Mary's age, loud and outgoing. Fanny felt left out, withdrawing into herself and growing melancholy and depressed. As they grew up, Mary continued to overlook her. Fanny felt invisible. It was Jane, later known as Claire, who would accompany Mary when she eloped to the Continent in the summer of 1814. Fanny had been packed off to Wales. Ever since they returned, Mary and Claire had been inseparable. Unlike Mary, Fanny didn't have a poet to sweep her off her feet. She was stuck at home. Fanny had found it really hard when Godwin and Mary Jane had forbidden her from seeing Mary and Percy. She felt alone. She visited them a few times in secret, but she had felt like an outsider. She felt awkward when she was around them. Mary also didn't seem to appreciate the risk she was taking to come over. Mary and Percy hadn't worried about their reputation when they eloped together and they questioned why she should be concerned about hers. They thought Fanny was weak. Some, like Godwin, thought she was in love with Percy and wanted to live with them. The poem Percy would write a few months after her death, *On Fanny Godwin*, leaves room for the possibility that she had asked to join them and he'd said no. Certain lines may allude to Percy and Fanny's last meeting. 'Her voice did quiver as we parted,' says the poem's persona, 'Yet knew I not that heart was broken / From which it came.'

Whatever they talked about in that final exchange, Fanny was not happy. She had not established a network of friends. She was not married. She was dependent on her stepfather, emotionally and financially, and it's not as if he had finances to spare. Mary didn't seem to care. On 8 October 1816, Fanny left Skinner Street and headed for Swansea. At a stopover in Bristol, she sent two goodbye letters: a 'very alarming' letter to Mary, now lost, and a letter to Godwin, saying she wished to 'depart immediately to the spot from which I hope never to remove'. Scared that Fanny might commit suicide, Godwin and Percy set off to look for her. It was too late. By the time Percy arrived in Swansea on 11 October, Fanny was dead. In *The Cambrian*, a local paper, he read that the body of a young woman of Fanny's description had been discovered in the Mackworth Arms. She had been wearing stays, a stiff laced bodice, embroidered with her mother's initials, and a gold Swiss watch Mary had bought her in Geneva that summer, and had overdosed on laudanum. Her suicide note talked of her 'unfortunate' birth and a life that had been 'a series of pain' to those close to her. In a plea full of self-loathing and desperation, Fanny wished anyone who knew her 'the blessing of forgetting that such a creature ever existed'.

Mary and Percy were devastated. It was 'a miserable day', Mary scribbled in her diary when she heard the news, too overwhelmed to write anything else. If there was one glimmer of hope it was that Godwin broke his silence and spoke to her. Perhaps he realized that with Fanny's death he had lost a link to his first wife. Perhaps he didn't want to lose another. Mary and Godwin would reunite in their shared grief. On 13 October 1815, Godwin wrote to Mary about Fanny's death. It had been the first letter he had written to her since she eloped with Percy two and a half years earlier. At first, Godwin was stoic. He thanked Mary for her 'strong expressions of sympathy' but added that he couldn't see it would help. By the following paragraph, he had softened: 'I said that your sympathy could be of no service to me, but I retract the assertion,' he said, 'it may be of infinite service.' Godwin may have thought it was the right thing to do to keep the manner of Fanny's death quiet. In *Political Justice*, he had defended suicide – he argued that it could be a rational decision – but society had yet to catch up. Suicide was illegal and his family had endured scandal enough. He didn't want Fanny's death to attract attention. Godwin arranged for Fanny to be buried in an unmarked grave and told people she had died of a fever on the way to see her aunts in Dublin.

The effect of hushing up Fanny's death would deeply affect Mary. If she couldn't talk about it, she might have wanted or needed to process her emotions and thoughts in another way. When Fanny died, she had been working on the ghost story she had written that summer at Byron's villa. As she worked through her grief, she continued to expand it. We've seen how Mary channelled some of her own feelings of being abandoned (by her mother) and then rejected and neglected (by her father) into the creature. Fanny's death may well have stirred up these feelings – Fanny had also left her. On a more generous reading, she might have also started to see Fanny's plight from her perspective. Fanny had felt abandoned by Mary. Maybe Fanny had thought that Mary had everything – from love to a future. As we know, that's not how Mary saw it: like Fanny, she was lonely, too. Mary might have empathized with her. She might have begun to realize how much these feelings – of abandonment, of rejection, of loneliness – can affect others as well. Fanny had felt so desperate that she would commit suicide. The creature would feel so desperate that he would kill other people.

The way Fanny had died may have also shaken Mary. Her mother, their mother, had tried to commit suicide in the same way by taking laudanum. Wollstonecraft's attempt, which was unsuccessful, seemed to foreshadow Fanny's fate. For Mary, the link, eerie and uncomfortable as it was, may well have stirred up feelings about her mother, particularly how much she missed her – not that she needed much of an excuse for that. Did Fanny's death trigger fears about loved ones leaving her? Did Wollstonecraft's suicide attempt give Fanny's death extra emotional force? Perhaps it made Mary think that suicide ran in the family. Percy had suggested suicide when her father had first separated them. Would she ever be afflicted by the desire to take her own life? Would her loneliness ever grow so unbearable that suicide would seem like the only option?

Suicide certainly seems to be on Mary's mind when she was writing *Frankenstein*. At times, both Victor and the creature are less than overjoyed at being alive. Lonely and rejected, the creature becomes thoroughly miserable. 'Did I request thee, Maker, from my clay / To mould me man?' he says to Victor, quoting Adam in Milton's *Paradise Lost*. 'Did I solicit thee / From darkness to promote me?' Life seems to be a burden to him. It is something he must endure. Victor feels trapped by the burden of living, too. After finding the corpse of his friend Henry Clerval, he falls ill for months and wakes up in a prison. 'I was overcome by gloom and misery, and often reflected I had better seek death than remain miserably pent up only to be let loose in a world replete with wretchedness,' he says. He feels 'doomed to live'.

Mary would be hit by waves of grief for the rest of the year. In December, she wrote to Percy to tell him that she had found a new home for them near Marlow in Buckinghamshire. She wished that Fanny was still alive so that the house could have been 'a proper assylum [sic] for her'. She felt guilty for not offering Fanny more support and providing her with a refuge. She felt 'so much agitated'. She may well have wanted to talk about it with Percy. That winter there would be other emotional challenges, too. Fanny's suicide wouldn't be the only one weighing on Mary's mind.

A Rash and Unfortunate Union

1816

Mary was still processing her grief over Fanny when she heard that Harriet, Percy's wife, had taken her own life. It was mid-December 1816. Harriet had also been thoroughly miserable. Percy, her first great love, had left her. She was a single mother. She had no career to distract or validate her. It was the nineteenth century. As a woman, her prospects were low. Life must have seemed daunting and overwhelming.

* * *

Despite her relatively comfortable start in life, Harriet had never been especially happy. She had been born on 1 August 1795 to John Westbrook, the owner of a popular coffeehouse in Mayfair, and a woman called Ann Elliott. Her father had high hopes for her and sent her to boarding school in Surrey. Harriet hated it. She didn't like her authoritarian father very much either. Teenage Harriet did all she could to manifest an escape from school until eventually one appeared. One chilly day in January 1811, 15-year-old Harriet met Percy, the brother of a couple of her school friends. Percy was 18 and good-looking. He had just been sent down from Oxford for writing a pamphlet promoting atheism. Like Harriet, he also didn't get on with his father, another domineering type. Percy thought Harriet was very pretty. She had light-brown hair, clear skin and a pleasant voice. Maybe, he ventured, he could help her run away from school. At last, Harriet thought, someone to rescue me. When would it happen? Harriet wrote to Percy threatening suicide if she had to stay at school a minute longer. Percy had a solution: they should get married. That August, Percy and Harriet eloped to Scotland. It was a typical Percy gesture. It was grand and romantic. It was also rash and ill-considered. 'If I know anything about love, I am not in love,' he had written to his friend Thomas Jefferson Hogg. Some people like Harriet, it turned out, thought differently. Harriet believed in lasting love. Marriage, she believed, was for life.

After the wedding, Percy and Harriet spent a few happy weeks in Edinburgh, before joining Hogg in York, where Hogg was interning with a solicitor. Within weeks, Percy left Harriet with Hogg while he visited his father. Sir Timothy had stopped his allowance – he hadn't approved of his son running off with a teenager. Percy wanted to sort things out. Harriet felt abandoned. She'd had a sheltered upbringing and wasn't comfortable exploring a new city on her own. During the day, she read, waiting for Hogg to come home from work. Without Percy, she was depressed. Again, she talked of suicide. Hogg suggested he cheer her up by having an affair with her. Alarmed, Harriet sent for her sister, Eliza. Eliza would protect her.

Eliza often accompanied Percy and Harriet even after they left Hogg in York. They went to Ireland, where Percy helped organize protests against British rule and then Wales. In June 1813, Harriet gave birth to their daughter, Eliza Ianthe, known by her middle name. But instead of bringing them closer, parenthood deepened the cracks in their marriage. Harriet struggled with breastfeeding and money was a constant worry. Percy felt frustrated and trapped. He hadn't enjoyed the influence in politics he would have liked – Ireland wouldn't gain independence from Britain for another 100 years – and he felt a lack of passion for Harriet. His marriage, he would tell Hogg, was 'a rash and heartless union'. Percy built up his support network, spending time with Thomas Turner, a lawyer and banker, his wife Cornelia and her mother, Mrs Boinville. By the end of the year, Percy and Harriet were spending longer and longer apart. In February 1814, Percy moved in with the Boinvilles. Percy and Harriet had an odd relationship. They were no longer living together, but they had yet to officially split up. In March, when questions arose over the validity of their marriage in Scotland, they decided to give it one last shot and married again in London. Perhaps Percy felt he should do the decent thing by Harriet. Perhaps he just wanted to legitimize their child. The following month, Percy and Harriet tried to live together again but were both unhappy. And so, when Percy and Hogg visited William Godwin that spring, Percy was primed to fall in love. Mary seemed perfect. Percy agonized for a bit, but there wasn't much of a decision. He knew which one to choose. After Percy and Harriet separated, Harriet returned to live with her father. Soon she would find out that she was pregnant with Percy's second child. She pleaded for Percy to come back, but it was too late. Percy had moved on.

Except he hadn't. Early on in Percy's relationship with Mary, he suggested to Harriet that they all live together in Switzerland. Percy had convinced himself that his connection with Harriet was never one of passion. It had always been one of friendship. Now, he said, he was 'more than a friend… far more – Brother, Father of your child'. In Harriet's eyes, Percy was deluded. How could he expect to have them both? For weeks, Harriet tried to convince herself that Percy's love for Mary was a phase, an infatuation. When Percy returned from his trip to Switzerland, he went straight to her – albeit for money. Percy would soon see, Harriet thought, that he was meant to be with her after all. But as the weeks turned into months, Harriet realized that she had been abandoned – and Percy had no idea he had done anything wrong. 'My attachment to Mary neither could nor ought to have been overcome,' he wrote to her in September 1814. 'Our spirits and [blank] are united. We met with passion, she has resigned all for me.'

That November Harriet had a son, giving Percy an heir. How happy he seemed. Perhaps Percy wasn't to blame for the breakdown in their relationship after all. Perhaps it was Mary. 'Mary was determined to secure him,' Harriet wrote to a friend. 'She heated his imagination by talking of her mother.' So really, it was Mary Wollstonecraft's fault. Harriet felt helpless. For the next two years, she remained at the family home in Belgravia, receiving missives from Percy usually when he wanted money. By the spring of 1816, Harriet was pregnant again. We don't know the father, but we do know that they weren't together. In the autumn, she would leave home and rent rooms in Knightsbridge under the name Harriet Smith. She told her landlady she was married and her husband was abroad. On 9 November, Harriet walked out of her lodgings for the last time. She left behind a note to Percy wishing him 'that happiness which you have deprived me of'. It would be another month before Harriet's body would be discovered.

It was early morning on 10 December when an elderly man going for a stroll in Hyde Park spotted something unusual floating in the Serpentine. A few days later, a short news story appeared in *The Times*, noting that 'a respectable female, far advanced in pregnancy' had been found in the river. 'A want of honour in her own conduct is supposed to have led to this fatal catastrophe,' added the reporter. Worried about the shame that suicide would bring on their family, the Westbrooks swiftly buried Harriet's body. Mary and Percy heard about Harriet's death ten days before Christmas in a letter from Percy's friend, Thomas Hookham. Mary was still grieving Fanny's death. Mary wouldn't grieve Harriet's in the same way. Harriet was her partner's ex. She was barely a friend, let alone a confidante. And yet Mary was the sensitive type. The death of anyone in her circle was likely to knock her a little. Mary might have also felt partly responsible for Harriet's misery. Had Percy not fallen for her, he might have made things work with Harriet and she could have been happy. One line in Harriet's suicide note was especially poignant. 'If you had never left me,' Harriet writes of Percy, 'I might have lived.' Ouch. Mary would have also known from press reports that Harriet had been pregnant. Harriet's suicide had resulted in the loss of two lives – her own and that of her unborn child. Once again, new life mingled uncomfortably with death. Perhaps Mary had started to understand Harriet's feelings a bit more, too. In the two years she had been with Percy, she had also begun to feel like an outsider in their relationship. How close Mary might have felt at times to wanting to escape like Fanny and now Harriet.

We have seen how Fanny's laudanum overdose may have stirred up feelings for Mary about her mother, who had tried to take her own life in a similar way. Wollstonecraft would try to commit suicide again a few months later – this time, by drowning. Mary had now witnessed two suicides within months of each other: Fanny's, then Harriet's, the methods echoing her mother's attempts. Did Mary spot the parallel? Did Harriet's death stir up feelings about her mother and half-sister again? Mary may well have wanted to talk through her feelings with someone close to her. Percy would seem the obvious choice – and yet he had his own agenda. A few days after they heard about Harriet's death, Percy wrote to Mary trying to absolve them of responsibility. He blamed Harriet's lifestyle. He suggested she had 'descended the steps of prostitution'. She was upset because she had met a man called Smith who left her. It is an intriguing theory, but there is one flaw: there is no evidence. Nor could Mary talk to Godwin, who also tried to blacken Harriet's name. He suggested that Harriet had been unfaithful to Percy. Harriet was the one who had acted unethically. Mary, as the other woman, was wholly innocent. He also said that Harriet might have been an alcoholic. But Mary couldn't push her feelings away like this. Guilt and sadness over Harriet's suicide clung to her for months. She would still be thinking of her more than twenty years later. 'Poor Harriet,' she would write in her diary in 1839, 'to whose sad fate I attribute so many of my own heavy sorrows, as the atonement claimed by fate for her death.'

Harriet's death did have one positive outcome for Mary. Mary had been calling herself Mrs Shelley for months. Now the title could be made official. Mary and Percy could marry. Marriage might have helped her feel more secure in her relationship, even if Percy's record suggested he didn't value marriage quite as much as she would have wished. At least their son, William, would feel he had a father. Mary might have also thought they would grow their family by looking after Percy and Harriet's children. This was what Percy wanted and expected. In other circumstances, he might not have been in such a hurry to marry again. He had never wanted to be tied down to anyone and being tethered to Harriet had been a huge mistake. He was already with Mary. He didn't need to offer her marriage to persuade them to be together. But marriage would strengthen a custody case over the guardianship of his children. Percy knew he faced competition from Harriet's parents, who had wanted to look after their grandchildren, Ianthe, now 3, and Charles, 2. In most cases, the father would have won the battle. The man's wife and their children would have been considered his property. But this situation was different. Percy held radical political views, was an atheist, had run off with another woman and had made little effort to look after his children since Charles had been born. As Percy saw it, he was still their father. If he were married, the courts might consider him a better prospect. He would be able to provide stability. William Godwin, who was beginning to sound surprisingly conventional, also thought that Mary and Percy should marry. They had been speaking more since Fanny's death, although their relationship was still fragile. And so Mary and Percy set a date. The ceremony was held on 30 December 1816 at St Mildred's Church in the City of London. It was small and simple, attended by Godwin, Mary Jane, and Mary and Percy's friends Leigh and Marianne Hunt. Mary noted it plainly in her diary as 'a marriage takes place'. Godwin bragged to friends that his daughter now had 'a station and character in society'.

Early the following year, while she was working on *Frankenstein*, Mary found out she was pregnant again. Her letters to Percy show she was anxious. She wanted his support. Towards the end of January, she would join him at a cottage in Hampstead rented by the Hunts. Percy channelled his energy into winning guardianship of his children. He wrote to influential friends, pleaded with Harriet's relatives and even plotted to kidnap them. In March, Mary and Percy moved into their own house with Claire and Alba in Marlow, beside the Thames. Percy would learn that neither he nor the Westbrooks had won custody. Instead, they would be handed to guardians. Percy wouldn't see Ianthe and Charles again. Mary had thought about the responsibilities of parenthood for years. Her ideas had been drawn into sharp relief in recent months. She was about to finish a draft of her first novel. *Frankenstein* would bear the mark of her experiences.

Life After Death

1816–1818

Women who wanted to slip away quietly from the world in the nineteenth century didn't plunge into the Serpentine like Harriet Westbrook. They took laudanum in a provincial hotel room like Fanny Imlay. There was less chance of being found before it was too late. The number of people who had drowned had been on the rise for some time. Many were accidents. There were labourers who worked beside the canal but couldn't swim. There were people going for evening strolls on badly lit riverside paths who missed their footing. Others were suicides. People lacked hope. They didn't want to go on. Drowning was an escape. Except it was far from fail-safe. Those hoping to drown could be unlucky. Others were looking out for people in trouble in the water. They would get paid for saving or trying to save them. Rescuers could earn four guineas if they were successful. They could still get two guineas if not.

The people behind this get-rich-quick scheme were from the Royal Humane Society (originally called the Humane Society). The organization had been established in 1774 by two doctors: William Hawes and Thomas Cogan. Their aim was to promote ways to provide 'immediate relief to persons apparently dead from drowning'. Cogan had been inspired by a visit to Amsterdam, where a similar group had been set up in 1767. According to the Royal Humane Society, 'relief' meant resuscitation and they issued clear directions on how to go about it. Rescuers should remove the body from the water, wrap the person in 'a great coat or two of the bystanders' and take them inside where they should dry them with 'warm flannels'. Someone should then blow air up the person's nostrils, while another presses gently on their chest to inflate their lungs. Others should rub the body with salt and dab it with rum, massage the person's temples with hartshorn and place hot water bottles – or bricks wrapped in more flannels – on the soles of the person's feet and palms of their hands. If the rescuers have a feather to hand, they might also like to tickle the person's nostrils. Finally, a jolt of electricity was recommended to 'render the plan of recovery more expeditiously and certainly efficacious'. The Royal Humane Society had some success and was well-regarded. The Princess of Wales was a patron. Franchises sprang up across the country.

Resuscitation was controversial because it threw up thorny questions about life and death. If drowned people were dead, resuscitation brought them back to life. In this case, the rescuer might be crossing a serious theological line. They were playing God. Perhaps it had been God's plan for that person to die. Perhaps, a rescuer might reply, it had been God's plan for them to be resuscitated. If the person had died, even temporarily, what happened to their soul? Did it slide into heaven or hell before trundling back to earth? Did it hang around in purgatory trying not to laugh as someone tickled the nose of its body with a feather?

To the casual observer, a lot of drowned people seemed dead. Even doctors struggled to say when someone was no longer alive. People knew the heart stopped beating, but it could be hard to detect a faint heartbeat (the stethoscope wouldn't be invented until 1819). So, it was little wonder that some believed resuscitation was more like resurrection. As one banner at the Humane Society's annual festival and procession in 1796 proclaimed, 'It was meet that we should make merry and be glad; for these / Thy sons were dead, / And are alive again.' What joy! Such statements, however, were also seen as dangerous. It was a grand claim to say you could bring someone back from the dead. Knowing this, the Royal Humane Society was careful about its language. It insisted resuscitation was successful only for people who were 'apparently dead' rather than clinically dead. '*Lateat scintillula forsan*,' read the motto on the back of the medal it gave to rescuers: 'A little spark may yet lie hid.' Yet what did it mean to be 'apparently dead'?

Some, like the Scottish surgeon John Hunter, said people who had apparently drowned were in a limbo state between life and death, when 'a suspension of the actions of life has taken place'. Fainting, comas and sleeping, he added, were also states of 'suspended animation'. Others, such as the doctor James Curry, distinguished between 'absolute' and 'apparent' death. His big work, *Observations on Apparent Death from Drowning, Hanging, Suffocation from Noxious Vapours*, wouldn't come out until 1819, after *Frankenstein* had been published. But Mary may well have heard about his ideas before then. In 1814, he had attended to Mary's stepsister, Claire. In 1817, he had attended to Percy. Any number of conversations could have taken place. People in both 'absolute' and 'apparent' states of death seemed dead, said Curry – their heart had stopped beating, they weren't breathing, they weren't moving and they couldn't feel anything. The difference was that 'absolute' death was permanent: the vital principle that had kept them alive wasn't just 'dormant' as in 'apparent' death; it was 'completely extinguished'. You could only really tell if someone was dead-dead – in a state of 'absolute' death – when their body started rotting away. If you had just pulled someone out the water and thought you could give them a chance of life, you probably wouldn't want to wait to see if that would happen.

Mary and Percy would have been aware of the Royal Humane Society and its recommended techniques. Percy mentioned the society by name in the notes to his poem *Queen Mab*, published in 1813, while Mary knew about resuscitation from hearing about her mother's second suicide attempt. She knew that after her mother had jumped into the Thames from Putney Bridge one rainy night in October 1795, she had been spotted by a boatman and revived. She might not have known the exact details of the resuscitation, but Godwin had said she was 'for a considerable time insensible'. Wollstonecraft would also later suggest she had, in some sense, died. She said she had been 'inhumanly [sic] brought back to life and misery'. To be 'brought back to life', she would have had to have gone from it. Wollstonecraft described her drowning ordeal before she had found happiness again. She was still depressed and was angry at her rescuers. Her wording, some say, was a dig at the Royal Humane

Society, who held that life was always worth living. Wollstonecraft disagreed. She had worried resuscitation would mean her 'poor body [would] be insulted by an endeavour to recall my hated existence'. She had opposed resuscitation, not on ethical grounds, but because she no longer wanted to live. Since her rescue, she felt condemned to 'a living death'. Could this episode in her mother's life have affected how Mary thought about resuscitation? Mary was the empathetic type and may well have understood her mother's pain of failing to escape her life. And yet, she loved her mother: she didn't necessarily wish she had died; she just wished she hadn't suffered. Wollstonecraft had conceived Mary after her second suicide attempt – years that wouldn't have belonged to her had her attempts succeeded. Had it not been for a chance rescue, Wollstonecraft would never have had another child. Wollstonecraft didn't feel she should have been alive. Mary might have felt that, in one sense, this made her a child of the dead. The success of resuscitation techniques suggested that the lines between life and death were not as clear as people thought. There could be life after death after all.

Perhaps Mary was thinking some of this when she included drowning and resuscitation in *Frankenstein*. The way Harriet had died, especially given that Mary's mother had almost died the same way, might not have given her the idea to write about drowning, but it might have affected how she did so. Mary may well have been dealing with her own emotions while she was writing. Drowning in icy waters is a looming threat in the framing narrative of *Frankenstein*. Victor tells his story while he is on Captain Walton's ship. Walton is aiming for the North Pole. His ship is trapped by pack ice in the Arctic Ocean. It's a treacherous voyage and Walton's goal could mean that they all drown. When we meet Victor, it seems as if he is just about to die this way, too. Walton and his sailors pull him up from the icy water. 'His limbs were nearly frozen,' Walton writes to his sister, Margaret, 'and his body dreadfully emaciated by fatigue and suffering. I never saw a man in so wretched a condition.' Victor soon faints. Walton describes how his crew 'restored him to animation'. They rubbed him with brandy, poured a few sips of it into his mouth and swaddled him in blankets. It's not full resuscitation like the Royal

Humane Society might have recommended – there's no breath of life and certainly no electricity, but the crew are following the initial steps. Mary had already started writing this part of her book before Harriet's death. She had been reading about 'old voyages' as research that November. But when she heard about Harriet, an idea might have taken a more definite shape in her mind. London in the winter wasn't the Arctic, but it was cold. How clearly she might have been able to imagine someone drowning in freezing waters now that the idea was so close to home.

Mary includes several references to drowning in the main story, too. One has a clear suicide link. After the creature kills Victor's brother, Victor spends time at the family home in Belrive, where he takes a boat out on the water. 'I was tempted to plunge into the silent lake,' he says, 'that the waters might close over me and my calamities for ever.' Miserable and guilty though he feels over his brother's death, the thought of Elizabeth, his father and his surviving brother stops him taking his own life. Dying could upset Elizabeth and leave her without a husband. It would also leave his relatives 'exposed and unprotected' to the creature. The creature might kill them, too. Later, after Victor has destroyed the creature's female companion on the Orkney Islands, Victor goes out to sea to get rid of the remains. He falls asleep and, when he wakes, finds his boat has veered off course. He fears he could 'be driven into the wide Atlantic, and… be swallowed up in the immeasurable waters that roared and buffeted around me.' This is how he will meet his end, he says. 'I looked upon the sea, it was to be my grave.'

Victor is ambivalent towards the power of water. At times, he longs to drown as an escape from the world. At other times, he fears the water will engulf him against his will. Mary might not have considered jumping off a boat or been scared she would ever be taken out to sea, but she could have understood that, depending on mood and circumstance, drowning could be seen as welcome – or a threat. For Harriet and her mother, it offered relief from suffering when they were desperately unhappy, although that didn't mean they hadn't feared it when things had been looking up. While Victor thinks he might drown, the creature saves a young girl from being subsumed by a 'rapid river'. The creature is brave and kind, dragging the girl from the water. The girl had been playing and slipped, a very different circumstance from Harriet or Mary Wollstonecraft. And yet, at some level, while Mary imagined the scene, she might have been thinking about her mother being saved. Maybe she was wishing someone had reached Harriet in time, too.

We don't know exactly what Mary was thinking. But the way Mary narrates the girl's rescue – through the voice of the creature – does give us some insight into her mind. Dragging the body from the water, the creature says: 'She was senseless; and I endeavoured, by every means in my power, to restore animation.' It sounds, we might think, as if she were dead. The creature is resuscitating the girl back to life. It taps into one of Mary's favourite themes: the blurring of boundaries between life and death. Just as Victor broke through the 'ideal bounds' of life and death to make the creature, the creature has broken through these bounds to help a young girl live. Unfortunately, it doesn't work out so well for the creature. 'A rustic' sees him, takes the girl and aims a gun at him. He gets little thanks for his good deed and ends up feeling more isolated than ever. So much of *Frankenstein* is about loneliness and loss. So much of Mary's life had featured similar themes. Fortunately, this wouldn't be the only thing that would inspire Mary. *Frankenstein* also features the new pioneers of science.

Section II

Men of Science

'It appeared to the uninformed part of the bystanders as if the wretched man were on the eve of being restored to life' - *The Times* on Giovanni Aldini's corpse experiment in 1803

The Owl in the Castle

On a hill near the city of Darmstadt in southern Germany, you will find the ruins of a medieval castle. Two turrets, their hats a gun-metal grey, stretch towards the sky, a reminder of their heyday hundreds of years ago. Moss has taken up residence in the cracks and crevices of ragged rock arches and walls with holes for windows. The castle is cloaked by coniferous forest. But on a clear, bright day, above the trees, you can see across the plains of the Rhine, the river a ribbon of spilled mercury. Nearby lies the town of Gernsheim, where Mary and Percy Shelley stopped in 1814 on their return from England by riverboat. They had run off to France, skipped into Switzerland and found they could go no further without the inconvenience of cold hard cash. It was time to go home.

You might be familiar with the name of the castle, even if Darmstadt or Gernsheim have only just appeared on your radar. It is Burg Frankenstein. Back then, Frankenstein didn't ring the bells it now does. In German, it meant 'stone of the Franks'. It might have been too far for the Shelleys to get to Castle Frankenstein on their trip, but they may well have heard about it and been attracted by the romance of the ruins, just as we might today. Mary Shelley, then Mary Wollstonecraft Godwin, might have written down the word 'Frankenstein'. Maybe she liked the sound of it. Two years later, she would give the name to the wildly ambitious scientist of her first novel – Victor Frankenstein. She might have thought the connection apt.

Castle Frankenstein had been built in about 1240 by Lord Conrad II Reiz von Breuberg, who later changed his name to 'von Frankenstein'. The castle, grand and imposing, was to be their family seat until 1662, when they sold it off. It would be one of the residents a decade later who would spark Mary's fertile imagination. By 1673, the castle had become a hospital for people injured and seeking refuge from the conflict with France. It was here, on 10 August, that Anna Eleonora Muenchmeyer and Johann Philip Dippel, a Lutheran minister, had a son, Johann Conrad Dippel. The younger Dippel went on to become an alchemist, rumoured to have discovered the elixir of life by experimenting with limbs stolen from graveyards in the dead of night and to have reanimated corpses. Dippel was brilliant, but like Victor Frankenstein, he baffled and terrified those around him. Both believed they could overcome death and create life. Both conducted dangerous experiments. Both worked in secrecy. Could Mary have been inspired by stories she heard about Dippel? Could he be the prototype for her protagonist?

* * *

Johann Conrad Dippel was never meant for greatness or notoriety. He was meant to be an ordinary pastor, like his father, grandfather and great-grandfather before him. He would be respected but unassuming, an upstanding member of the community. To prepare him, his father had him homeschooled, before sending him to Darmstadt Gymnasium. He was considered a strange boy. Other children called him 'the owl' because he liked to spend time alone and read by candlelight in the castle towers at night. Aged 9, Dippel was showing signs that he was a freethinker, too: he questioned the Catechism. By his teens, he had begun to think he was above others, guided by a higher spirit, which gave him an insight into the mysteries of the world. The young Dippel was smart and self-assured – when he wasn't being precocious or a little lofty.

At 17, Dippel scooted off to the University of Giessen, about sixty miles north of his home, to study theology, registering under the name 'Frankensteina'. He often dazzled his tutors and fellow students with his searing intellect and had no qualms about challenging convention. His thesis was titled *De Nihilo* or *On Nothing*. Dippel would go on to publish more than seventy works under the pseudonym 'Christianus Democritus' or the 'Christian Democritus' (an ancient Greek thinker).

After graduating in 1693, Dippel went to the Imperial University of Strasbourg. He lectured everywhere he could, from taverns to churches. But while his courses in astrology and palmistry were a hit, his theological views drew some serious critics. In arguing that Christianity was more about ethics than rules, Dippel attacked so many sects that he vexed almost everyone. He also seemed to change his position a lot. One critic called him '*ein indifferentistischer Schwärmer*' or 'an indifferent enthusiast' for his flipflopping, while the Swedish theologian and philosopher Emanuel Swedenborg, initially a Dippel super-fan, said it made him a 'most vile devil… who attempted wicked things'. Within two years, Dippel was accused of killing a man in a duel and was forced to flee. Now on the run, Dippel moved back in with his parents near Darmstadt and threw himself into the latest craze: alchemy. Laboratories had been springing up across the country at the behest of Count Ernst Ludwig of Hesse. The prince had been trying to turn his court at Darmstadt into a mini-Versailles and, like many overseeing a DIY makeover, had gone over budget. He nearly bankrupted the treasury. He hoped alchemists at these new laboratories, at Dornberg and Arheilgen, Giessen and Castle Frankenstein, would find the philosopher's stone, a formula that would turn base metals such as lead and copper into gold, so that he could repay his debts.

True alchemists were not just in it for the money. In its purest form, alchemy, which had been around for thousands of years, was a quest for knowledge. It was a way to understand the world better. Not only would the philosopher's stone (usually described as a heavy red powder) produce gold, it would also prolong life. Anyone who possessed it would become immortal. While exciting, alchemy was time-consuming and perilous. Alchemists could inhale the toxic vapours of mercury and charcoal and die. They were also at risk of kidnap and torture from those desperate for their secrets. Dippel had decided to join them after a trip to Giessen, where he met a Lutheran minister who had shown him chemistry books from his personal library. In all or nothing fashion, on his return, Dippel bought a property near Darmstadt on credit for 50,000 guilders. In 1701, after several months of mixing and heating and distilling and waiting, he claimed success. But the joy wasn't to last. Dippel's crucible cracked and his magic potion was lost. Pursued by creditors, he went into hiding once more, eventually settling in Berlin.

Berlin was the capital of the newly founded Kingdom of Prussia and came under the rule of Frederick I. Like Count Ernst Ludwig of Hesse in Darmstadt, the king had also begun various extravagant building projects, including Charlottenburg Palace. He too had overspent and needed to pay back his debts. The king was inundated with alchemists offering him boundless riches in return for his patronage. They said they could turn base metals into gold. Dippel had come to the attention of Count August of Sayn-Wittgenstein, one of the king's ministers, and was asked to judge the veracity of their claims. The minister also convinced the king to give Dippel a mansion and laboratory to do his own work. Having already tried to transform base metals into gold, Dippel set his sights on another, no less ambitious goal. He decided to find the elixir of life, a remedy that would cure all ills. Dippel gathered horns, bones and dried blood, and repeatedly distilled them. 'The work is messy and arduous,' he wrote. First, the liquid was thick, sticky and black. Then, after more distilling, it turned pale yellow. Dippel's Oil or *Oleum Animale Dippelli* smelled putrid and tasted even worse. Contemporaries described it as 'stink medicine'. But that didn't put everyone off. Dippel claimed it could fix fevers, clean up colds and erase epilepsy. If you took it regularly, he added, it would make you immortal. Some people rubbed it on their skin. Others drank it. For the rest of the century, it would be included in pharmacopeias, respected bibles of medicine, for its healing properties. Doubts about its health benefits set in from the end of the eighteenth century, but it didn't disappear entirely. In the Second World War, British troops coated North African wells with Dippel's Oil to make the water undrinkable. Today, some people rub it on horses to repel insects and soak fences in it to protect them from damage by wild animals. According to legend, Dippel tried to sell the formula to buy Castle Frankenstein. His offer was turned down.

For a while, Dippel shared his laboratory with a Swiss dye producer called Johann Jacob von Diesbach. One day in 1704, Diesbach was cooking up purple Florentine lake, a deep red pigment made of cochineal (derived from dried bodies of insects), alum, iron vitriol and, in usual circumstances, potash – except he had run out. Dippel gave him a generous helping of it from the batch he had been using to distil his animal oil. The resulting dye looked a bit off: it wasn't a reddish purple; it was a rich blue. Pure blue colours had been hard to produce and work with until now. Woad faded, indigo ran when it was washed and ultramarine was made by crushing rock from the mountains of Badakhshan (modern-day Afghanistan), making it prohibitively expensive. Dippel and Diesbach's dye, initially known as Berliner *blau* or Berlin blue, was highly sought-after. Used to dye the uniforms of the Prussian army, it was soon dubbed Prussian blue and was later used by photographers for tinctures to produce cyanotypes, as well as French Impressionists in their paintings. Pathologists still use it today to detect lead poisoning. Dye success aside, Dippel was still not safe from detractors. According to some reports, he was accused of being a Swedish spy and thrown briefly in jail. In 1707, he was on the move again, a little like the itinerant Victor Frankenstein. This time, he was off to Holland.

In 1707, Dippel began studying medicine at the university at Leyden. He would use findings from his earlier experiments for his thesis, *Maladies and Remedies of the Life of the Flesh*. To some, his claims here would have been startling. Dippel not only believed he had found the elixir of life and could exorcise demons; he also said he could transfer souls between bodies using a funnel. The rumours about his methods were even more extreme. It was widely accepted that Dippel experimented with dead animals, but some believed he experimented with human bodies, too. Dippel was accused of robbing graves and trying to bring bodies back to life. Mary Shelley might have captured some of these elements for her own creation, Victor Frankenstein, who also cut up bodies. 'I collected bones from charnel-houses,' says Victor. 'The dissecting room and the slaughterhouse furnished many of my materials.' In the early 1800s, when Mary was writing, people in Britain were captivated by human anatomy and Mary would have been well aware of the practice. There is no evidence Dippel used cadavers in his experiments, let alone tried to bring them alive, but both Victor and Dippel believed they could.

In 1714, Dippel went to Denmark. At first, things went well – Dippel was named Royal Councillor – but they quickly soured. Dippel wrote pamphlets that annoyed local rulers and Count Reventlow, a former patron, put him in jail for life. A hangman burned Dippel's works in front of him and he was thrown – tied, hand and foot – into a dank cell in Hammarshus, a medieval fortress on the island of Bornholm in the Baltic. It would be the Queen of Denmark, wife of Frederick IV, who would come to his rescue a year later in 1726. She thought Dippel might be able to cure her husband's illness. Dippel's method, which included healing the spirit before repairing the body, is said to have worked. Dippel's reputation as a doctor grew and, in 1727, he went to Stockholm as a physician to the Swedish court. Yet again, he attracted critics. One Swedish bishop referred to him disparagingly as 'the Messiah of the nobility', while a Swedish baron wrote he was 'the bane of the Bishops, since on his coming to Sweden he made as much noise as if a Russian army of 100,000 had invaded the country'. Rumours also circulated that Dippel was a Russian spy.

In 1729, Dippel returned home to Germany. He bought a house in the village of Berleburg, near Castle Frankenstein, and worked from a laboratory in a mansion owned by his brother, Heinrich Adam, near the village of Traisa. A hotel and restaurant called The Dippelshof now stands on the site of the mansion, which was destroyed in the Thirty Years' War in the seventeenth century. Dippel continued to keep his work secret, doing little to quash rumours that spread about him, which included the idea that he had sold his soul to the devil. Dippel was convinced he had seventy-five more years to live, a belief he put down in a pamphlet where he talked about his secret elixir. It wasn't to be. The following spring, on 25 April 1734, Dippel was found dead in his study. He was 60 years old. Some say his body was found cold and rigid. He had been foaming at the mouth. The right side of his face was blue. They claimed he had been poisoned by people for his secrets or by mistake because he had drunk his blue dye. Others say he was killed by the devil for breaking a bargain. He probably died of a stroke. Dippel was buried in a chapel in Bad Laasphe nearby, although his remains are said to have vanished. Only his reputation, sketchy in parts but controversial to the core, lives on.

Some of the material that could help confirm the truth about Dippel's life might have been destroyed by the bombings of Darmstadt, where he lived, and Giessen, where he studied, during the Second World War. Any biographical gaps and discrepancies might never be resolved. And yet this hasn't stopped efforts to connect Johann Conrad Dippel, of Frankenstein Castle, and Victor Frankenstein, of Mary Shelley's novel. Some scholars speculate that Mary and Percy visited the castle on their travels. The castle did appear in nineteenth-century guidebooks and may well have been known to English travellers on the Rhine. However, it wasn't one of the hilltop castles commonly painted by English visitors; it would have been a schlep to get there – and, crucially, there is no record of a visit. Mary could have still seen it from afar. In her diary, she mentions 'a ruined tower with its tessellated windows… on the summit of [a] hill'. Was this Castle Frankenstein? The outline would have been visible from Gernsheim, where their boat was moored.

Even while admitting there is no castle in *Frankenstein* (a later addition from dramatizations), there are other clues to a connection between Mary and Dippel. One passage in Mary's writing suggests that she spoke to students from the University of Strasbourg when Mary and Percy were in the area. Dippel had studied there, the argument goes, so they may well have told the couple about a famous alumnus. Dippel was known about by many, his life already enshrined in myth. Locals on land or fellow travellers on the boat Mary was taking along the Rhine may well have told her about the castle and Dippel, too. Another line in Mary's later diaries suggests she wanted to spend a full summer in the area 'to linger among the ruins, to hear still more of its legends'. This could also mean she knew of the legend about Dippel. The castle ruins may well have been on her radar.

There is a little bit more. From 1769 to 1773, a small group of writers and composers, known as the *Kreis der Empfindsamen* or the Circle of the Sentimentalists, would meet in Darmstadt for readings, nature walks and discussions. The group, which included Johann Wolfgang von Goethe, were especially drawn to ruins and would spend weekends at Castle Frankenstein, singing under the linden tree. This was before

Mary's time, but she may well have known about the group. They were mentioned in the *Edinburgh Review*, which she liked to browse, while members such as Goethe were part of her world. Mary's mother, Mary Wollstonecraft, championed Goethe's work, while *The Sorrows of the Young Werther* (1774), his first novel, is central to *Frankenstein* as one of the books read by the creature. Could Mary have heard about Castle Frankenstein and Dippel in this roundabout way?

And what of the influence of Dippel himself? Is it just coincidence that Mary writes of 'gods [making entirely] new men' in her diary soon after visiting the area? Did she have stories of Dippel trying to create life in her mind at the time? If Mary hadn't heard of Dippel or the castle, where did she get the name 'Frankenstein'? While 'Frank' might have been a common German name, it has a much stronger connection to the region of the Rhine, where Mary travelled in 1814, than Geneva, where she started her story in 1816. Dippel's experiments might have been typical of scientists in the late eighteenth century, but perhaps Mary heard about his work, too. Today, Dippel's ghost is said to lurk in the castle grounds, especially around Christmas and New Year. He wears a long black coat, carries a flask of elixir and howls outside the chapel. Perhaps it would be strong proof that Dippel influenced Mary if he called out her name or cried out for the creature. He does not. But a link between them is hard to shake off. Dippel's experiments pave the way for a man Mary may have met in a more conventional setting, Humphry Davy.

The Celebrity Chemist

In the early nineteenth century, Mayfair had a real problem with traffic jams. You would want to leave extra time if you planned to go anywhere near the Royal Institution at 21 Albermarle Street on lecture days. The organization had been founded in 1799 to show people how science applied to their lives. For some, that was interesting enough, but one lecturer attracted especially large crowds. Everyone wanted to see Humphry Davy, assistant lecturer in chemistry. Davy's first series was on galvanism, when electricity is produced by a chemical action. He conducted explosions with the flair of a performer, sending sparks a-flying. 'Mr Davy… acquitted himself admirably well,' a reviewer would later write for the *Philosophical Magazine*. 'From the sparkling intelligence of his eye, his animated manner, and the *tout ensemble*, we have no doubt of him attaining distinguished excellence.' Later in 1801, Davy would publish his first paper in the *Philosophical Transactions*, the Royal Society's journal, about a new type of voltaic battery. He was just 22.

Charismatic and self-assured, Sir Humphry Davy helped secure the shift in scientific circles from the old ways of alchemy, which focused on finding the philosopher's stone, a substance that could turn base metals into gold and make people immortal, to the new ways of chemistry, which was concerned with examining the structure of substances using the modern method of testing hypotheses through observation. Alchemy had been on the way out for a while but had been hard for many to shake off. For years, some natural philosophers had been alchemists and chemists. Robert Boyle, the seventeenth-century Anglo-Irish natural philosopher, is a good example. As one of the first real chemists, he pioneered the modern scientific method of testing a hypothesis. He also defined what we understand today as an element. But while he questioned some forms of alchemy in his book *The Sceptical Chemist* (1661), he also spent a lot of time trying to find the philosopher's stone. He believed it could not only transmute base metals into gold but also conjure up angels.

Mary was aware of the allure of alchemy and its dangers. She had read her father's 1799 novel *St Leon*, following an alchemist, who having succeeded in his quest, ends up with riches and eternal life, but is thoroughly unhappy. In *Frankenstein*, the young Victor is swept up by alchemy when he comes across a volume by Cornelius Agrippa, a sixteenth-century polymath. His father dismisses the work as 'sad trash', but that doesn't stop Victor reading more of it, as well as work by Paracelsus and Albertus Magnus. Victor recalls that, as a child, he 'had not been content with the results promised by the modern professors of natural science', turning to the 'dreams of forgotten alchemists'. He says he suffered from 'a confusion of ideas' due to his 'extreme youth and my want of a guide'. Mary's choice of Victor's reading material may well be significant. Paracelsus, a German-Swiss physician and alchemist of the Renaissance, had come up with a simple recipe to create a homunculus, a small man, in *De Natura Rerum* or *Essay on the Nature of Things* (1537). All you had to do was put human semen in a flask, simmer it on a low heat, wait forty days until it started to take the shape of a man and then feed the little creature for forty weeks with human blood. The result would look like a human child but have 'great knowledge and powers'. Albertus Magnus, a thirteenth-century Dominican friar, bishop, theologian and philosopher, was also interested in DIY man-making, at least as legends go. In one account, he built a man from brass. In another, he made a mechanical man from flesh and bone. Agrippa was in on the act, too: he tried to germinate life from dead flesh. Victor may well have been inspired.

Mary suggests Victor was educated out of his old views about alchemy at university in Ingolstadt. There, he meets Professor Krempe, a 'little squat man with a gruff voice', who believes alchemists rely on 'exploded systems', peddling 'fancies… [that] are a thousand years old, and as musty as they are ancient'. Victor takes this on board but doesn't necessarily accept that he has been wasting his time by paying them attention. He prefers the views of the more moderate Professor Waldman, who gives alchemists credit for laying the foundations for modern chemists, even if their theories have now been superseded. 'The modern masters,' he says, 'penetrate into the recesses of nature… They have acquired new and almost unlimited powers; they can command the thunders of heaven, mimic the earthquake, and even mock the invisible word with its shadows.'

Humphry Davy was a full-on chemist. 'Chemistry,' he wrote in a notebook, has arisen from 'the ruins of alchemy'. For Davy, 'The dim and uncertain twilight of discovery… has been succeeded by the steady light of truth.' The new science revealed 'the composition of the atmosphere, and the properties of gases', while scientists had developed 'the phenomenon of electricity'. 'A new influence has been discovered,' he continued, 'which has enabled man to produce from combinations of dead matter effects which were formerly occasioned only by animal organs.' Man can even use science to change his environment and future. It has enabled man to practise powers that 'may almost be called creative'. He can now 'modify and change the beings surrounding him'. The scientist is no longer 'a scholar, passive and seeking only to understand her operations, but rather… a master, active with his own instruments'. This idea might have resonated with Victor, who took an active role in shaping the world around him. He used chemistry, some might say, to achieve the goals of the alchemists. Like Agrippa, Paracelsus and Albertus Magnus, he sought to master nature and create life.

* * *

Penzance wasn't the obvious birthplace in 1778 for a celebrity chemist. The tiny town on the southwest coast of Cornwall took three days to get to by coach from London and depended on fishing and tin mining. But no one asked whether Penzance was ready for fame. It just had to step up to the mark. Humphry Davy's parents came from respectable, traditional backgrounds. His father, Robert, was a woodcarver and gilder. His mother, Grace, was from a mining family. Grace's parents had died of a fever when she was 7 and she had been adopted by John Tonkin, a local surgeon, philanthropist and mayor. Tonkin would go on to pay for Davy's schooling and encourage his love of nature and chemistry. When Humphry was young, his father inherited a seventy-nine-acre estate in the depths of the countryside. He built a house there, giving Humphry and his four younger siblings the chance to explore the woods and marshland and go shooting and fishing. The young Davy loved exploring and telling stories. But when he was 16, his father died of a stroke and he needed a way to provide for the family. Davy became an apprentice to John Bingham Borlase, a surgeon-apothecary and friend of Tonkin's. He borrowed books from Tonkin, poring over William Nicholson's *Dictionary of Chemistry* (1795), which showed how chemistry had arisen from alchemy, and Antoine Lavoisier's *Le Traité élémentaire de chimie* (1789), translated into English the following year as *Elements of Chemistry*, which detailed the new theories of oxygen, a new table of elements and the value of close observation and precise measurements. As Davy mixed lotions and potions, he became enthralled with the structure of substances and how they reacted to each other.

Davy did his own experiments in his room with wine glasses, teacups, and mineral acids and alkalis. He made friends with a new lodger of his mother's, Gregory Watt, son of James Watt, the engineer – a friendship that led, via Gregory's father, to a job in 1798 as superintendent of the Pneumatic Medical Institute in Bristol, run by Dr Thomas Beddoes. As part of his job, Davy examined the healing potential of gasses, often experimenting on himself. In 1799, he inhaled carbon monoxide. 'I seemed [to be] sinking into annihilation,' he recorded as he breathed in the third quart, 'and had just power enough to drop the mouthpiece from my unclosed lips… I faintly articulated, "I do not think I shall die".' He then took his pulse, collapsed outside the laboratory with chest pains and had to be helped into bed. A week later, Davy breathed in carbonic acid, burned his throat and choked. Further experiments with nitrous oxide, or laughing gas, were more pleasurable. 'The objects around me became dazzling, and my hearing more acute,' he said, writing up his results in the poem *On Breathing Nitrous Oxide*. At the turn of the century, Davy heard about the invention of the battery, which could produce a sustained electrical current. He found that substances could be broken down into parts when a current was passed through them – the process we now call electrolysis. After reading a paper about William Nicholson and Anthony Carlisle's experiment using a voltaic pile to decompose water, Davy wrote to his friend, the poet Samuel Taylor Coleridge: 'I have made some important galvanic discoveries which seem to lead to the door of the temple of life.' He would later employ electrolysis to discover elements, such as sodium and potassium, recreating his experiments in front of rapt audiences.

People loved Davy's Royal Institution lectures. He was full of energy and charming with it. His galvanism series gained rave reviews in the press. Women made up half the audience. Fascinated, they took notes. Transcripts of Davy's lectures were published to spread the word to more people. In 1802, he delivered a second series of lectures, this time on agricultural chemistry, and was soon promoted to a full lecturer position, before being appointed professor of chemistry. In 1805, Davy lectured on geology using a large model of a volcano that produced smoke, caught fire and emitted a cloud of ash. That year, the Royal Institution gave him the Copley Medal for outstanding work and elected him to the council. In the first of four lectures at the Royal Society, Davy looked into the nature of electricity again; this time showing that the electrical charge from batteries was the same as lightning, that electricity was a form of energy rather than being a type of matter and that chemical materials were held together by positive and negative energy. He would go on to develop the Davy lamp, a lamp for miners that wouldn't explode in the presence of gasses like methane. Davy's work helped people see science as a serious profession rather than merely the hobby of wealthy gentlemen.

Davy didn't just mix with scientists. He was also friends with poets, including Robert Southey. Connections were important. Southey would introduce Davy to Coleridge. They would become close friends. Coleridge went to Davy's lectures to replenish his supply of metaphors. He admired his scientific knowledge and his creativity. 'Living thoughts spring up like Turf under his feet,' said Coleridge, coming up with a plan for them to stay at Southey's house in Keswick in the Lake District. They could invite Southey's neighbours, Dorothy and William Wordsworth, and

Davy could teach them all chemistry. The plan never came off, although Coleridge did take Davy to dine with William Godwin in 1799. Davy then became a regular at the Godwin household, where he may well have met a young Mary Shelley. Godwin attended Davy's lectures, too, and while there is no certainty that Mary tagged along, there is evidence of one 9-year-old girl in the audience. Even if Mary didn't go to the lectures – she would have been very young to take everything in – she would have heard about Davy later from Percy, who was also an admirer. He bought *Davy's Elements of Chemical Philosophy* when it was published in 1812 and, in 1820, would write lengthy notes in his copy of *Elements of Agricultural Chemistry*.

In autumn 1816, while Mary was writing *Frankenstein*, she read Davy's work, too – probably *A Discourse, Introductory to A Course of Lectures on Chemistry*, a printed copy of one of Davy's 1802 lectures. She mentioned it five times in her diary. It was the only strictly scientific work she read during this period. Some might say it shows. Davy's ideas and approach to science are echoed by Professor Waldman and Victor. First, there is Waldman's similar approach to Davy on society's transition from alchemy to chemistry. Waldman says: 'The ancient teachers of this science… promised impossibilities, and performed nothing. The modern masters promise very little… [but] have indeed performed miracles.' Davy says: '[The alchemists'] view of things have passed away, and a new science has gradually arisen.' Waldman talks of 'modern masters' discovering 'the nature of the air we breathe' and 'command[ing] the thunders of heaven'. Davy talks of the practitioners of modern science finding out 'the composition of the atmosphere' and 'the lightnings… [being] taken from the clouds'. Both Waldman and Davy talk about chemists having 'powers' to change the world, too. Waldman and Davy also believe in the value of studying all branches of science. Waldman advises Victor to 'apply [himself] to every branch of natural philosophy'. Davy says: 'The man of true genius… will combine together mechanical, chemical, and physiological knowledge.'

Victor also shares some of Davy's scientific views. Victor describes his discovery about how to make a creature as a 'sudden light' emerging 'from the midst of this darkness'. Davy believed that science offered a 'steady light of truth'. Victor believes that 'to examine the causes of life, we must first have recourse to death'. Davy thought that the 'powers of life' could only be found after studying the 'simple and unvarying agencies of death matter'. Victor aims to make new life from dead body parts. Davy talked of chemistry being concerned with 'the conversion of dead matter into living matter'. Victor implies that 'the principle of life' might be electricity, especially when read with Mary's 1831 preface where she mentions galvanism. Early on, Davy believed that electricity was connected to life: studying galvanism, he thought, could help us understand how life worked. In 1800, he wrote to Coleridge: 'I have made some important galvanic discoveries, which seem to lead to the door of the temple of the mysterious god of Life.' In the *Discourse*, Davy talked about one of man's greatest achievements being the discovery of 'a new influence' – probably electricity, which was central to so many of his experiments. Modern science, he said, would help man understand the 'powers of life'. The pace of their work was similar, too. Victor proceeded slowly with his work: 'I hesitated a long time concerning the manner in which I should employ [the life force]', he says. Davy believed a gradual approach was more likely to lead to success; modern scientists often fail, he said, because they try to make discoveries too quickly rather than 'slowly endeavouring to lift up the veil concealing the wonderful phenomena of living nature'.

Furthermore, both Victor and Davy were optimistic about what science could achieve, and as confident men at the helm of this discipline, verged on arrogance. 'So much has been done, exclaimed the soul of Frankenstein, – more, far more, will I achieve,' wrote Mary in an addition to the 1831 version of her novel. 'Science has done much for man,' said Davy, 'but it is capable of doing still more.' Davy believed science was 'necessarily performed with the passion of Hope'. Both Victor and Davy believed that the scientific pursuit makes men happy because there was always something to learn. Victor talks of there being 'continual food for discovery and wonder' in science. Davy said science 'is eminently calculated to gratify and to keep alive the more powerful passions and ambitions of the soul'. Both saw science as increasing others' happiness, too. Victor says that 'a new species would bless me as its creator and source.' Davy believed that science would rid society of divisions: 'the different parts of the great whole of society should be intimately united together by means of knowledge and the useful arts'. Science, he said, was a 'great parent', giving her children 'dignity', 'power', 'consolation', 'happiness', 'tranquillity' and 'order'.

This is where the world of *Frankenstein* then differs. Making a creature using the wonders of modern science does not make Victor happy; it makes him utterly miserable. He talks of his soul being 'torn by remorse, horror, and despair' when he realizes his 'unhallowed arts' have led to the deaths of William, his brother, and Justine. Rather than science being a 'great parent', offering a community, it isolates him, making him feel lonely. Victor hides away while he is working and withdraws while his creature is on the rampage. After making the creature, Victor can't bear to even think about his work. He dreads the prospect of repeating it to make a female companion for the creature and loses hope. Victor's scientific endeavours lead to the destruction of those he loves, as well as his downfall. Science alone, Mary suggests, is not inherently good. It will not necessarily benefit the individual or society. The outcome depends on what people do with it. Had Victor taken responsibility for his work, offering the creature love and support, things could have turned out very differently. Victor might have continued to love his work, enjoyed a long, happy marriage to Elizabeth, be praised by his family and gone down in history as the greatest scientist of his day. The only downside would have been for Mary Shelley. Her tale might have been quite hollow without the horror and terror and fear that results from the blind ambition of her modern Prometheus. At best, it might have been a celebration of man's ambition and a feel-good story of paternal love.

Did Humphry Davy read *Frankenstein*? He had a good ten years to do so before he died in 1829. If he did, he may well have recognized elements of himself in Waldman and Victor. He might also have recognized some of the phrases as ones he used in his own work. The similarity is too striking to ignore. And yet, Davy would have had a weak case for claiming close identification or plagiarism. For Mary, Davy was more an example of the men of science at the time than a model to copy in too much detail. Davy's dedication to science, especially chemistry, in an age of change, as well as his optimism for its potential, offered ideas for her to explore, but they weren't unique. Davy had made sure plenty of people knew about them. His talks were so popular that Albemarle Street, where the Royal Institution was based, was turned into a one-way thoroughfare to ease congestion on his lecture days. We never hear of Victor's wildly popular lectures or of the times he caused a traffic jam or of the day he was created a baronet like Davy for his contribution to science. We can imagine, however, that Mary's protagonist might have quite liked it.

Grandfather of the More Famous Charles

All brands benefit from the occasional update and the Darwin family was no exception. In the late eighteenth century, the naturalist Erasmus Darwin decided to spruce up his family coat of arms. The original design featured a shield sporting a sash with three scallops. Darwin, who was fascinated by fossils, added a slogan: '*E conchis omnia*' or 'everything from shells'. It captured one of his big ideas: the theory of evolution. All life, he said, had one common ancestor. Species had developed in complexity over time. He had trumped his grandson, Charles, by fifty years.

* * *

Erasmus and Charles Darwin were born at Elston Hall in Nottinghamshire, near Newark-on-Trent, eighty years apart. Erasmus was born in 1731. His parents were well-to-do, but they also believed in hard work. His father, Robert, was a doctor and a lawyer. Erasmus, the seventh and youngest child, would similarly refuse to stick to one lane. He would become a doctor, naturalist, philosopher and poet. He was, said fellow poet Samuel Taylor Coleridge, 'the most inventive of philosophical men… He thinks in a new train on every subject.'

Erasmus started his career in a conventional fashion. After reading maths and classics at Cambridge, he went to medical school in Edinburgh. In 1757, he set himself up as a doctor in Lichfield in Staffordshire, where he was soon hailed a hero for rescuing a young fisherman from death's door. He would go on to practise medicine in the area for fifty years and become so acclaimed that King George III would ask him to be his physician, a role he politely declined. He was busy in his personal life, too.

The frontispiece to the 1831 edition of *Frankenstein* by Theodor von Holst. (*Tate Britain*)

Mary Shelley by Richard Rothwell, circa 1831–1840. (*National Portrait Gallery, London*)

T. P. Cooke as the creature in *Presumption; or, the Fate of Frankenstein*, a dramatization by Richard Brinsley Peake, 1823. (*New York Public Library*)

Boris Karloff as the creature in *The Bride of Frankenstein* directed by James Whale, 1935.

Mary Wollstonecraft by James Heath, after John Opie stipple engraving, circa 1797.

William Godwin by James Northcote, 1802. (*National Portrait Gallery, London*)

Claire Clairmont by Amelia Curran, 1819. (*Art UK*)

Percy Bysshe Shelley by Amelia Curran, 1819. (*National Portrait Gallery, London*)

JD Cooper's wood engraving of the Mer de Glace in the Alps, after P. Justyne, 1896. (*Wellcome Collection*

The Royal Humane Society established a hut next to the Serpentine in Hyde Park, London. (*Wellcome Collection*)

Men of Science Living in 1807–8 by Sir John Gilbert, featuring Sir Humphry Davy. (*National Portrait Gallery, London*)

Alchemist Joseph Conrad Dippel lived in Castle Frankenstein. (*Frank Vincentz*)

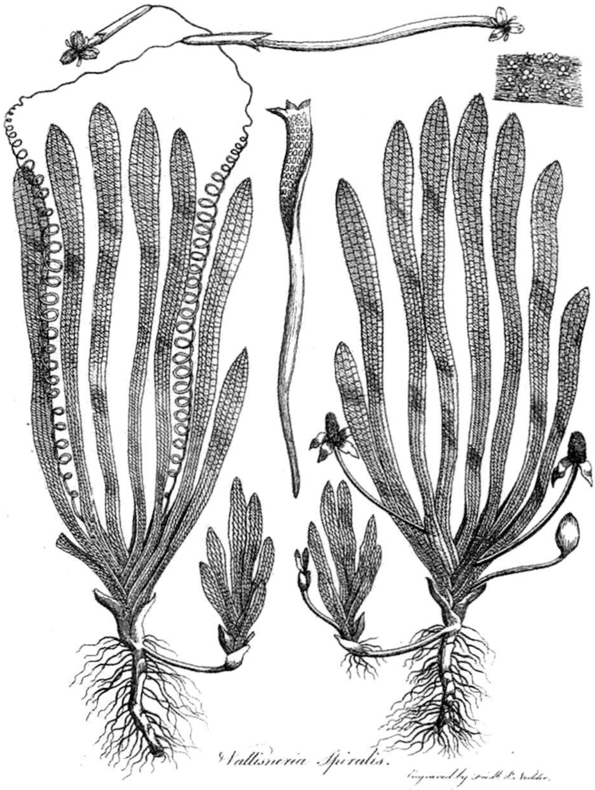

An illustration from Erasmus Darwin's poem *The Botanic Garden*, 1791.

Benjamin Franklin flew a kite in a storm to show that lightning was an electrical charge (or so it is said). (*The Pennsylvania State University*)

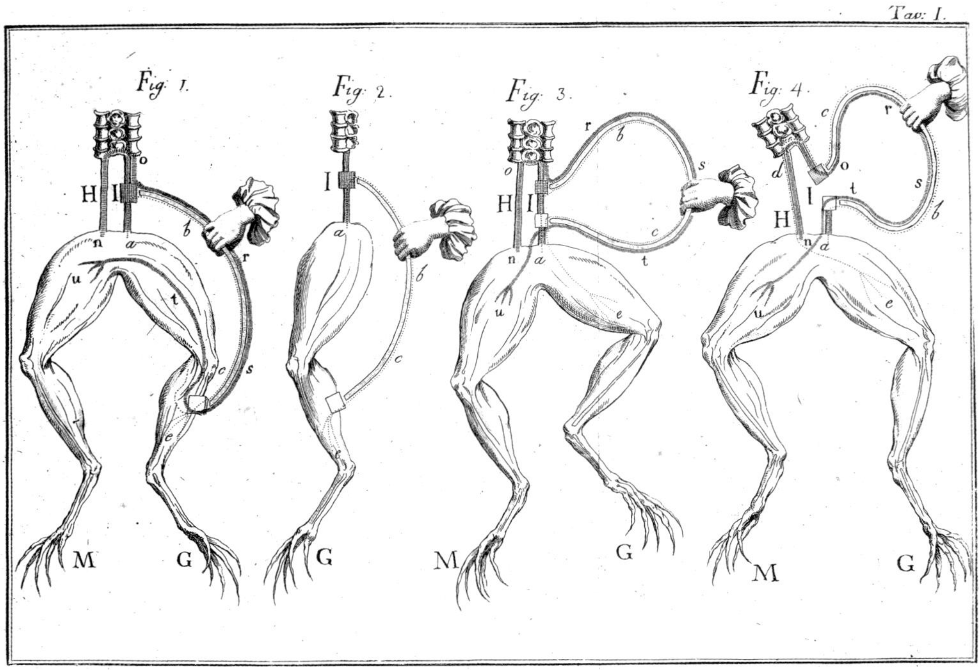

Luigi Galvani connected metal rods to frogs' legs to try to prove the existence of animal electricity. (*Wellcome Images*)

Giovanni Aldini used electricity to stimulate the muscles in severed ox heads, causing their eyes and mouth to move. (*Wellcome Images*)

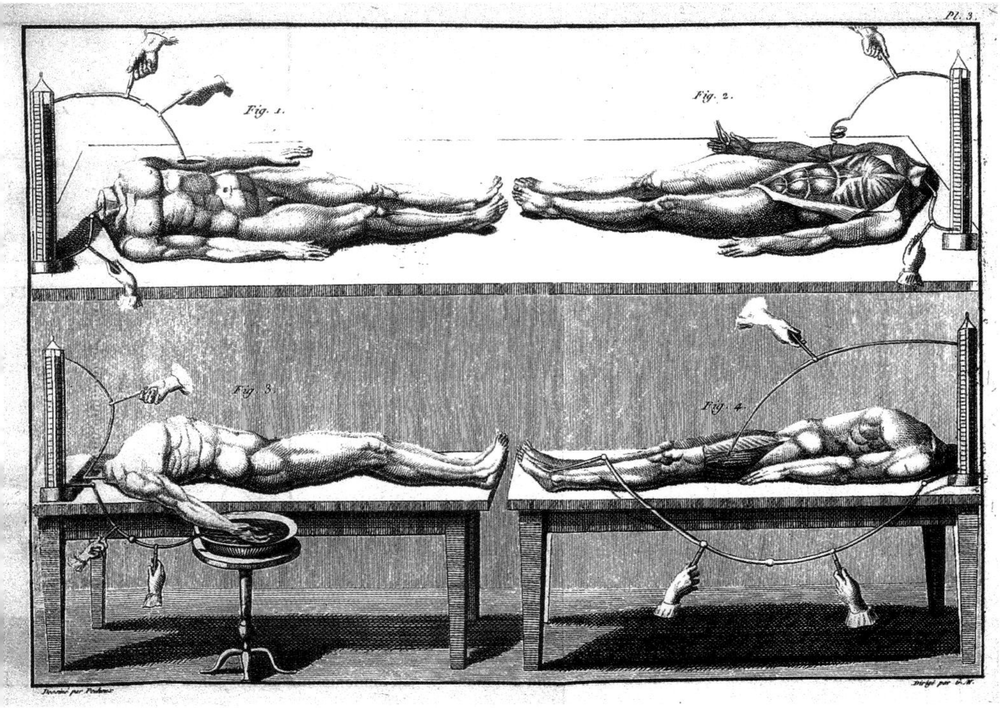

Giovanni Aldini ran an electrical charge through the corpse of George Foster, shocking his audience. (*Wellcome Images*)

Anatomist John Hunter in his study, with the skeleton of the Irish Giant behind him, after an oil painting by Sir Joshua Reynolds. (*Wellcome Images*)

Charles Byrne, a giant; George Cranstoun, a dwarf; and three regular-sized men. Etching by J. Kay, 1794. (*Wellcome Images*)

Lord Byron by Jean-Baptiste Mauzaisse.

Lord Byron's Villa Diodati by Lake Geneva, 1833, where Mary started *Frankenstein*. (*New York Public Library*)

Samuel Taylor Coleridge by William Say, after James Northcote. (*Yale Center for British Art*)

The Nightmare by Henry Fuseli, 1781. (*Tulip Hysteria*)

The Storming of the Bastille on 14 July 1789, in a line engraving with etching, after H. Singleton (*Wellcome Collection*)

The Declaration of Independence, July 4, 1776 by John Trumbull, 1843. (*New York Public Library*)

John Locke, after Godfrey Kneller. (*Art UK*)

David Hartley, 1791. (*Wellcome Images*)

The Sorrows of Young Werther by Johann Wolfgang von Goethe, 1774. (*Free German Foundation / Frankfurt Goethe Museum*)

(199)

Paradiſe Loſt.

BOOK VIII.

THE ARGUMENT.

Adam *inquires concerning celeſtial Motions, is doubtfully anſwer'd, and exhorted to ſearch rather things more worthy of knowledge:* Adam *aſſents, and ſtill deſirous to detain* Raphael, *relates to him what he remember'd ſince his own Creation, his placing in Paradiſe, his talk with God concerning ſolitude and fit ſociety, his firſt meeting and Nuptials with* Eve, *his diſcourſe with the Angel thereupon; who after admonitions repeated departs.*

THE Angel ended, and in *Adam's* Ear
So charming left his voice, that he a while
Thought him ſtill ſpeaking, ſtill ſtood fixt to hear;
Then as new wak'd thus gratefully reply'd.
What thanks ſufficient, or what recompence
Equal have I to render thee, Divine
Hiſtorian, who thus largely haſt allay'd
The thirſt I had of knowledge, and vouchſaf'd
This friendly condeſcenſion to relate
Things elſe by me unſearchable, now heard
With wonder, but delight, and, as is due,
With glory attributed to the high
Creatour? ſomething yet of doubt remains,
Which onely thy ſolution can reſolve.
When I behold this goodly Frame, this World

Dd 2 Of

Paradise Lost by John Milton, 1688. (*Folger Shakespeare Library*)

Jean-Jacques Rousseau by Maurice Quentin de La Tour, 1753.

Omai by Joshua Reynolds, 1776. (*Sotheby's*)

Prometheus by the workshop of Hendrick Goltzius, 1589. (*Rijksmuseum*)

The year he moved to Lichfield, he married Mary Howard, also known as Polly. They would have one daughter and four sons, including Robert Waring Darwin, father of Charles. When his wife died in 1770, he hired a governess to look after Robert and had a couple of daughters by her. In 1781, Darwin married again; this time to Elizabeth Pole, daughter of Charles Colyear, 2nd Earl of Portmore. They would have four sons and three daughters, bringing Erasmus' children up to fourteen. Erasmus was popular – not just with women. He was kind, sociable, enthusiastic and a great conversationalist. He wasn't, however, much of a looker. His friend, the poet Anna Seward, described him as 'above the middle size… and inclined to corpulence'. (A practical man, he had a semi-circle carved out of his dining table so that he could at least sit at it in comfort.) He also had 'a stoop in the shoulders' and a 'large full-buttoned wig' that made him look 'nearly twice the years he bore'. His mind, however, was in fine form. Darwin had a huge influence on the ideas of his day, as well as having an impact on Mary Shelley a generation or two later as she gathered material for *Frankenstein*.

The Midlands, where Darwin lived, was a hotbed of new thinking and proved a fitting home for the Lunar Society, an intellectual circle founded by Darwin in 1765 with the entrepreneur Matthew Boulton. The supergroup, which never numbered more than fourteen, often met at Boulton's home, Soho House, in Handsworth. Each member or 'lunatick', as they called themselves, was appreciated for their expertise. There was James Watt, the engineer; Joseph Priestly, the chemist; and Josiah Wedgwood, the pottery manufacturer (and Charles Darwin's other grandfather). Meetings were held on the Sunday or Monday closest to the full moon so that attendees could ride home easily by moonlight. They were lively affairs. After dinner, members would thrash out the latest scientific developments and brainstorm ways to use them to advance manufacturing and society. They would talk about everything from minerals to magnetism, often giving demonstrations and doing experiments together. The Lunar Society captured the spirit of the Enlightenment. The lunaticks valued reason and freedom. They questioned authority. They sought progress. They also put ideas into practice, helping to advance the Industrial Revolution.

As well as the latest news from the world of medicine, Darwin had much to contribute. He was interested in geology and paleontology, meteorology, anatomy and botany (he'd even planted a garden a mile from his house to keep his supplies fresh). No question was too daunting for him to tackle – not even the origin of life. As creative as he was conscientious, Darwin couldn't help but think outside the box. Using his knowledge of many different disciplines, he came up with an early theory of evolution, leading to the slogan on his coat of arms.

Darwin first aired his thoughts in his poetry. *The Loves of the Plants* (1789) is a popular interpretation of some of the ideas of the Swedish botanist Carl Linnaeus, whose work Darwin had helped translate from Latin into English. Its rhyming couplets personify plants in an erotic way that horrified more conservative members of society and made it hot-off-the-press popular with everyone else. For those with learned tendencies, it also had considerable footnotes. In Darwin's 1803 poem, *The Temple of Nature*, published after his death, he developed his ideas, tracing life from microorganisms to civilized society. 'As successive generations bloom,' he wrote, 'New powers acquire and larger limbs assume.' Wordsworth, who took the popularity of Darwin's poetry about the natural world as a sign he could have similar success, loved it. Coleridge not so much: 'I absolutely nauseate Darwin's poem,' he said.

Realizing that poetry wasn't always the best platform for scientific thought, Darwin further explored the theory of evolution in prose. In the first volume of *Zoonomia or the Laws of Organic Life* (1794), he categorized animal life to learn more about diseases, proposing towards the end that 'all warm-blooded animals have arisen from one living filament'. Preempting Charles Darwin's theory of the survival of the fittest, he suggested that every organism is propelled by 'lust, hunger and security', with 'the strongest and most active animal [propagating] the species, which should thence become improved'. Erasmus Darwin's theory of evolution reflected the optimism of the Enlightenment – that species, like society, improved with each generation. Charles would read *Zoonomia* when he was 16, although it would take a while for his grandfather's conclusions to sink in. Charles began his voyage on the HMS *Beagle* believing in special creation, where each species has been made as it is. It was only on his return that the idea of evolution took hold. Was it just coincidence that Charles gave his first notebook the title 'Zoonomia'? And that *On the Origin of Species* had a similar ring to a work of his grandfather? The subtitle of Erasmus's poem *The Temple of Nature*, as Charles would have known, was 'The Origin of Society'.

Evolution didn't quite solve the mystery of life for Erasmus. If all life came from one microorganism, there was still the question of how that microorganism came into being. In *Zoonomia*, Darwin suggested 'the great first cause [has] endued [the original living filament] with animality'. Darwin may have been vague about the nature of this first cause to allow some readers to believe it was God, absolving him of accusations of atheism. Did he believe it might be something else?

A note Darwin added to *The Temple of Nature* under the title 'Spontaneous Vitality of Microscopic Animals', suggested the microorganism might have come into being through spontaneous generation, an idea put forward by Aristotle in about 350 BC. In *On the Generation of Animals*, Aristotle described how animals and plants could appear from non-living matter. Slime, he thought, created oysters and sand produced the Darwin family favourite, scallops. The generation of life depended on particular conditions. For Aristotle, non-living matter contained 'vital heat' or 'pneuma'. The theory was widely held through the ages and into the seventeenth century, when Jan Baptista von Helmont, a Flemish scientist, suggested that mice could be produced by stuffing dirty rags into a container of wheat and waiting for three weeks. Perhaps this was taking the theory a bit too far. Some scientists then started to voice their scepticism. In the early days, it might have been enough to observe such a spectacle and gaze in wonder. Now, with the burgeoning Enlightenment values, which encouraged theories like these to be verified by experiments, it had to be tested. The big spontaneous generation debate in the eighteenth century was between Comte de Buffon and John Needham, a Catholic priest and microscopist, on one side, and Lazzaro Spallanzani, an Italian priest and biologist, on the other. In 1748, Needham, spurred on by Buffon, tried to show that life would arise in sealed, sterilized flasks of broth. In 1767, Spallanzani published experiments to show that any life in the broth was due to contamination – the longer the flask was boiled, the less growth, until it was eventually killed off. But even this wasn't seen as conclusive. The debate raged on.

In 1815, Mary and Percy spent some time in the West Country, where they might have visited a man called Andrew Crosse. Crosse lived in a large house called Fyne Court in the Quantock Hills near Somerset. Born in 1784, he had always been fascinated by science, especially the new developments in electricity. Aged 12, he went to science lectures; in his teens, he experimented with Leyden jars and later, he built a voltaic pile at home. When he was 21, his parents died and he inherited the family estate, allowing him to swap his studies in law for a life pursuing his scientific interests. He turned the ballroom into a laboratory, complete with fifty Leyden jars and bowls of crystals, and, in his grounds, he attached 1,800ft of copper wire to trees and fixed a lightning conductor. He invited anyone who was interested to pop round for a tour. Locals called him 'the thunder and lightning man' and 'the Wizard of the Quantocks'. Crosse was especially interested in whether crystals and minerals in caves and rocks were caused by electrical occurrences, and it was during one of these experiments, in 1836, that he observed the appearance of tiny insect-like creatures, which a local paper dubbed *Acarus crossii*. 'I was not a little astonished,' said Crosse, who believed he had witnessed spontaneous generation.

Erasmus Darwin is unique among Mary Shelley's men of science as the only named scientist in the preface to the first and third editions of *Frankenstein*. In the first, written by Percy, he features in the opening line: 'The event on which this fiction is founded has been supposed, by Dr Darwin… as not of impossible occurrence.' In the third, written by Mary, his experiments – or those he is 'supposed' to have carried out – are talked about by Percy and Byron. Here, it becomes clear that Mary is referring to the theory of spontaneous generation – the idea that animals and plants could appear from non-living matter. In the experiment attributed to Darwin, 'a piece of vermicelli [was preserved] in a glass case, till by some extraordinary means it began to move with voluntary motion'. 'Vermicelli' might be a type of pasta. In a note to his poem *The Temple of Nature*, Darwin refers to 'the experiments of Buffon… [in which] microscopic animals are produced in three or four days' from a paste of flour and water in a glass phial. They 'appear to be produced by a spontaneous vital process', he says. In the poem, he writes: 'Without parent by spontaneous birth / Rise the first specks of animated earth.' In another reading, 'vermicelli' is Mary's misspelling of '*vorticellae*', a microscopic animal Darwin also talks about in these notes, saying that they appeared to come alive even after they had been dried. In both cases, Darwin's conclusion still stands. 'The most simple animals and vegetables may be produced by the congress of the parts of decomposing organic matter,' he writes. The theory of spontaneous generation, he believed, was true.

In the 1818 introduction to *Frankenstein*, Percy asks readers to entertain the idea of spontaneous generation, inviting them to imagine that a creature made from the 'bones from charnel-houses' could be brought to life under the right conditions. By 1831, however, Mary has begun to doubt Darwin's theory. After expounding the vermicelli experiment, Mary appears to reject it: 'Not thus, after all, would life be given.' Why then was she telling us about it? Did she expect readers to compare introductions and want to clarify that this one overrides Percy's? Or did she want to emphasize what came next about the importance of electricity in the process of bringing the creature alive? Spontaneous generation, an older idea, could not explain how the creature was given life, but a jolt of electricity, a newly fashionable idea, could: 'galvanism had given token of such things'? Alternatively, could there be a glimmer of reservation in Mary's dismissal – that she believes there might be some truth in it? Could electricity, internal or external, trigger spontaneous generation? The language Mary uses to describe the corpse being 'endued with vital warmth' is remarkably like that of Aristotle, the original proponent of spontaneous generation, when he talks about non-living matter containing 'vital heat'. In the pages of *Frankenstein*, Mary tells us that Victor has discovered 'the cause of the generation of life' but keeps it vague.

If she is not talking about spontaneous generation, could Mary be commenting on Darwin's theory of evolution elsewhere in *Frankenstein*? Victor's experiment goes against evolution by missing it out altogether – he tries to create a complex organism from dead matter and then faces the consequences. In one way, his experiment was a success – he brought inorganic matter to life, resulting in the creature. In another, it was a disaster – he abhorred his creation, abandoned it and it turned on him. This is what could happen, Mary might be suggesting, if we defy nature. The idea of evolution appears again later in the novel when Victor considers creating a female companion. The theory of evolution suggests that species could mutate. Each generation will get stronger with weaker members of the species dying out. Victor fears that a female companion will have a 'wickedness [that] might desolate the world'. Together, the male and female creature might have children creating 'a race of devils… on the earth', threatening the future of mankind.

Darwin was full of ideas, writing six papers for the *Philosophical Transactions* of the Royal Society, where he was a fellow, including one describing for the first time how clouds form. As a doctor, he was compassionate towards his patients, treating poorer ones for free, and showing remarkable accuracy in diagnosing illnesses and predicting the outcome. His prescriptions were sometimes unconventional for the time (he advocated exercise) and sometimes unconventional for any time (he tried to remedy a 5-year-old's squint by asking him to wear a large false nose). But a large false nose was little surprise to anyone who had heard about Darwin's inventions away from his medical practice. These included a copying machine, a speaking machine, a carriage that wouldn't tip over (later giving car manufacturers a template for a steering mechanism), a horizontal windmill for his friend Josiah Wedgwood to grind pigments for his pottery, and a tiny mechanical bird. He even sketched a rocket engine.

Erasmus was also progressive in his views on women's education. Most girls at the time were taught at home. Adamant they should go to school, Darwin set one up. In *A Plan for the Conduct of Female Education in Boarding Schools* (1797), he proposed that girls should study botany and chemistry, physiognomy and philosophy, modern languages and the arts. They could even learn about manufacturing. How much they might glean from a school trip to the Wedgwood potteries. He would have been able to discuss his ideas with Mary Wollstonecraft at a supper held by the publisher Joseph Johnson. Wollstonecraft was a little more radical. She believed women should be educated so that they could contribute to society. Darwin believed that women should be educated so that they could better support men. Even so, given the thinking of the day, Darwin's view was generous. It reflected his stance that everyone had rights. Like his friend Benjamin Franklin, Darwin supported the American and French revolutions. He also opposed the slave trade, lambasting it in his poems *The Loves of Plants and The Economy of Vegetation*.

Darwin died in 1802, probably of a lung infection, and soon fell into obscurity because of his provocative views. Many of his ideas were seen as dangerous. Even in his lifetime, he'd had to be careful. In 1770, he'd had his motto '*E conchis omnia*' painted on his carriage. This infuriated the canon of Lichfield Cathedral, the Revd Thomas Seward, father of Anna, so much that Seward composed a satirical verse accusing Darwin of atheism. If Darwin didn't change his motto, he said, he would lose many of his patients. As much as Darwin liked his design, he covered the words up. It took his grandson Charles to restore his reputation. *The Life of Erasmus Darwin* (1879) omitted – by accident or design – his key idea of evolution but talked of his character in glowing terms. 'His energy was unbounded,' wrote Charles. 'As a physician, he was eminent in the noble art of alleviating suffering… He was highly benevolent and retained the friendship of many distinguished men during his whole life.'

The theory of spontaneous generation didn't fare quite as well. French chemist Louis Pasteur confined it to history in the mid-nineteenth century when he conducted an experiment with broth in swan-necked flasks. When he put yeast water in the flask and allowed only air in, the water remained clear. When he let in microorganisms, fermentation took place. Life, he proved, emerged only from other life. Pasteur's conclusions would come too late for Mary. But she may well have been aware that the theory of spontaneous generation was about to take its last gasp. Despite Andrew Crosse's discovery of mites, which would come after the third edition of *Frankenstein*, there were plenty of doubts around while Mary was writing. Which side was she on? A comparison of the 1818 and 1831 introductions suggests she may have changed her mind in the intervening years or she envisaged that many of her readers had done so. In the first preface, Darwin – linked presumably to the theory of spontaneous generation – is cited clearly as an influence to suggest the plausibility of Victor's experiment. In the latter, he is dismissed – and yet, he is still named, still in the background, still part of Mary's sprawling mix.

The Vitalist and His Opponent

The early nineteenth century was a good time for lectures. One day in 1816, William Lawrence, the new anatomy professor at the Royal College of Surgeons, took the stage for his debut talk. A flamboyant man, lithe and eloquent, he had drawn quite the crowd. His lectures followed a series by John Abernethy. Abernethy had been an anatomy professor at the Royal College for a couple of years. He was stocky and plain-spoken. Most new kids on the block would begin a talk like this by praising the previous speaker, especially when the speaker had been their mentor. In excited tones, they would thank them for helping them get where they are today. On the social scene, Lawrence was a charmer. He would have no trouble thanking someone before claiming the limelight for himself. But this lecture series was work, not play. Today, he had other ideas.

* * *

William Lawrence had been born in 1783 in Cirencester, Gloucestershire. At home, science and medicine were common topics – Lawrence's father, also called William, was the top doctor and surgeon in town. The young William was bright. Showing promise that he would excel at his father's profession, he scooted off to London when he was 15 to start an apprenticeship with the surgeon John Abernethy. Lawrence would train under Abernethy for the next five years. Although they got on at work, the two men were very different. Lawrence was flamboyant; Abernethy was brusque. Abernethy had been born in 1764 in London and was the son of a merchant. Having excelled at school, Abernethy completed an apprenticeship in surgery and whizzed up the ranks. In 1787, at just 23, he was appointed assistant surgeon at Barts hospital, becoming a surgeon there in 1815, a role he maintained until he retired twelve years later.

On the side, Abernethy ran a successful private practice as a doctor, where he was known for his blunt bedside manner and for diagnosing his patients whatever their symptoms with digestive issues. At least his prescription was palatable. He often recommended a dose of biscuits. The biscuits, sold at his local bakery, contained sugar and caraway seeds. The Abernethy biscuit is still popular today. Abernethy also lectured, first at his home and then, when his audience outgrew the space, at a lecture theatre Barts built for him. He had inadvertently started the hospital's medical school. Abernethy wrote on medical matters, too, and was the first person to classify tumours. From 1814 to 1817, Abernethy was an anatomy professor at the Royal College of Surgeons. Back in the day, he had been a fan of the anatomist John Hunter and had listened closely to his talks. When Hunter died in 1793, Abernethy vowed to pass on his ideas to a new generation. In the spring of 1814, he delivered a lecture at the Royal College with the title 'An Enquiry into the Probability and Rationality of Mr Hunter's Theory of Life'. He could have no idea that, two years later, he would be challenged by his former apprentice and be the centre of a major debate. Hunter had proposed that blood was 'endowed with the principle of life' and might be the key to vitality. Abernethy thought blood couldn't wholly explain life, but it might be closely associated with whatever the vital principle may be. Abernathy described 'vitality' as a 'subtle, mobile, invisible substance, super-added to the evident structure of muscles, or other form of vegetable and animal matter'.

Abernethy, like Hunter before him, was a vitalist. He believed that some kind of substance, a vital principle, gave an organism life. The mere organization and function of living bodies couldn't explain it. The theory had been doing the rounds in some form since ancient times. In the third century BC, Galen, a Greek doctor and philosopher, had argued that life depended on certain vital spirits. But then people went quiet on the topic. Few paid it much attention until the seventeenth century, when the French philosopher Rene Descartes described human bodies as automata. They were mechanical devices, he said, albeit sophisticated ones. Lots of thinkers reacted badly. Biology, they protested, didn't seem sufficient to explain perception or movement or development or life. And what did this mean for the soul? Did it exist? By the late eighteenth century, the issue had been formulated along particular lines. What made organic matter different from dead matter, and vegetable life different from animal life, asked natural philosophers? Did organic matter need a vital principle to bring it alive or for it to stay alive? If so, what was this principle like?

The debate reached new heights on the Continent with the claims of Franz Mesmer, a German doctor. Mesmer had proposed that every living thing has an invisible force, which could be used for healing. The force was 'animal magnetism'. His theory became known as 'mesmerism'. In 1784, King Louis XVI of France decided to investigate whether it was true. Researchers, who included the American polymath Benjamin Franklin and the chemist Antoine Lavoisier, refuted the theory. An invisible force, they said, didn't exist. Similar conclusions undermining vitalism were being reached across the Channel. In 1793, John Thelwall, a political orator and friend of Samuel Taylor Coleridge, gave a lecture on animal vitality at Guy's Hospital in London. The talk resulted in a series of follow-up meetings full of fascinated medical students. Thelwall dismissed Hunter's mysterious idea of a 'spark of life'. As a materialist, he said that life could be explained by the physical make-up of the body.

If Abernethy's 'invisible substance' did exist, what was it? Abernethy said it was 'analogous on the one hand to the soul and on the other to electricity'. Abernethy stopped short of saying that the vital principle was electricity, but he did think electricity formed an 'important link in the connexion [sic] of our knowledge of dead and living matter'. He referred to the experiments of Humphry Davy as proof. In his lecture, William Lawrence, like Thelwall, claimed there was no evidence of a 'super-added' substance. Well-read in French and German medicine, Lawrence had been influenced by the French anatomist and pathologist Xavier Bichat, who also held a materialist view of life. In Bichat's lectures, *Physiological Researches on Life and Death*, translated into English in 1816, he had defined life as 'the sum of the functions by which death is resisted'.

Similarly for Lawrence, life was the 'assemblage of all the functions' of a living body. Scientists have 'observe[d] living bodies in the moment of their formation... when matter may be supposed to receive the stamp of life... [but] we have not been able to catch nature in the fact'. All people have seen is that animals 'have participated in the existence of other living beings... the motion proper to living bodies, or in one word, life, has its origin in that of its parents'. Lawrence was a radical materialist. He said you couldn't separate life from a living being. The human body was merely a complex organism. You could observe its organization 'from an oyster to a man'. Life came about as a result of its complexity and could be explained in purely physical terms. Lawrence questioned what Abernethy's 'substance' could be. 'For subtle matter is still matter,' he said, 'and if this fine stuff can possess vital properties, surely they may reside in a fabric which differs only in being a little coarser.'

When Lawrence attacked Abernethy's theories in 1816, Abernethy felt slighted, horribly so. Lawrence had been his assistant. They had lived together while Lawrence was training. Lawrence had been his protégé. Now Lawrence was arguing with him – in public. Lawrence's lectures attracted media attention not so much for his denial of a vital spark but for his claim that the development of species could be seen 'from an oyster to a man'. This was alarming to a Christian audience, pre-Darwin, who believed in special creation, the idea that God designed all life directly as it is today. Charles Darwin's *On the Origin of the Species* wouldn't be published for another three decades, but scientists already seemed to be trying to topple man from his pedestal. How special was man if he originated from – or was at least remarkably similar to – other forms of life? *The Quarterly Review*, a conservative periodical, reflected people's fears. Lawrence asked his audience, they said, to believe 'that there is no difference between a man and an oyster... That all the eminent powers of reason, reflexion, imagination, and memory... are merely the function of a few ounces of organized matter called the brain!' And if that wasn't enough, 'Mr Lawrence strives with all his powers to prove that men have no souls!' Lawrence's stance was reductive and had dangerous overtones of atheism.

Lawrence was not the first to propose a proto-evolutionary theory. Decades earlier, Erasmus Darwin – Charles' grandfather – introduced the concept in the first volume of *Zoonomia* (1794). Similar ideas had emerged on the Continent. The question was whether anyone thought it involved a vital principle. Were scientists and philosophers on the side of Abernethy or Lawrence? Lawrence used evolution to refute its existence. Others claimed the vital principle was responsible for evolution. Several theories were doing the rounds. In 1780, Johann Friedrich Blumenbach, a German physician and anthropologist, put forward the theory of '*Bildungstrieb*', a 'formative drive' essential for 'generation, growth, nutrition and reproduction' in all living things. Blumenbach's ideas were widely debated in Romantic circles. He may well have been one of the 'physiological writers of Germany' Percy refers to in his introduction to the first edition of *Frankenstein*. Coleridge had heard Blumenbach's lectures at Göttingen University. 'I wish much to investigate the connection of the imagination with the *Bildungstrieb*,' he wrote later in a notebook dated 1810. Coleridge also knew Abernethy – he had consulted him about his stomach complaints and nightmares – and staked his own claim in the vitalism debate. Coleridge's poetry suggests he sided with Abernethy as a vitalist. In *Conversation Poems* (1795–1807), he refers to the idea of 'one life' in all living beings. As a poet, this is how he perceived the world. His scientific work is more ambiguous. In *Hints Towards the Formation of a More Comprehensive Theory of Life (*1818), a paper he wrote with his doctor James Gillman, he denied that life depended on something external and mystical. 'I must reject fluids and ethers of all kinds, magnetical, electrical, and universal to whatever quintessential thinness they may be treble-distilled and (as it were) super-substantiated!' said Coleridge. Yet the pair also tried to avoid a materialistic standpoint, where life was explained merely by a being's physical organization. They argued instead that 'a life principle' was an inherent drive towards 'individuation' in all things. In humans, it appeared as 'self-consciousness', including a sense of morality and the soul.

Coleridge and Gillman's theory had echoes of *Naturphilosophie*, an idea put forward by Friedrich Wilhelm Joseph von Schelling, another contender for Percy's gang of 'physiological writers of Germany'. The theory was trending among a group of writers and thinkers that met from 1794 to 1806 in the university town of Jena to discuss the latest ideas. Like the vitalists, Schelling argued you couldn't explain life in a purely mechanistic way. Organisms, he said, contained certain organic forces. Schelling saw the natural world as a network of invisible powers and energies; it had a spiritual energy or soul. Each being had an inherent drive to get to the next, higher stage: plants, for example, wanted to become sentient animals and animals wanted to become men. The concept intrigued people and invited ridicule. A diamond, said one geologist who supported *Naturphilosophie*, was 'a piece of carbon that has come to its senses'. Another one replied: 'Then a quartz... must be a diamond run mad.'

These ideas shaped the landscape in which Mary Shelley was writing her novel. Lawrence's attacks were becoming pointed. It was no longer enough for him just to state his case. Now he felt the need to be sarcastic about his opponent and parody the opposition. 'To make the matter more intelligible, this vital principle is compared to magnetism, to electricity, and to galvanism; or it is roundly stated to be oxygen,' he said. ''Tis like a camel, or like a whale, or like what you please.' Lawrence seemed to adopt a more conciliatory tone when he acknowledged that the vitalist perspective was understandable, attributing it to a 'propensity in the human mind'. However, he trod dangerous ground by suggesting the same propensity drives men's belief in 'higher and imaginary beings', especially when they witness unexplained phenomena. Lawrence wasn't just attacking vitalism; he was also undermining religion, the bedrock of society. Over the next few years, Lawrence and Abernethy would trade barbed insults in their lectures at the Royal College, captivating the public who could follow the debate in literary periodicals like the *Quarterly Review* and the *Edinburgh Review*. There was no easy way to shut down the argument. It began to have a life of its own.

Who did Mary side with in *Frankenstein*? Did she believe that the creature comes alive because of the mere organization of his body parts from 'vaults and charnel houses' in line with Lawrence? Or must Victor imbue the corpse with a vital spark for it to join the realms of the living? Victor confronts the subject early in the story. 'Whence, I often asked myself,' he says, 'did the principle of life proceed?' Mary and Percy asked each other the same question. They mentioned it in their joint journal when they were travelling on the Continent in 1814. A year later, John Polidori, Lord Byron's doctor, recalled in his diary that he talked with Percy 'about principles – whether man was to be thought merely an instrument' in the summer of 1816, while they were all in Geneva. Mary confirms this in her preface to the 1831 edition of *Frankenstein*, telling us that she listened to a conversation along these lines at the villa in Geneva between Byron and Percy on 'the nature of the principle of life, and whether there was any probability of its ever being discovered and communicated'.

Mary wrote this preface years after the Lawrence–Abernethy row, but she had been composing her story at its peak. Did Mary think the answer had been settled when she wrote the draft? Did she later? Mary may well have learned the intricacies of the debate from Lawrence. Lawrence had been one of Godwin's visitors when Mary was growing up and Percy consulted him about his stomach and kidney pains for three years from 1815, while the vitalism debate raged on. Suspecting that Percy had TB, Lawrence recommended the couple live in a warmer climate. They took his advice after *Frankenstein* was published in 1818 and left for Italy. But just because Mary knew Lawrence, it doesn't mean she agreed with him. Mary has Victor take a stance much closer to that of Abernethy: that inanimate matter needs to be imbued with something to make it come alive. Victor tells Walton that he worked for two years with the 'sole purpose of infusing life into an inanimate body'. He describes the churchyard as containing 'the receptacle of bodies deprived of life' and, after years of study, says: 'I became myself capable of bestowing animation upon lifeless matter.' Finally, he is ready to transform it: 'I collected the instruments of life around me that I might infuse a spark of being into the lifeless thing that lay at my feet.' There are further hints throughout the novel that Mary, aligning herself with the creature, subscribed to a vitalist rather than materialist view of man. Here, vitalism would be aligned with dualism, where men were seen to have a mind or soul comprising a non-physical substance (related to the vital principle) and a body made up of a physical substance or matter. Thinking about what will happen to him after he dies, the creature says: 'my ashes will be swept into the sea by the winds'. But that won't be the end of him: 'My spirit,' he says, 'will sleep in peace.'

The Abernethy versus Lawrence row pitting vitalists against materialists is only one way of answering Victor Frankenstein's question: 'Whence... did the principle of life proceed?' or what makes matter organic or alive? Today, vitalism, as it is traditionally defined, is largely discredited because it relies on a belief in an invisible, unknown force – 'the vital principle'. Instead, the debate has been reframed to focus on the nature of consciousness. What is it? If we create a sophisticated enough machine, will it become aware of its surroundings and have a life of its own? How far could artificial intelligence take us?

Lawrence's materialist view was too daring if you wanted to get far in society – and he did. In 1819, his lectures were published as *Natural History of Man*. Under pressure from the Royal College of Surgeons, which had a more conservative stance, Lawrence withdrew them from circulation. He made it clear, however, that he wasn't happy about it, writing: 'I take the opportunity of protesting, in the strongest possible terms... against the attempt to stifle impartial enquiry by an outcry of pernicious tendency.' The publisher Richard Carlile also issued a copy under the radar, which proved so popular that it ran to nine editions. Carlile was a handy supporter. In 1821, he brought out a pamphlet, *Address to the Men of Science*, in which he urged people like Lawrence not to be cowed into submission. Thomas Wakley, editor of *The Lancet*, also initially backed Lawrence and had a dig at Abernethy for bringing theology into science. Wakley's support floundered, however, when Lawrence, who had now publicly withdrawn his materialist views, stood for the council of the Royal College of Surgeons. It was 1825. Wakley objected and forced his way into the council chamber. Lawrence helped carry him out. Lawrence's reputation among the establishment had been restored. In 1846, he was appointed president of the Royal College, taking up the post again in

1855. In 1858, he became Serjeant Surgeon to Queen Victoria and was rewarded with a baronetcy in 1867 just before he died.

Abernethy, the more overtly conservative of the two, had been president of the Royal College, back in 1826. He had also had a run-in with Thomas Wakley. In 1824, Wakley published Abernethy's lectures without his consent. Still annoyed about it years later, Abernethy included a dig at Wakley in his book, *The surgical and physiological works of John Abernethy*, which came out in 1830, the year before he died. 'Who would labour in this manner,' he writes, 'under the persuasion that the fruits of his exertions might be surreptitiously taken from him?' While Lawrence had denounced his views, Abernethy had to accept that his views were 'stolen' from him. Neither surgeon, however, would be forgotten. Mary Shelley – and Victor Frankenstein's quest to create life – would make sure of that.

The Man with the Kite

You didn't need much equipment to be a scientist in the eighteenth century. It was very lo-fi. In the summer of 1752, Benjamin Franklin conducted a landmark experiment with a silk handkerchief and a couple of sticks. He used them to make a kite. Franklin fixed a metal spike to the top and a hempen thread with a key at the end to the bottom and waited with his son William for a storm. At the first crackle of thunder, the pair fetched their notepads and rushed outside with the kite to see if the key would conduct an electrical charge. William was in his early twenties. Kites were no longer playthings. They were scientific instruments. What science they would witness today! As the storm played out, the hairs of the hempen thread stood on end as if to attention. They seemed to be electrified. With a jolt of excitement, Franklin approached the key with his knuckles and felt a twinge. Lightning, he discovered, was electrical. His sandy hair soaked through, Franklin scribbled down some immediate observations and skipped back inside. Had lightning struck the kite itself, Franklin and William may well have been dead.

* * *

We know Benjamin Franklin today as one of the Founding Fathers of the United States, but he wouldn't have known back then that this was his destiny. Franklin had been born in 1706 in Boston, Massachusetts, then a British colony, and was the fifteenth child of seventeen. After a short spell at school, where he came top in English but was mystified by maths, he helped his father, Josiah, make candles and soap. The young Benjamin daydreamed about becoming a sailor like one of his older brothers, but his father, fearing he might suffer the same fate and never return, sought an alternative pursuit for him closer to home. Benjamin loved reading, so his father arranged for him to undertake an apprenticeship with another brother, James, who was a printer. Benjamin joined James in his print shop when he was 12. Like many a publishing intern, Benjamin wanted to write. His brother had founded *The New-England Courant.* Couldn't he write for that? James, however, refused to publish anything with his name on, so Benjamin did what any imaginative writer would do: he adopted a pen name and assumed a different identity. 'Silence Dogood' was a middle-aged widow. In fourteen letters, Benjamin – or Silence – mocked elements of colonial life. No topic was off-limits. In one letter, he / she / they ridiculed the hoop petticoat, a 'monstrous topsy-turvy Mortar Piece[s]'. When James discovered Ms Dogood was little Benjamin, he wasn't best pleased. The brothers fell out and, in 1723, Franklin left to pursue new opportunities. He settled in Philadelphia, bought the *Pennsylvania Gazette*, which he edited, and wrote and published an astronomy journal called *Poor Richard's Almanack*, again under a pseudonym. He was 'Poor Richard' or 'Richard Saunders'.

In Philadelphia, Franklin met the woman who after a bit of a hoo-ha would become his wife. Deborah Reed, the 15-year-old daughter of a builder and his future fiancé, first spotted Franklin, then 17, sauntering down the road eating a 'puffy' roll and carrying two more, one under each arm (he didn't have any pockets). How funny this man looked, thought Deborah as she stood in the doorway of her home. Benjamin and 'Debby' soon began courting. They thought about marriage but held off while Franklin went to England. Once there, Franklin decided he wasn't coming back and put an end to the relationship. What was a girl to do? In 1725, Debby's mother, Sarah, encouraged her to marry someone else, a Mr John Rogers. But Rogers was in debt and failed to keep down a job. Their marriage quickly fell apart. Franklin then decided he wasn't going to stay in London forever after all and, in 1727, returned to Philadelphia. The pair got back together and, in 1730, married under common law. They would go on to have two children together. They would also raise a third, William, fathered by Franklin and born to an unknown woman around the time of his marriage.

Franklin was so successful in business that he took early retirement in 1748. Now, he could focus on his hobbies: science and inventing. Franklin had come up with his first invention when he was just 11 – a pair of swimming fins for the hands. He described them as looking like painter's palettes; the swimmer put their thumb in the hole and held the paddle in their palm. 'I pushed the edges of these forward and I struck the water with their flat surfaces as I drew them back,' recalled Franklin in a letter in 1773 to the French doctor Jacques Barbeu-Dubourg. 'I swam faster by means of these [palettes], but they fatigued my wrists.' Franklin would go on to invent a metal-plated fireplace; the glass armonica, a musical instrument made up of different-sized bowls; and 'double spectacles' or bifocals so that he could read and see into the distance without switching his frames.

But now, in the late 1740s, Franklin's main interest was electricity. He did experiments in his home laboratory. Once, he gave himself an electric shock by mistake, which he felt as 'a universal blow throughout my whole body from head to foot'. This was followed by 'violent shaking'. He also experienced numbness in his arms and neck. Undeterred, Franklin continued with his electrical experiments. In 1749, in a letter to a friend in London, Franklin described the idea of an electrical battery. This was decades before the Italian physicist Alessandro Volta introduced the 'voltaic pile' at the turn of the century. Franklin also had a theory that lightning and electricity were the same – both appeared as a flash of yellow and crackled. He wasn't the only one. The English surgeon John Freke had suggested it in his 1746 treatise on electricity. But few had been as interested by lightning as Franklin to fully investigate its nature and its force. Lightning fascinated him. To protect people – and buildings – from the destructive power of lightning during storms, Franklin developed an iron rod eight to ten feet long with a point at the end. 'The electrical fire would, I think, be drawn out of a cloud silently before it could come near enough to strike,' he wrote. In 1752, Franklin tested the theory that lightning was a form of electricity with a kite – or so the legend goes. Some historians aren't quite so sure he ever stood in the rain with his son and a silk handkerchief, but Joseph Priestley, the English chemist, was adamant in his book *History and Present Status of Electricity* (1767) that he did, and Franklin had described a similar experiment in a letter to a friend the year he was said to try it himself. A couple of years earlier, Franklin had also proposed an experiment using a lightning rod in a letter to the Royal Society in London, which may well have started the rumours. That suggestion had been taken up in northern France by Thomas-François Dalibard, a physicist, who put a 40-foot metal pole on a stool supported by three wine bottles – it was France, what else? – during a storm and found he could draw off sparks from the rod. A local priest was summoned as a witness, a crowd gathered in awe and a craze took hold: people across Europe tried it themselves. Percy Shelley was among them. He was said to have attempted Franklin's version at Eton with a kite and almost electrocuted himself. Very Franklin-eseque.

What significance would this have for *Frankenstein*? Even without Percy's near-electrocution and interest in Franklin's experiments, lightning held literary appeal for Mary Shelley. First, it was a vivid motif – one associated with the Gothic. It could convey power, the supernatural, anger, revenge, destruction, fear. Writers had used it for thousands of years. In ancient Greece, Zeus, the head god, stood on Mount Olympus, hurling lightning bolts at anyone who displeased him. In the Bible, God similarly 'shot out lightnings, and discomfited [David's enemies]' (Psalm 18.14). Lightning could also signal God's approach. In the Old Testament, just before God gives Moses the Ten Commandments, 'there were thunders and lightnings' (Exodus 19.16). In the New Testament, it heralds the Second Coming. 'For as the lightning cometh out of the east, and shineth even unto the west,' proclaimed Jesus, 'so shall also the coming of the Son of Man be' (Matthew 24.27). Elsewhere in the Gospels, it has dangerous connotations. 'And he said unto them, I beheld Satan as lightning fall from heaven.' (Luke 10.18). Here, Jesus sees Satan, an archangel, fall from grace just as lightning falls from the sky. Lightning and Satan are linked.

Mary came up with the idea for *Frankenstein* in Geneva in 1816 on a dark and stormy night. She was living through a thunderstorm. 'The thunderstorms that visit us are grander and more terrific than I have ever seen before,' she wrote in her journal. 'We watch them approach from the other side of the lake, observing the lightning play among the clouds in various parts of the heaven, and dart in jagged figures upon the piny heights of Jura, dark with the shadow of the overhanging cloud.' Of course, we may think, storms and lightning are likely to appear in her novel.

Lightning appears a couple of times in *Frankenstein.* Perhaps the most striking is in the run-up to the midpoint of the story when Victor is returning to Switzerland. He has just found out that his brother William has been murdered. As he nears Geneva, a storm has gathered, and he sees 'lightning playing on the summit of Mont Blanc in the most beautiful figures', echoing the language of Mary's journal. As he walks on, 'vivid flashes of lightning dazzled my eyes, illuminating the lake, making it appear like a vast sheet of fire'. Then, just as Victor is equating the sound of the weather with William's funeral dirge, 'a flash of lightning illuminated... the wretch'. The storm reflects the turbulence in Victor's heart and mind and mirrors how Victor's world is being torn apart by the creature. It also creates terror in the reader. Lightning has brightened the sky enough for Victor to see 'the filthy daemon'. This electric flash of light, with its connotations of power and destruction, is Victor's connection to the creature. Realising the creature is a murderer, Victor becomes set on revenge. It brings him closer to his downfall.

This episode has extra weight because of an experience Victor had as a boy. As a teenager, Victor 'witnessed a most violent and terrible thunderstorm' with his father at their house near Geneva. 'Dazzling light', he tells Captain Walton, reduced 'an old and beautiful oak' to a 'blasted stump'. The next morning, the tree was 'thin ribbands of wood'. The story appears in both the 1818 and 1831 editions of Mary's novel with a few minor differences. In the earlier version, Victor learns the science behind the tree's destruction from his father. In the later version, he learns about it by a 'man of great research in natural philosophy'. Victor finds it 'new and astonishing'. In both cases, Victor then questions the work of alchemists that had gripped his imagination. In the 1818 version, Victor's new understanding of electricity leads him to 'overthrow' his old beliefs. In 1831, it puts them 'greatly into the shade'. In both, he starts to direct his studies towards 'natural philosophy'. (In Mary's draft, this was 'chemistry', a slightly narrower field.) Mary's first version goes into more detail about the link between lightning and electricity. Victor directly asks his father about 'the nature and origin of thunder and lightning' and gets the answer 'electricity'. His father shows him its effects using 'a small electrical machine', as well as 'a kite, with a wire and string, which drew down that fluid from the clouds'. Mary might not mention Franklin here, but given the scientific context, he was surely in her mind. Would it be pushing it to go further, to suggest that Franklin is hovering above the pages, influencing elements of Mary's characters? It is Victor's father, Alphonse, who carries out the experiment Franklin is known for. This might make Victor the natural successor to Franklin, pushing the next frontier in electricity. Frankenstein and Franklin do share some characteristics – most obviously the sound and spelling of the first part of their names. Was Mary making a conscious or subconscious connection between her protagonist and the scientist? Did the words 'Castle Frankenstein', which she might have encountered on her travels, stick because the name 'Franklin' was already there?

Fuelled by curiosity, both Victor and Franklin pushed the boundaries of science – and Mary wasn't the only one to suggest they did so to a Promethean extent. The German philosopher Immanuel Kant made the connection too, describing Franklin, in an essay published in the 1750s, as 'the Prometheus of modern times'. For Mary, Victor was the 'modern Prometheus'. Was anyone who experimented with electricity, especially those who drew fire, or lightning from the sky, Promethean? Given that Mary was well-versed in the classics, there is little to suggest that she borrowed Kant's appellation, but it is intriguing that they both alighted upon a similar title. Perhaps Kant's description suggests that it was natural at the time to think that Franklin had shades of Prometheus about him so that when Mary came to write about a man experimenting with a kite, Franklin, quickly followed by Prometheus, sprung to mind.

Whatever film directors might have us believe, Victor didn't bring his creature to life with lightning; nor was there lightning at the time of the creature's birth. But there is a link between Victor witnessing lightning and creating a living being. It is how he learns about electricity.

Lightning, a middle English word, comes from the word '*lightnen*', to make bright. At its root is the word 'light', which, according to the Bible, is a prerequisite for God creating life. 'Let there be light and there was light,' proclaims God (Genesis 1.3), before going on to separate the light from the darkness and calling the light 'day'. Victor might not have used lightning to bring his corpse to life, but he does 'infuse a spark of being' into it. What is lightning, if not a great spark of light? They are surely related. Science tells us so. When Victor creates life, Mary may well have had galvanism in mind.

* * *

In 1753, the Royal Society awarded Franklin the Copley Medal for his work in electricity. Alongside his interest in science, he would maintain a lively sideline in politics. In 1757, he moved to London as the colonial representative for Pennsylvania, Georgia, New Jersey and Massachusetts. He was unable, however, to get the British government and colonies to warm to each other, testifying in Parliament about the colony's opposition to the Stamp Act. When he returned to America, the War of Independence was getting into its stride. Debby had not been keen on ocean travel and when Franklin started making trips to Europe in the 1750s, she had remained at home, running his businesses and looking after the children. Franklin had tried to persuade her to change her mind when he popped back in 1762, but she refused. They would never see each other again. By the time Franklin next returned home in 1774, Debby had been dead for three months. She had suffered for years from a series of strokes. Franklin was now deep in American politics. In 1776, he helped draft and then signed the Declaration of Independence, before scooting off to France, again representing America, to negotiate an alliance between France and America against Britain. By now, he had attained almost cult status, with women wearing a copy of his bearskin cap. His next significant step was negotiating the Treaty of Paris in 1783, finally ending the American War of Independence. Franklin returned home in 1785, where he helped draft the Constitution. Franklin disagreed with just one key point related to the new American identity: the appointment of the bald eagle as a national symbol. In a letter to his daughter, he said the eagle had 'a bad moral character'. A turkey would have been better. It was 'a much more respectable bird' and 'a bird of courage'.

Franklin's final mission was to help get rid of slavery. In the past, he had profited from it, but now he was firmly against it, becoming president of the Pennsylvania Society for Promoting the Abolition of Slavery. He presented a petition calling for an end to the slave trade to congress in 1790, just months before he died of complications from lung disease. Franklin had been born an Englishman but was now heralded as a true American and honoured with public tributes. He didn't, of course, achieve everything on his own. John Adams, then vice president of America, was exaggerating only slightly when he said future generations would believe 'the essence of the [American Revolution was] that Dr Franklin's electrical rod smote the earth and out sprung General Washington. That Franklin electrified him with his rod and thence forward these two conducted all the policy, negotiation, legislation, and war.' Adams had a complicated relationship with Franklin and was making a point that history wasn't quite as simple as all that. It is an arresting image, nonetheless.

The Great Promoters of Galvanism

Monday, 17 January 1803 would be marked in the diary of two men in London for very different reasons. For George Forster, 26, it was the day he was to be hanged. Forster had drowned his wife and child in Paddington Canal. He would meet his end at Newgate Prison. How he wished this fateful date would never come. The same could not be said for Giovanni Aldini, an Italian physicist. Aldini had been looking forward to this date as much as Forster had been dreading it. He was on the frontier of research into electricity. Under the 1752 Murder Act, bodies of executed criminals could be used for science. The Royal College of Surgeons had offered this one to him. Aldini had conducted plenty of experiments on the effects of electricity on animal parts. Now he could find out its effects on the human body.

After the execution, Forster's body was extracted from the gallows and carted across London to the Royal College's home at Lincoln Inn Fields. Aldini then set to work. He used three troughs, each containing forty discs of copper and forty discs of zinc to generate electricity, conducting the current through metal rods inserted into Forster's corpse. First, he conducted a current to a rod attached to Forster's head. The jaws quaked, nearby muscles contorted into uncomfortable-looking positions and one eye popped open. Conductors attached to Forster's body produced even stronger contractions of the muscles. 'The arms alternately rose and fell... the fists clenched and beat violently the table,' Aldini later recorded. 'A lighted candle placed before the mouth was several times extinguished.' What strange goings-on! A reporter from *The Times* was there to record events. 'It appeared to the uninformed part of the bystanders as if the wretched man were on the eve of being restored to life,' he said. It was all so alarming that Mr Pass, a Beadle of the Royal

College, didn't just pass out; he died of fright. The Royal Humane Society had been recommending electric shocks for resuscitation since the late eighteenth century. Aldini had said he wanted to show that the method had potential – although not necessarily to the extent of raising Forster from the dead. 'I… did not aim at reanimating the cadaver,' he claimed a year later, perhaps to allay any allegations that he had been trying to cause a scandal. He was too late. Aldini's experiment caused enough of an outcry for similar demonstrations to be banned. In 1805, Aldini felt so hounded that he left the country.

The previous month, Aldini had carried out another experiment in front of the Royal Highnesses the Prince of Wales, the Duke of York, the Duke of Clarence and the Duke of Cumberland. This time, his prop had been an ox head, fresh from the abattoir. Aldini had fixed metallic wires from a voltaic pile to different parts of the bull's head, causing its tongue to loll, its eyes to roll and its lips to curl back. The ox looked like it was alive and annoyed – perhaps at being disturbed from its eternal slumber to find it lacked a torso and limbs. Theatrical as he was, Aldini hadn't been conducting these spectacles as mere entertainment. He had wanted to spread the word about the work of his uncle, Aloisio Luigi Galvani, another Italian physicist. The two had been close and had followed similar career paths. Aldini had been born in 1762 in Bologna, Galvani's hometown. In 1782, after graduating in physics from the city's university, he worked as an assistant in his uncle's home laboratory, experimenting with electricity. He then returned to the university as a professor of experimental physics. Galvani had worked there as a professor of medicine, surgery, anatomy and obstetrics.

* * *

Aloisio Luigi Galvani had been born twenty-five years earlier in 1737. The son of a goldsmith, he was mild-mannered, kind and modest. After gaining degrees in medicine and philosophy at the University of Bologna, he joined its academic ranks. Unable to leave his work behind, he did experiments at home, keeping a range of Leyden jars (a jar that could store electric charge) and machines to produce electricity by friction to hand. Galvani was also interested in the human skeleton and comparative anatomy, combining his interests when he made his major discovery: animal electricity by chance. Inspiration came from some soup. One day, Galvani's wife Lucia Galeazzi was preparing frogs' legs for the broth. When her knife touched one of the frog's nerves, it twitched. Lunch would have to wait. Galvani and Lucia, who would often assist him in experiments, set out to understand why. Galvani would go on to conduct a series of experiments throughout the 1780s on the effect of electricity on frogs' legs. In one instance, he planned to examine the effects of atmospheric electricity on frogs and had hung them, spinal nerves exposed, on brass hooks from an iron rail. When one hook brushed against the rail, the leg jerked. Galvani and his assistants placed the legs and hooks on other metals, producing similar results. When they placed them on wood or glass, non-conducting materials, very little happened.

Scientists already knew that electricity could make muscles move. Galvani wanted to find out more about the nature of that electricity and how it was produced. Watching a frog's leg kick, Galvani was reminded of the Leyden jar, which had been invented just forty years earlier, in 1745. Scientists could store electricity in it by filling it with water and then directing an electrical current into it through a metal cap. The water's charge would then generate an opposing electrical charge in an outer metal plate. Galvani envisaged a frog's muscle and nerve as two sides of the jar. When the circuit in the animal was completed, animal electricity was produced – a bit like the artificial electricity in the vessel. 'These results surprised us greatly,' he later wrote, 'and led us to suspect that the electricity was inherent in the animal itself.' Galvani believed animal electricity was distinct from the kind of electricity that flows through metal. He published his findings in *Commentary on the Effect of Electricity on Muscular Motion* (1791), expounding his theory that animal electricity was secreted by the brain and distributed through the inner core of nerves to muscles. For Galvani, electricity was the life principle that John Abernethy had talked about. To mix fact with fiction, Victor may well have thought that stimulating animal electricity in a body of 'bones from charnel-houses' could bring that body alive.

But not everyone agreed with Galvani's findings. Alessandro Volta, another Italian physicist, repeated Galvani's experiments. At first, he was impressed. Then he began to doubt Galvani's interpretations. Volta had been born in 1745 in Como, northern Italy and was the son of a nobleman. He was expected to go into the church, but was waylaid by science and in 1779, became chair of natural philosophy at the University of Pavia. Volta, who coined the term 'galvanism' to refer to Galvani's animal electricity theory, believed that two dissimilar metals caused the electric charge and explained Galvani's findings. Galvani could show only that electricity was the stimulus for nerves and muscles. His experiments didn't show muscles contracted because of electricity in the animals' bodies. Galvani shunned controversy, but bolstered by his nephew's support, he defended his work. Challenging Volta's point that the muscle contractions in the frogs' legs had been caused by two dissimilar metals, he tried to show that they could also be stimulated with just one metal or none at all. In one experiment, he dipped the end of a nerve and its detached leg muscle in mercury, showing the nerve could still stimulate the muscle. He may also have conducted another experiment where he exposed a frog muscle and cut its spinal cord. When the end of the spinal cord brushed against the muscle, it twitched. Then, in 1797, he showed that the nerve of one frog's leg could stimulate the nerve in another one, making the muscle contract. His evidence was mounting, but Galvani was about to lose his career. That year, Napoleon created the Cisalpine Republic in Italy. Galvani refused to take the oath of allegiance to the new state and soon lost his appointments. The following year, he died.

Galvani might have lost his legacy, too, had it not been for Aldini, who would go on to champion his work. It was just as well. Volta wasn't going to give up his side of the row. Between 1793 and 1800, Volta wrote twenty memoirs and many letters arguing that animals did not have their own intrinsic electricity. Any evidence Galvani or Aldini had offered could be explained away, he said, by metals or other factors. Something good, however, was to come of Volta's work. In trying to disprove Galvani,

Volta developed an early battery. The Voltaic pile, which dates back to 1799, comprised a stack of alternating discs of zinc and copper divided by brine-soaked paper and could produce a continuous electrical charge. William Godwin's friends, William Nicholson, a physicist, and Anthony Carlisle, a chemist and surgeon, followed Volta's work closely. After refereeing Volta's paper about his early battery for the Royal Society, they constructed one themselves, passing an electric current through water and decomposing water into oxygen and hydrogen. Humphry Davy would use a similar method, known as electrolysis, to isolate nine new elements, including magnesium and potassium. Volta would also lend his name to a unit of electricity – the volt.

Scientists clamoured to weigh in on the Galvani versus Volta debate. Victor Frankenstein would have plenty to say decades later. For now, people had to make do with the experiments of physicists like Christian Gottlieb Kratzenstein. Kratzenstein had been born in 1723 in Wernigerode, in what is now central Germany, and would spend much of his life collecting academic posts, teaching medicine, the natural sciences, maths, mechanics and finally, experimental physics. His disciplines might have been varied, but they all fed into his big passion in life: discovering how electricity affected the human body. He was delighted to find that applying a low-voltage electrical current to the body could make paralyzed fingers move. He also found that applying a current to his body helped him sleep better at night, leading to treatment that would later be used for insomnia and depression. Kratzenstein died in 1795, two years before Mary would be born, but his name lived on. Kratzenstein would become known as a founder of electrotherapy. His name also sounds remarkably similar to the protagonist in Mary's novel.

In the preface to the 1818 edition of *Frankenstein*, Percy says that the 'physiological writers of Germany' suggested the premise of the story was possible – you could create life. We can only guess who he had in mind, but certain names have been proposed again and again. Perhaps Percy was talking about Alexander von Humboldt, a German explorer and natural philosopher. Humboldt had been born in 1769 in Berlin and was from aristocratic stock. His father was an army officer. His godfather would become King Friedrich Wilhelm II. He wasn't just well-connected from birth; he was also well-educated. Humboldt's private tutors were top-notch. Markus Herz, a former student of Kant, taught him geography, while Karl Ludwig Willdenow, one of the founders of phytogeography, the study of the geographic distribution of plants, would introduce him to botany. Humboldt's mother, however, was less interested in her son becoming a scientist and more interested in him going into politics. To please her, he read law at university. But he couldn't stay away from science for long. He went on to train in geology, before taking up a post in the Prussian Department of Mines. He would eventually be seen as one of the founders of modern geography.

Humboldt heard about the disagreement between Galvani and Volta on a visit to Vienna in 1792 and conducted hundreds of experiments to determine who was right. Sometimes he went to extraordinary lengths. Once, he experimented on a dead bird he found in his garden, placing a zinc blade in its beak and a silver one in its rectum to induce an electric shock. The bird flapped its wings and, it is said, walked. To push the experiment further, Humboldt tried this test on himself. In 1797, Humboldt published his findings, claiming that there was some truth to both Galvani and Volta's arguments. Humboldt believed that the nervous system generated a substance that made the muscles contract (Galvani's animal electricity) and that metal electrodes exacerbated it but didn't produce it (bimetallic electricity). Volta, however, would not be pacified. He was insistent that animal electricity did not exist. We now know that both arguments had something going for them. Animals are inherently electrical: the heart produces an electrical pulse that keeps them going, while two dissimilar metals can be used to produce electricity.

As for Humboldt, he had dreams to chase. His mother had died in 1796, leaving him enough money to quit his job and plan a trip. In 1799, he embarked on a long-distance voyage with the botanist and doctor Aime Bonpland, starting in South America. On his travels, Humboldt delved into botany and zoology, geology and geography, and developed his views on slavery and colonialism. Electricity was still in his thoughts. At the Orinoco River, he had the bright idea of experimenting with electric eels that swam in the water. To catch them, he sought the help of local fishermen and a pack of thirty horses and mules, sending the animals into the water first to tire the eels out. Humboldt then dissected the eels. His experiments proved his hypothesis that the eels released their shocks intentionally and that shocks would only be transmitted through certain materials like metal rods and human contact. When Humboldt returned five years later, in 1804, he found he was famous. He would go on to deliver highly popular lectures, initially at the University of Berlin, in 1827 and 1828, and then in a music hall to accommodate the thousands of people who clamoured to see him. He would gather and expand his notes into five hefty volumes. The first lecture was published in 1845. The fifth, which was half-finished when Humboldt died in 1859, had an index more than 1,000 pages long.

If indices were any measure of intellect, Humboldt was up there with the best. You could also judge him by the company he kept. His circle included the writer Johann Wolfgang von Goethe and the physicist Johann Wilhelm Ritter – another contender for Percy's 'physiological writers of Germany'. Ritter had been born in 1776 in Silesia, then in Prussia, now in Poland, and studied medicine at the University of Jena. He would become best known for discovering ultraviolet light in 1801, but he was also immersed in the discussions over electricity that were happening in the early nineteenth century. Ritter discovered that water could be decomposed by electricity. He invented the process of electroplating and, in 1802, built the first dry-cell battery (Volta's had been the first wet-cell version). He would build the first electrical storage battery a year later. Ritter, like Galvani, ran electric currents through frogs' legs to observe what would happen, concluding that the effects of galvanic electricity were caused by chemical reactions rather than Galvani's animal electricity or Volta's theory of electricity generated by the contact between metals. Like Humboldt, he was also interested in the effects of electricity on the human body and thought there was no better subject than himself. On several occasions, Ritter applied electricity to his hands, ears, nose, eyes and tongue. Whatever contribution these experiments made to science, the effects on Ritter may have been detrimental, contributing to his poor health. He died in 1810, aged just 33.

Ritter had been interested in how animal electricity differed from bimetallic electricity. The same question had kept Karl August Weinhold up at night – and it was his experiments that would have the most in common with Victor's. The work of Galvani, Aldini, Kratzenstein and Ritter might all have been useful to Mary, but if we're casting for the 'physiological writers of Germany', Weinhold is a shoo-in. Unlike the other scientists, Weinhold claimed you could use electricity to create life rather than just renew it. Weinhold had been born in 1782 in Halle. After a stint as an army surgeon, he would become a professor of medicine. He would published an account of his work in 1817, the year before *Frankenstein* came out. Weinhold thought the brain was like a battery with wires attached and set out to prove it. In a series of experiments on dead kittens, he removed their spinal cords and brains, replacing them with a mixture of zinc and silver. His observations were startling. In one, 'the animal... raised its head, opened its eyes, stared for a time... hopped around, and then sank down exhausted'. In another, he claims the kitten could see and hear. Life, for a time, seems to have been restored. Weinhold said the kittens were alive because of bimetallic electricity. We don't know for certain that the kittens did hop around. He only had one witness – an unnamed assistant. But the image was hard to shake off, especially given Weinhold's profile – he would go on to become the Prussian royal physician. Weinhold had few reservations about the scare or scandal he might have caused. He would later argue for population control in the poor by suggesting compulsory infibulation, sewing the foreskin shut. If Victor had thought of this for the creature, he might not have been so concerned about him becoming the father of a super-race.

* * *

Mary would have been too young to have heard about some of the experiments in galvanism. When Aldini had made Forster's eye pop open, she would have been just 5. But the debate about the effect of electricity on the body continued while she was growing up. She may well have heard about it from her father. She would learn more about it when she left home. We know she went to at least one lecture on the topic. In December 1814, she attended a talk in London by Andre-Jacques Garnerin, a French inventor and the first man to descend successfully in a parachute. In Geneva, a couple of years later, she may well have heard more about electricity's therapeutic effects from John Polidori, Byron's doctor. Aldini's work had big implications for medicine – he had suggested his techniques could treat conditions like 'melancholy madness' or clinical depression, laying the foundations for what we now know as electro-convulsive therapy. When Mary returned from her 1816 trip to the Continent with Percy, she would have a direct line to one of Aldini's assistants, Charles Hunnings Wilkinson. Mary and Percy had settled in Bath. Wilkinson also lived there and had continued to push Aldini's work. Galvanism was 'an energizing principle', he said, 'which forms the line of distinction between matter and spirit, constituting in the great chain of the creation, the intervening link between corporeal substance and the essence of vitality'. Mary may well have gone to his talks at Kingston Lecture Room. Wilkinson, by coincidence, had a second home in Geneva, where Victor Frankenstein was raised.

There are parallels between Aldini and Victor, too. Both were repulsed by their work. Conducting his initial experiments, Victor often turned 'with loathing from my occupation'. Not that this stops him. When he considers creating a female companion, he talks about facing 'repugnance to the task', which then becomes overwhelming. Aldini also felt 'repugnance' over his work, although he is able to continue, too. His 'love of truth' gets him through. The creature also describes the process of creation as a 'series of disgusting circumstances'. Similar words would appear in the *Edinburgh Review* in 1815 referring to the work Aldini. 'The accounts that he gives of his results,' it reads, 'are rather disgusting than instructive.' The descriptions of the creature coming alive and Forster's body moving also have uncanny similarities. 'I saw the dull yellow eye of the creature open,' Victor tells Captain Walton, 'and a convulsive motion agitated its limbs.' *The Times* reporter had written about Forster's muscles being contorted, while 'the left eye actually opened'. Both Victor and Aldini wanted to take control of nature – although perhaps to different extents.

Aldini had said he had no desire to create life and did fear scandal. Victor admits he wanted to 'command the vital powers'. Victor is a more extreme version of Aldini with less showmanship.

This all assumes that the creature was brought alive by electricity. Mary is vague – and yet, in fact and fiction, one word keeps appearing. Try as we might, we can't escape the word 'spark'. The Royal Humane Society had used it to describe life in its motto: '*lateat scintillula forsan*' or 'a small spark may perhaps lie hid'. *The Times* reporter had used it to suggest Aldini's methods could be useful in 'rekindling the expiring spark of vitality'. Victor talks about infusing 'a spark of being' into the creature to bring him alive, later wishing he could 'extinguish the spark, which [he] had so negligently bestowed'. At the end of the story, the creature asks himself why he didn't 'extinguish the spark of existence' that Victor had given him after he was rejected by the De Laceys. Was the spark figurative or do Victor, the creature and Mary equate the principle of life with a spark of electricity?

In the year *Frankenstein* was published, Aldini's corpse experiment had a dramatic reboot. That autumn, James Jeffray and Andrew Ure, professors at the University of Glasgow, tried to resurrect Matthew Clydesdale, a father-of-two who, in a drunken fury, had murdered an elderly man. Jeffray and Ure ran an electrical current through his body using rods and a voltaic pile. 'Rage, horror, despair, anguish and ghastly smiles, united their hideous expressions in the murderer's face,' wrote Ure. Clydesdale even started to breathe. One report has him standing up, with Jeffrey plunging a lancet into his jugular to stop him in his tracks. Spectators ran from the scene out of fear.

Today, Mary's 1831 preface tends to inform our reading of *Frankenstein*, although biographers have warned that some details might not be strictly accurate. What of the crucial conversation between Byron and Percy about galvanism? Was galvanism mentioned at the villa in Geneva, as Mary alleges? John Polidori said it was. 'Shelley and I had a conversation about principles,' he writes in his diary, 'whether man was to be thought merely an instrument.' Was Mary a 'nearly silent listener', as she claims? Perhaps she was at the time, preferring to listen and observe. But she wouldn't be silent on the page, as readers were to find out eighteen months later.

The Devious Dissector

In the top right-hand corner of an oil painting of the surgeon John Hunter, glowing with an aura of the uncanny against the smoky cedar walls, is a pair of dangling feet. The toes are long, the ankle bones thick, the skeleton oversized. The picture is by Sir Joshua Reynolds. Hunter's companion, hanging up beside him, is Charles Byrne or the Irish Giant. Charles Byrne – or O'Brien as he was before taking on his stage name – was born in 1761. His father is thought to have been a weaver. His mother may well have been Scottish. Both were of regular build. Their son was different. There was no difficulty reaching the top shelf in their house. They just asked Charles. He would grow to just over 7ft 7in (2.31m). The family lived in a remote hamlet in County Londonderry, Ulster. His parents were content. But Charles dreamed of greater things. He longed for mass adoration. In his late teens, he packed his bags and sailed to Scotland to make his name – and make his name he did.

Byrne, who liked to dress in a natty frockcoat with a waistcoat, knee breeches, silk stockings and frilled cuffs, was a one-man novelty act. In Edinburgh, he gave the night watchman something to talk about by nonchalantly lighting his pipe one foggy morning on a streetlamp because it was at the perfect height. With a canny sense of what sells, he put himself on display at country fairs and village greens for money across Scotland and northern England, where he was an instant hit. He reached London in spring 1782, where he quickly attracted curious and delighted audiences, as well as the king and queen. One reviewer praised his 'elegance, symmetry and proportion', while the diarist Silas Neville noted with enthusiasm that 'nature has exceeded her usual limits in a most astonishing degree'. Byrne, a gentle, amiable man, was even celebrated in a stage show at the Theatre Royal, Haymarket – *Harlequin Teague; or the Giant's Causeway.*

* * *

But although fame was welcome when it came with acclaim and respect, Byrne also attracted the attention of another celebrity of the day, the surgeon John Hunter. Hunter was as feared in some quarters as he was revered. He had always been the determined sort. He was born in 1728 near East Kilbride in Scotland. His father, also called John, was a grain merchant. His mother, Agnes, was the well-educated daughter of a Glasgow magistrate. The youngest of ten children, John was anything but studious. Fascinated by nature, he preferred scampering about the outdoors. What trade could he ply? A vocation was far from obvious. First, he was sent to Glasgow to complete an apprenticeship in cabinet making, but that didn't work out. Next, he was sent to London to help his brother William, a surgeon, at his anatomy school. John turned out to be surprisingly good at it – and good, too, at finding bodies for William to study.

Believing he had found his vocation, John decided to become a surgeon. He started a medical course at St Mary Hall, Oxford, but baulked at learning Greek and Latin and poring over dusty old medical texts. He was better at practical tasks and turned instead to different surgeons, helping them out until he got a role as an assistant at St George's Hospital. Yet this job would only take him so far. John's experience still wasn't enough for him to join the Company of Surgeons and practise fully in his own right in London. There was, however, an alternative. John could practise in his chosen field if he was prepared for conflict. In 1760, he became an army surgeon.

John had an instructive few years working in France and Portugal, but on his return home, he still couldn't penetrate the London surgical clique. Needing a job, he turned to an adjacent field and got a position with a dentist, where he learned about tooth transplants. His reputation strengthened. In 1767, Hunter became a fellow of the Royal Society, and a year later, finally got a post as a surgeon at St George's Hospital. He soon set up his own anatomy school and delivered lectures, just not very successfully. He often got caught up in detail and lost his audience. He was, however, revered as a mentor and practitioner for his dedication and meticulousness, becoming a surgeon extraordinary to George III in 1776. Prime Minister William Pitt and economist Adam Smith also sought out his services. His workdays began at five in the morning, allowing him to dissect for a few hours before breakfast. He would then see patients at home or in hospital, operating on the poorer ones for free, before having dinner at 4pm. In the evening, he would write. Hunter died in 1793 during a meeting at St George's Board of Governors, where they had been discussing student admissions. As part of his legacy, he left 14,000 specimens, including animal tissue and organs that he had collected for dissection and close study, which would be bought by the government. It was a collection that a lot of people admired, but few – least of all Charles Byrne – wanted to end up in. About 3,000 specimens have survived and are housed at the Royal College of Surgeons in London.

The eighteenth century saw a surge of interest in anatomy. Anatomy schools sprung up in the big cities across Europe and surgeons now had to pass exams in the subject before they qualified. It was useful, physicians realized, to examine a dead body before operating on a live one. While some felt queasy at the idea of anatomy (studying the body) or dissection (cutting up flesh to get to the bones), others were fascinated. Between 1793 and 1796, Sir Astley Cooper, a bright young surgeon, who attended lectures by John Hunter, performed public dissections in the anatomy theatre of the Royal College of Surgeons. They were the hot ticket of the day. But surgeons didn't see dissections as mere performance. They took their work seriously and realized that their understanding of the body could mean the difference between life and death. Total concentration was involved, as the surgeon John Abernethy suggested when he described his mentor John Hunter at work. Hunter stood for hours almost stock-still, said Abernethy, carefully unpicking connecting tissue, 'patient and watchful as a prophet, sure that the truth would come'.

Herophilus, a Greek doctor, had performed the first public dissection in the early third century BC, but many people still felt uneasy about it hundreds of years later. The religious concerns can't be overstated. Some feared that dissection could harm the soul and that people wouldn't be recognizable in the afterlife. Dissection was banned in England until 1540, when the Companies of Barbers and Surgeons in London, later the Royal College of Surgeons, was given a licence to dissect four executed criminals a year. Rapt students would watch a tutor dissect a body in an anatomy theatre, perhaps pointing to a medical textbook as he did so. Yet these rare occasions weren't considered enough. Medical schools and students wanted a more hands-on approach – why could they not touch the bodies themselves? Some areas had their own laws: from 1694 in Edinburgh, anatomists could use corpses of people found dead in the street or those who had died by suicide. But the rules were often hard to enforce. The 1751 Murder Act, allowing the bodies of killers to be made available for dissection, helped a little, but demand still outstripped supply. If you were as keen to work with a dead body as Hunter, you would do anything to get one.

Some anatomists became savvy if slightly underhand businessmen, offering prisoners money to pay their funeral costs or bribing the hangman at the gallows to give them the body. Others were more patient, waiting until people were buried and paying men to steal them from the grave. Bodysnatching was big business. Gangs of six or seven men – known as body snatchers, grave robbers, resurrectionists or sack-'em'up men – trawled churchyards when it got dark and became so adept at the task that they could remove a body from a grave in fifteen minutes, carting away up to ten a night. Sometimes they stole from dead houses, too, where corpses were kept before they were buried, and homes. They sold the teeth to dentists, who turned them into dentures; the hair to perruquiers, who made flowing locks into wigs; and body fat to manufacturers of candles and soap. Then, they put the body in a sack and dropped it off at an anatomy school or rooms kept by a surgeon. Hunter was thought to be among the recipients, while the London Borough Gang, which ran from about 1802 to 1825, was behind the supply to a lot of the big London anatomy schools, after doing a deal with Astley Cooper.

Body snatchers could make good money. You could get as much for a fresh corpse as you could for taking a job as a labourer for several months. Corpses of people who had died of unusual illnesses fetched more, while children or 'smalls' were sold by the inch. Churchyards became dangerous places. Bodysnatching wasn't a clear crime – a dead person wasn't property, so their body couldn't be stolen – but it was considered unsavoury. It wouldn't do for dead bodies to be seen merely as material for anatomists or for people to go round digging up graves as and when they liked for a bit of cash (as tempting as it might be). Sometimes, officials would whip a body snatcher in public to set an example. At other times, a mourner spotting a body snatcher might take the law into their own hands and start a fight or a riot. Friends and relatives opposed to dissection sometimes went straight for the anatomist. Some despised surgeons for being able to cut up a body dispassionately as illustrated in William Hogarth's *The Four Stages of Cruelty*. The engravings, made in 1751, show a surgeon as a magistrate, overseeing the anatomization of a murderer's body. People opposed the idea that corpses and body parts now seemed to be traded like other commodities.

Mourners often tried to protect the dead from an undignified end. The cheapest option was to place flowers or rocks on a freshly dug grave so that they would notice if a body snatcher had been snooping around. The problem was that body snatchers could easily replace them – or, if you did notice a misplaced rock, it could mean that it was too late. Placing a slab of heavy stone on the coffin was little deterrent either – the body snatcher could dig down at one end to the coffin and drag the corpse out. Some had a patent coffin, which had hidden springs to stop anyone opening the lid. Other corpses were tied down by iron straps. Watchtowers appeared in churchyards, where guards would sit at night, although if you were really concerned, you might hold a vigil over a newly dug grave as freshly buried bodies were worth more. Others took even more drastic measures and buried pistols attached to trip wires just below the ground designed to shoot anyone who tried their luck. Coffins with iron lids, several layers and big, jangling locks were a safer bet, as were cages over coffins or mortsafes, which were used in Scotland after 1816. Sir Astley Cooper, a keen anatomist, was buried in several coffins in a stone sarcophagus, when he died in 1841, keeping body snatchers out.

Demand for bodies from graveyards increased after 1823, when the Judgment of Death Act came in. Fewer crimes were now punishable by death. Knowing how much anatomists wanted corpses, William Burke and William Hare skipped the bodysnatching process altogether. Hare ran a boarding house. When one of his elderly lodgers died without paying his rent, the pair sold his body to an anatomy school in Edinburgh to cover the shortfall. It was only a short leap to kill off other lodgers and invite people over who might never leave. The pair killed sixteen people. Hare eventually testified against Burke, who was found guilty and sentenced to death. After he was hanged in 1829, his body was anatomized and dissected. Burke and Hare's success led to a run of copycat crimes across the country, including a gang known as the London Burkers. To enforce a modicum of order, Parliament established the 1828 Select Committee on Anatomy to look into the situation, discussing the value of anatomy, examining the supply of bodies for dissection and looking at the relationship between anatomists and body snatchers. This finally gave rise to the Anatomy Act of 1832, which Abernethy had campaigned for, allowing anatomists to use unclaimed corpses from prisons, workhouses and hospitals. People could also donate the body of their next of kin.

Bodysnatching – and killing for corpses – slowly faded out, with few reported cases after 1844. But that was decades after *Frankenstein*. At the time Mary Shelley wrote her novel, bodysnatching – and the mutilation of the body after death – was a real fear. A natural sciences student at the University of Ingolstadt in Bavaria, Victor tells us he 'became acquainted with the science of anatomy'. Yet it isn't enough. He also wants to 'observe the natural decay and corruption of the human body'. Decay may be 'natural', but the body, he notes, is corrupting. It sounds like an unpleasant, debased process. Victor's desire to get close to the dead echoes Abernethy's approach. 'To obtain knowledge [of human anatomy],' he said in a lecture that may have been attended by Percy Shelley, 'we must be companions with the dead.' Abernethy knew his medical students might need a bit of persuading to fully embrace dissection. 'We have need of enthusiasm, or of some strong incentive, to induce us to spend our nights in study, and our days in the disgusting and health-destroying avocations of the dissecting-room,' he said in a lecture. Giovanni Aldini, the Italian physicist who had once wired up a corpse and suggested he could bring it alive, had also been aware that dabbling in death could be contentious: 'The spectacle of death has always brought fear to the heart of sensitive man; the philosopher, however, is obliged to stifle this painful feeling in the desire to be useful to his fellow men.' Victor echoes these sentiments when he talks about his experiments to bring a corpse to life: 'Who shall conceive the horrors of my secret toil,' he says, 'as I dabbled among the unhallowed damps of the grave, or tortured the living animal to animate the lifeless clay?' To persevere with his research, he says he had to have been 'animated by an almost supernatural enthusiasm'.

Mary had grown up close to corpses, too – the family home in Skinner Street was near the Smithfield slaughterhouses. Every time she stepped outside, she would have seen and breathed in the fetid smells of cattle corpses and fresh meat. The idea that Victor 'collected bones from charnel-houses' would have been easy for her to imagine. Victor found his 'materials' in 'the dissecting room and the slaughterhouse'. In Germany, where Victor studied, surgeons could dissect the bodies of anyone who had died in prison or by suicide – the laws were more relaxed than those in the UK. But that wouldn't have stopped British readers asking where the bodies in this dissecting room came from. Could some have been taken from a grave?

Victor performs a sort of reverse dissection, assembling a body from discarded parts. When the creature comes alive, Victor cries: 'Great God! His yellow skin scarcely covered the work of muscles and arteries beneath.' He not only knows the make-up of a human body, its physical workings; he can still see it. The creature is exposed. Victor tells us that the creature's limbs were 'in proportion' and that he chose the parts for their beauty. The creature should be beautiful, but he is not. He is monstrous and 8ft tall. John Hunter, the most celebrated surgeon of Mary's day, was also after the corpse of a very tall man – Charles Byrne. Some records say he was 8ft 4in (2.54m). Could Mary have been inspired by Charles Byrne as she envisaged the creature and John Hunter as she created Victor?

Byrne knew that, after his death, anatomists would want his corpse. Terrified his body would be dissected, he arranged to be buried at sea. When he died in 1783, aged 22, his body was placed in a lead coffin and taken to Margate. But Hunter was determined to get his hands on Byrne's body and, it is said, paid the men in charge of the coffin £500 to give it to him on its way to the coast. He was successful. After dissecting Byrne's body, Hunter proudly added the skeleton to his collection of bones and tissue, where it went on display at what would become the Hunterian Museum at the Royal College of Surgeons. It stayed on show for 200 years – although today, after protests that Hunter should have followed Byrne's wishes and left him alone, it is available only to people studying Byrne's unusual condition, gigantism. In its place hangs the portrait by Sir Joshua Reynolds, painted in 1785, with the dangling feet in the background. The day after John Hunter died, his body was dissected, too. It was just as he wanted.

A Wizard with Words

At the turn of the nineteenth century, at Field Place in West Sussex, there were strange goings-on. A young Percy Shelley and his four sisters – his brother would be born later – could be found leaping about in floaty gowns and silk scarfs in the grounds of the mansion pretending they were spirits or fiends. On some days, Percy filled a fire-stove with flammable liquid. The children's hearts would skip a beat at the explosion. They were terrified and delighted. Percy had been born in 1792. As the eldest, he would tell his sisters stories to entertain and scare them. A favourite character was an old alchemist with a long beard who lives in a garret of their house. Alongside Percy's preoccupations with a man in the attic and various psychic phenomena was a passion for science, especially the burgeoning field of electricity. 'When my brother commenced his studies in chemistry, and practised electricity upon us, I confess my pleasure in it was entirely negatived by terror at its effects,' recalled his sister Hellen. 'Whenever he came to me with his piece of folded brown packing paper under his arm, and a bit of wire and a bottle… my heart would sink with fear at his approach.'

Percy's schooling had much to answer for. At first, he was home-educated. Then, aged 10, he went to Syon House Academy in Brentford, Middlesex. The strict environment came as a shock. How different it was from his comfortable home life, where he had bathed in the love and attention of his parents, the servants and siblings, even if he occasionally sent them scurrying off in fear. He wasn't so adored here. At school, he was ribbed for his countryside accent and bullied by his classmates for his dreaminess. He also lacked the survival skills needed for a young boy among his boisterous peers, losing his temper as often as he lost a fight. There was one highlight: a series of lectures by a man called Adam Walker about electricity, astronomy and chemistry.

Adam Walker had been born in the Lake District in 1731. The son of a woollen manufacturer, his start in life was aeons away from aristocratic Percy's. He could hardly read when he left school but still managed to throw himself into books as he grew up to learn more. He also loved building models, creating miniature versions of nearby mills and factories. In the 1760s, Walker started a school in Manchester and became a teacher. From there, he developed a career as a travelling lecturer, touring England, Scotland and Ireland and demonstrating scientific ideas. His stops included Syon House, where Percy would have encountered him. Visual aids were his thing. Part of his act in later years included an eidouranion, a transparent orrery he invented to show the movement of the planets. It was more engaging than PowerPoint and didn't crash as often. Sometimes, his eidouranion display would be accompanied by the tinkling of a celestina, a mechanical harpsichord he had also devised. Walker published transcripts of his talks, which Percy may well have read, too. His *Analysis of a Course of Lectures on Natural and Experimental Philosophy*, first out in 1766, was so popular that it went through twenty editions. The last was published in 1827. Walker often described in his work how he carried out his experiments, so that readers could follow along at home. Percy, an avid fan, was keen to have a go and had his own galvanic battery. Experimenting with electricity on his sisters, he suggested to one that he could use it to get rid of her chilblains. She was terrified. He also tied a cat to a kite to be flown in a storm. We can imagine the cat would have been terrified, too.

Walker's influence would have an influence on Percy for years to come. Percy's cousin Thomas Edwin noted in his 1847 biography *Life of Shelley* that when he visited him at Oxford, he discovered 'he had not forgotten our Walker's Lectures, and was deep in the mysteries of chemistry'. At Oxford, Percy used teacups as equipment – an idea he may well have got from Walker who, like the chemist Joseph Priestly, wanted science to be available to all and believed that you didn't need technical apparatus to take part.

Walker's ideas might even have made their way into *Frankenstein*. In line with ideas of the time, Walker saw electricity as the spark of life. In *A System of Familiar Philosophy* (1799), he wrote about 'its power of exciting muscular motion in apparently dead animals'. Percy takes a similar position in some of his poems. The imagery in *Prometheus Unbound*, for example, links electricity with love, light and life. And, as for Mary, we know that Victor imbued 'a spark of being' into inanimate matter to make the creature and that there is evidence to suggest this is electricity.

There is also a connection between Mary and Walker, some say, in their use of the Prometheus myth. 'The flame of Prometheus's torch was the expression of a philosophical truth which did not escape the ancients,' Walker says. 'Without light, nature would be lifeless.' And then there is the overlap in Walker's ideas about man's relationship to nature and Mary's attitude. Walker talks about nature trying to restore the balance between elements like air and fire when humans meddle in them. When nature as we know it can't win, he says, it is replaced by 'an artificial nature' led by 'unhappy passions'. Could the creature, a result of meddling in the extreme, be an example of 'artificial nature'? It certainly has one. Could he be led by 'unhappy passions'? And could Victor Frankenstein also be seen as being fuelled by miserable desires, now that he has won over nature and destroyed the natural order?

In 1805, Percy was sent to Eton, where he fared little better in the social stakes. He loathed sports and led a revolt against fagging, where the younger boys were expected to do tasks for the older ones. Pupils would gang up on him, engaging in 'Shelley-baiting' and calling him 'Mad Shelley'. Again, Percy found solace in science, a subject yet to find its way onto the core curriculum. Perhaps that was part of its appeal. But Eton hadn't closed its doors against it: the school had approved certain science mentors – including James Lind, cousin of the surgeon by the same name who discovered the causes of scurvy. Lind tutored Percy between 1809 and 1810, his last two years there. He had been physician to the royal household in Windsor nearby and would become a close friend and mentor to Percy. Later, Percy would tell Mary about their long walks together. 'I owe that man far – oh! Far more than I owe my father,' he would say, recalling Lind's 'tolerance' and 'wisdom'.

Born in 1736, Lind was educated in Scotland, before travelling the world as a ship's surgeon. He journeyed to Iceland, China and South Africa. Back home, he carried out Luigi Galvani's experiments with electricity, writing about his findings to his friend, Tiberius Cavallo, an Italian physicist, between 1782 and 1809. 'Have you made any dead frogs jump up like live ones?' Cavallo once asked him. 'I am glad to hear of your success in the new experiments on muscular motion,' he wrote a month later, 'and earnestly entreat you to prosecute them to the *ne plus ultra* of possible means.' Later that year, Lind wrote to Sir Joseph Banks, president of the Royal Society, to thank him for supplying frogs that allowed him to carry out experiments towards 'the unravelling of that extraordinary and as yet inexplicable phenomenon, Animal Electricity'. They were experiments he carried out in front of the king and queen. Supremely well-connected, Lind earned enough respect among his peers to mix with many of the big thinkers and natural philosophers of the day, from Benjamin Franklin, of kite fame, to the empiricist David Hume. He followed their work and the latest scientific developments with interest. Percy benefited from his knowledge, his kindness and his library, comprising books on science, magic, philosophy and literature.

At Eton, Percy kept scientific equipment like Leyden jars, which stored electricity, in his rooms. Once, he charged his door handle with electricity, giving a shock to the next tutor who touched it. Another time, a tutor found him standing on a chair, surrounded by blue sparks. When the tutor asked him what was going on, Percy said he was raising the devil. The tutor grabbed an object on the table, perhaps to steady himself, and received an electric shock in return. Science, for Percy, didn't mean an end to the occult. Writing to a friend while at Eton to arrange to meet him in the holidays, he warned that he might meet 'death-demons, & skeletons dripping with the putrefaction of the grave' on the way and 'at the frightful hour of midnight' awake to see 'the Hell-Demon lean[ing] over your sleeping form'. At Eton, Percy blew up the stump of a willow with gunpowder in the grounds. The effect would have been familiar to Victor, who witnessed the destruction of a tree stump in a storm at a similar age. He also brought a brass canon at an auction. It wasn't, however, in line with school policy. Tutors quickly confiscated it before Percy could put it to use.

Lind may have taught Percy about other areas of science as well. There's a good chance, for example, that he was well-versed in artificial respiration as a way to bring the near-dead back to life. He was a surgeon after all. In Edinburgh, he had studied under the Scottish physician William Cullen, who had been key in putting together the official methods for reviving people who had recently drowned or suffocated. Could similar discussions have later cropped up between Mary and Percy? Cullen might have been especially interested in two cases in *Frankenstein*. The first happens early on, when Victor is saved from the perishingly cold waters of the ice floe in the Arctic Ocean. 'We accordingly brought him back to the deck, and restored him to animation by rubbing him with brandy, and forcing him to swallow a small quantity,' says Captain Walton. 'As soon as he showed signs of life, we wrapped him up in blankets.' The second is the creature's efforts to save a young girl he has found in a river. 'She was senseless,' he says, 'and I endeavoured, by every means in my power, to restore animation.'

Is it too much of a stretch to say that Lind influenced *Frankenstein* through Percy, either in the discussions he had with Mary while, or before, she was writing her story or in the revisions he made to the draft? We know that Lind had an effect on him – partly through Mary's notes and partly from Percy's poems. In *Prince Athanese*, a fragment written in Marlow in late 1817, Zonoras, who imparts 'philosophic wisdom, clear and mild' to Shelley's hero is widely seen as Lind. But how much of Lind in particular, rather than just general scientific thought at the time, can be found in the pages of Mary's novel? Some say quite a bit. The description in the novel of Victor Frankenstein's studies at University of Ingolstadt could be a version of Percy's scientific education, with Waldman, Victor's chemistry lecturer, standing in for his teachers. To go further, 'Waldman', some argue, is an amalgam, albeit a rough-and-ready one, of 'Walker' and 'Lind'.

Back home in Sussex, Percy conducted his own versions of some of the grand electrical experiments that had made the headlines over the past half century or so. In 1747, a group of scientists, including Martin Folkes, president of the Royal Society, and Sir William Watson, an English doctor, decided to test the velocity of electricity in a stunt over the River Thames. First, they connected a Leyden jar to a 1,200-foot wire stretched across Westminster Bridge. They asked one man to hold one end of the wire and touch the river and another to hold the other end of the wire at the opposite end of the bridge, with the Leyden jar. They then asked a third to touch the jar and the water. When the circuit had been completed, all three men received an electric shock. Percy Shelley had a go, too, with the tools he had available. He persuaded his family to sit around the dining room table holding hands. He then electrocuted them with brown paper, a bottle and a wire.

Percy's science education didn't stop at school. In 1810, he went up to University College, Oxford to study the physical sciences and metaphysics. He would soon meet Thomas Jefferson Hogg, who would become a close friend and Percy's biographer. Hogg describes Percy as 'the chemist in the laboratory, the alchemist in his study, the wizard in his cave'. Like Lind, Percy had amassed books on magic and witchcraft, galvanism and electricity. Like Victor, both start university giving weight to both alchemy and modern science. Hogg says Percy's room looked as though he 'had endeavoured first to reconstruct the primaeval chaos'. There were burn marks on the carpets and scientific equipment wherever you looked: 'an electrical machine, an air-pump, the galvanic trough [and] a solar microscope'. Percy sometimes asked Hogg, he recalls, to help him with his experiments. Once, he got Hogg to operate an electrical generator, while Percy stood on a glass-legged stool, enabling a current to flow through him. He then used the generated sparks to set dishes of alcohol alight or create explosions with gunpowder. At one point, he was said to electrify a college servant. That didn't seem to trouble the authorities as much as a pamphlet Percy circulated in his second term. *The Necessity of Atheism*, which he published with Hogg, looked at the nature of belief, and its title caused enough controversy for them to be sent down or expelled.

Percy's father was so furious that he threatened to cut Percy off with just £200 a year (£13,200 today), if Percy refused to retract his views. Percy held fast, setting himself up for a lifetime of financial stress. While he might have doubted the existence of God, or so it would appear from his controversial publication, his imagination held onto the possibility of darker forces at work. During a midnight walk, Percy told Hogg that he heard a devil pursuing him, swishing through the grass.

Science had been a significant part of Percy's life during his formative years, his interest in chemistry, electricity and astronomy infusing his poetry. Hogg said Percy felt he wasn't so hot on maths and 'treated the whole notion of [its] paramount importance with contempt', but from his schooling, Percy would have been fluent in the basic axioms and terms and alludes frequently to shapes, surfaces, angles and symmetries in his poetry. He also freely cited ideas from those of the astronomer William Herschel to Erasmus Darwin in his work. He even said once that he saw poets as 'men of science' and considered the 'science of things' more important than 'the science of words'.

In the 1818 preface to *Frankenstein*, Percy says: 'The event on which this fiction is founded has been supposed, by Dr Darwin, and some of the physiological writers of Germany, as not of impossible occurrence', showing that at least Percy or Mary had a solid knowledge of the science of the time. How much did Percy's interest rub off on his wife? If it's too much of a stretch to say Lind or Walker appear in the novel, can we identify traces of Percy himself? Some parallels seem coincidental. Is it really significant that both Percy and Victor, for example, were born to wealthy families or is it just necessary so that they have enough free time and resources to allow them to indulge their passion for science? How important is it that both Percy and Victor were fascinated by alchemy and chemistry, reading the works of Albertus Magnus, Paracelsus and Pliny, or is that just typical of the time? Percy seems to have given weight to both for longer than Victor, who at least ostensibly slides from the ways of old to the methods of modern scientists at university. Both Percy and Victor, point out some scholars, were also brilliant at languages, from French and German to Latin and Greek, but wasn't anyone who was bright? And what of their characters? Like Victor, Percy could be moody, get obsessed with projects and need time alone. Unlike Victor, he was a university dropout and a poet. Was Mary suggesting that had Percy continued with his studies, he too might have made a creature? It seems unlikely, but that isn't to say she didn't use some of Percy's background and interests in her work. She was just selective.

One neat link can be found in Percy's first collection of poems. *Original Poetry: by Victor and Cazire* (1810) comprised sixteen poems and a fragment of one written by Percy (going by the pen-name Victor) and his sister Elizabeth (going by the name Cazire). Was Mary making a point calling her main character Percy's pen-name? Is she suggesting that Victor has some of Percy's traits? Or is it an in-joke or coincidence? And what of Elizabeth or Cazire? Cazire may well come from Charlotte Dacre's 1805 novel *Confessions of the Nun of St Omer* about a woman called Cazire who grows up in a convent, is swept up in female desire and then becomes a nun. There might not be a Cazire in *Frankenstein*, but there is an Elizabeth. And if we see *Original Poetry* as important to Mary, how obliged are we to accept other similarities between the poems and *Frankenstein*? Is it significant that Percy also explores the theme of vengeance? 'Alone will I glut its all conquering maw,' reads a line in the poem *Revenge*. 'I will glut the maw of death,' cries Frankenstein's creature. Is this a coincidence or a connection? Percy might not have written *Frankenstein*, whatever early critics thought, but he still made his mark. It would be up to Mary to decide what to do with her material. She might not have any characters skip around the grounds of a mansion in floaty gowns and silk scarves, yet there would be an alchemist in the attic.

Section III

The World of Ideas

'Everything is good as it leaves the hands of the Author of things; everything degenerates in the hands of man' – ***Emile, or On Education*** **by Jean-Jacques Rousseau**

The New Romantics

Mary Shelley wasn't a born Romantic. Her parents were icons of the Enlightenment. Enlightenment thinkers believed that reason could uncover objective truths. But Mary was a rebel. She was drawn to a new movement that valued emotion and celebrated individuality and creativity. Romantics believed that the imagination could reveal hidden insights into our experiences. Like Enlightenment thinkers, they questioned the role of God. The Romantics knew exactly what they would put in his place. They bowed to the majesty of nature. The thinker Edmund Burke had put it best in *A Philosophical Enquiry into the Origin of Our Ideas of the Sublime and Beautiful* (1757) when he described nature as the greatest example of the 'sublime', a concept that could stir feelings of awe and terror. These were exciting and alarming times.

Despite their different views on life, the Romantics and the thinkers of the Enlightenment weren't sworn enemies. They all championed freedom and tolerance and were open to new ideas. They often crossed paths. The major Romantics would later be lassoed together as the Big Six. Mary would be connected to all of them. One worked with her mother. William Blake had illustrated Wollstonecraft's *Original Stories from Real Life*, while his poem *Visions of the Daughters of Albion* (1793) was partly inspired by her major work, *A Vindication of the Rights of Woman*. They may well have met, too, at one of Joseph Johnson's literary gatherings. Other Romantics had met her father or at least had something to say about his work. There was John Keats, William Wordsworth, Samuel Taylor Coleridge and Percy Shelley, who Mary would go on to marry. The final one, Lord Byron, had a child with Mary's stepsister, Claire. Mary would even begin *Frankenstein* at Byron's suggestion at his villa in Geneva.

Long before Mary met Byron or Percy, she would meet Coleridge. She was 8 when she would have an encounter with him that would change her life. That encounter would involve a sailor, a sofa, a squabble and a squawk. We need to go back to August 1806. Godwin's friend Samuel Taylor Coleridge was over for supper at Mary's house. Coleridge had pretty much launched the Romantic movement with Wordsworth when they published their poetry collection, *Lyrical Ballads* (1798). He had long admired Godwin and had been a fan of Wollstonecraft. He had known Mary since she was 2. Mary had heard some people say that Coleridge wasn't very attractive. He had puffy skin, bulbous eyes, pudgy lips and hair like a bird's nest. But Mary didn't care. He was fun. He played with her and told her stories. Coleridge held Mary in huge affection, too. He had always found her very well-behaved, unnervingly so.

But Mary was developing a defiant streak. That evening Coleridge was going to recite *The Rime of the Ancient Mariner*, a narrative poem in *Lyrical Ballads*. It was full of big themes – sin and suffering and redemption. The poem follows a sailor who had shot an albatross, bringing a curse on his ship and its crew. Mary longed to hear it. It was late and past Mary's bedtime. Mary had an idea. She would pretend to go upstairs but hide behind the sofa in the parlour where the recital was going to take place so that she wouldn't miss out. Mary and her stepsister Jane tried to be as quiet as possible so that they wouldn't be discovered. They were not quiet enough. When Mary Jane, Mary's stepmother, found them, she was furious. They must be scolded!

The recital would have a lasting effect on Mary, perhaps even more so for its context. This was a prime example, Mary might have thought, of her stepmother failing to see what was important in life and what really made Mary happy. How hurt Mary felt, how misunderstood. It was so unfair. Fortunately, this would not be the last time she would cross paths with Coleridge. Her father had realized that he had made an impression on her and would take her to one of his Shakespeare lectures when Mary was 14. Mary would continue to read Coleridge's poems throughout her teenage years. When she met Percy, she found that he too was a fan. In the autumn of 1814, they would read *The Rime of the Ancient Mariner* together. When she wrote *Frankenstein* two years later, she would return again to the poem that had caused her to create such a scene as a child.

The *Ancient Mariner* and *Frankenstein* have strong parallels. First, there is the similarity between their narrative structures: both tell a story within a story. The mariner tells his tale to a wedding guest. Victor tells his tale to Captain Walton. Both works also offer warnings about what happens when someone dares to go against nature. The mariner ends life by killing an albatross. Victor creates life but he does so by artificial means. In both stories, the inciting incidents set off a chain of events, causing the protagonists – the mariner and Victor – to suffer. After the sailor kills the albatross in the *Ancient Mariner*, his ship meets another carrying Death and 'Nightmare Life-in-Death'. They gamble for people's souls. Death wins the souls of the crew. Life-in-Death wins the soul of the mariner. As the crew dies, the mariner grows increasingly lonely. The bodies of the crew then rise again using their 'limbs like lifeless tools' to help him return home. In *Frankenstein*, the catalyst for the ensuing catastrophe is Victor's creation of the monster. The creature embodies a different sort of 'Life in Death': his limbs are made of old bones, once 'lifeless tools'. After Victor abandons the creature, he even cites Coleridge's poem, describing how he 'doth walk in fear and dread… Because he knows a frightful fiend / Doth close behind him tread.' Like the mariner, Victor will soon feel horribly lonely. Everyone around him will start to die. Only he knows why. The creature is Victor's albatross, an idea Mary alludes to when she describes how Victor felt the 'deadly weight' of his promise to make the creature a mate 'hanging round his neck' and 'bowing [him] to the ground'.

Victor and the mariner are a little like each other, too. Their actions can both be seen as cruel or at least thoughtless. The mariner killed a 'sweet bird', 'a Christian soul'. Victor never considers he might have a responsibility to the creature, turning his back on him just because he didn't like the way he looked. The creature's ugly appearance suggested to Victor that he was ugly inside. Victor is unable to show kindness to the creature to try to understand him and realize he might be good. Victor and the mariner both end up alone because of how they have behaved.

Mary might not just have had Victor in mind when she was thinking of the mariner. The sailor in Coleridge's poem also resembles Captain Walton in Mary's framing narrative. They were both journeying across polar seas. The mariner had been in the Antarctic. Walton was in the Arctic. The mariner's description of his ship being surrounded by ice that 'cracked and growled, and roared and howled' could easily apply to Walton's ship, especially as he draws closer to the Arctic, a place he imagines to be of 'frost and desolation'. Mary highlights the parallels by having Walton quote directly from the poem. Both the mariner and Walton describe the landscape as 'the land of mist and snow'. 'But', adds Walton, 'I shall kill no albatross.' He blames the appeal of 'the dangerous mysteries of the ocean' to 'that production of the most imaginative of modern poets' (Coleridge's *The Rime of the Ancient Mariner*), mentioning 'the Ancient Mariner' explicitly in case we miss the reference. Walton does not kill an albatross like the mariner, but he does nearly violate nature in another way – through reckless exploration. He does, however, eventually turn back, saving his life and the lives of his crew. He has learned something from the poem.

Coleridge would be with Mary when she started *Frankenstein* – not in person, but through his work. One evening during the summer of 1816, when Mary and Percy were staying at the Villa Diodati, Byron recited the opening verses of Coleridge's poem *Christabel* (1816), a companion piece to the *Ancient Mariner*. In the poem, 'sweet Christabel' falls under the spell of a demonic woman called Geraldine. In one section, Geraldine disrobes, exposing 'her bosom and half her side'. It was 'A sight to dream of, not to tell!' When Byron reached these lines, Percy screamed, put his hands to his head and scarpered out the room. Polidori and Byron found him leaning against the mantelpiece in a cold sweat. Percy had been looking at Mary at the time and had seen her as Geraldine, with her nipples as eyes. The image had a touch of the Gothic about it. It was fantastical and terrifying – and had probably come from Mary, who had told Percy earlier that Coleridge had initially imagined Geraldine with 'two eyes in her bosom'. The Romantics were often having visions. That summer, Mary and her friends would also read Coleridge's *Kubla*

Khan: or A Vision in a Dream (1816). Coleridge had said that in creating it, images appeared 'without any sensation or consciousness of effort'. The 'anodyne', probably opium, he had taken that afternoon might have helped, too. By December 1834, Mary was describing her imagination as her 'Kubla Khan', her 'stately pleasure ground'. Gothic writers had fruitful visions, too. Horace Walpole had said he had the idea for *The Castle of Otranto* (1764), when he dreamed of a huge suit of armor, helmet included, heading his way. Robert Louis Stevenson would say that was how he'd had the idea for the *Strange Case of Dr Jekyll and Mr Hyde* (1886). Bram Stoker would say that was how he came up with *Dracula* (1897).

Mary would say a vision is how she came up with the idea for *Frankenstein*. One night after Byron had set them all the challenge to write a ghost story, Mary had a waking dream. 'My imagination, unbidden, possessed and guided me,' she says in her 1831 preface, 'gifting the successive images that arose in my mind with a vividness far beyond the usual bounds of reverie.' In Mary's vision, she would see 'the pale student of unhallowed arts kneeling beside the thing he had put together'. Mary was awake but not in control of what she was thinking. Her imagination was 'possessed' in a way the Romantics, who sought out just these sorts of experiences, would have been proud of.

Some doubt whether Mary really did have a vision at the Villa Diodati. If she did, she doesn't seem to have told Polidori. Byron's doctor kept a detailed diary of the trip and was particularly interested in anything Mary had to say (he had a bit of a crush). Mary did have strong reasons, though, for telling her readers that she had one. By 1831, when Mary wrote her preface, she needed money. She was a single mother – Percy had died nine years earlier and his family were unwilling to help her out. She wanted *Frankenstein* to sell. Mary's claim rooted her in the Romantic tradition. It also absolved her if readers thought her story was too shocking. It wasn't really her idea, she might say. It came to her in a dream. In a similar way, she could pacify conservative readers who thought that women should be mothers rather than writers. Where would they get the time or talent to create art? The only way for a woman to have written *Frankenstein* was if she had been visited by a muse who had influenced her, they might say, if not forced her hand. When *Frankenstein* was published anonymously in 1818, some people thought Percy had written it. Perhaps a strong origin story also helped persuade any doubters that Mary was the author. In her preface, Mary goes into detail about her creative process. Surely no one could doubt her after that.

We can still allow room for Percy to have had an influence on *Frankenstein*. They were together when she wrote it after all. He read drafts and made edits, contributing about 4,000 of the total 72,000 words of the original manuscript. Sometimes Percy corrected factual errors and spelling mistakes. Sometimes he changed Mary's language, preferring a more ornate style. Rather than 'talked', he suggested 'conversed'. Rather than 'caused', he proposed 'derive their origin from'. Rather than 'we were all equal', he put 'neither of us possessed the slightest pre-eminence over the other'. He also changed sentences like 'I did not despair', which might be clear and direct but is rather plain, to the wordier 'I doubted not that I should ultimately succeed'. Percy sometimes suggested more specific terms, too, replacing 'smallness' with 'minuteness', or adding that the creature had 'lustrous black' hair instead of just 'flowing' hair, enhancing the image we have of him today.

But perhaps the biggest change that Percy made was in the last line. Mary had written that Walton 'soon lost sight of [the creature] in the darkness and distance'. Percy altered this so that the creature was 'lost in darkness and distance', suggesting that he was lost for good. He has met his end. Percy may have killed the creature off. Percy had never liked the creature, some might say. It was Percy who introduced the description of the creature as an 'abortion'. His sympathies lay with Victor. Perhaps Percy recognized parts of himself in Mary's main character. He too was interested in science. He too was idealistic. Both, observers might point out, were self-absorbed. Both, they might continue, neglected a key relationship: Victor abandoned the creature; Percy abandoned Mary by paying more attention to her stepsister Claire. Not that Percy would have seen it like that. Percy believed you should be free to love anyone you wanted. Percy might have thought Victor had just got a bit carried away with his project. Victor was a tragic hero, a man who was merely a little too ambitious for his own good. Mary saw things differently. For her, Victor was capable of evil. He was an agent of chaos. Mary's sympathies lay not with Victor, but with the creature.

When Mary wrote the short story that was to become *Frankenstein*, however, her thoughts might have been in a very different place. She had written it at Byron's villa in Lake Geneva in response to his suggestion that they all write a ghost story. She was trying to write something thrilling. It didn't have to be full of angst and deep psychological meaning. But Byron didn't just provide the initial prompt. He also influenced the content. Polidori would later describe how, on that dark and stormy night, the friends 'began to talk ghostly' as they debated whether the dead could come back to life. In her 1831 preface, Mary would recall hearing chats between Byron and Shelley about 'philosophical doctrines' and 'the nature of the principle of life', ideas she would explore in *Frankenstein*. In telling her story, Mary makes two small but intriguing references to Byron. Victor's brother, William, Mary tells us, loved playing with his friend 'Louise Biron'. The name seems too close to be mere coincidence. But why does Mary include it? Perhaps, we might think, it was an in-joke – Byron would get it, as would his many fans. Then, after Victor discovers his younger brother William has been murdered, he travels to Geneva. On the way, he stops in Lausanne, where he describes the snowy mountains as 'the palaces of nature', a phrase that also appears in *Childe Harold's Pilgrimage* (1812–1818), the poem that catapulted Byron to rock-star status. Was the phrase just in Mary's mind or did she deliberately include it to acknowledge a friend?

Byron – or his absence – may have also influenced Mary as she developed Victor's character. In January 1817, Mary's stepsister Claire would have Byron's child, Alba (later called Allegra). Claire had been pregnant over the summer when the group were in Geneva. On Claire's return to England, she wrote to Byron several times, asking him to care for her and their baby. Byron ignored her. Mary looked after Claire instead. Byron was a little like Victor Frankenstein, a man neglecting his responsibility towards his child. Mary already had a sense of what it was like to grow up without one parent and then have another not speak to her. Byron was absent before his child was even born.

However annoyed or dismayed Mary might have been at Byron's behaviour, they kept in touch. In March 1818, a couple of months after *Frankenstein* had been published, Mary and Percy travelled to Italy, where they hoped to see Byron. Mary had taken a copy of her book to pass on. They didn't, however, meet up. The following month, Percy sent Byron a package containing a novel by 'an old friend of yours', who Percy reveals in secret is 'Mrs S'. Although her book had been a hit in England, Mary says she would 'regard [Byron's] approbation as a more flattering testimony of its merit'. In May 1819, Byron praised the book in a letter as 'a wonderful work for a Girl of nineteen – not nineteen indeed – at that time'. What makes it wonderful, we might say later, isn't just the story; it's also how Mary synthesizes ideas of the time. The ideas of the Romantic poets were just the start. For another influence from the cultural milieu, we swivel our attention from the book of poems on the shelf towards an oil painting on the wall by the Swiss artist Henry Fuseli.

The Nightmare

In 1782, the curators of the annual Summer Exhibition at the Royal Academy decided to shake things up a bit. Alongside the standard portraits (*Portrait of a Gentleman*, *Portrait of a Naval Officer*, *Portrait of a Dog*) and landscapes (*Landscape with a Fox Basking in the Sun*, *View of the Peak of Tenerife, Morning with a Fog*), they would hang an oil painting with a less decorous subject. *The Nightmare* by Henry Fuseli, a Swiss artist, shows a depraved-looking imp crouching oppressively on the breast of a woman, supine and helpless. From the red velvet curtains pokes the head of a gigantic horse. The vision is terrifying and titillating. It is all about power and submission, anxiety and trauma, conflict and death. The curators knew it was daring. It was Gothic in extremis. It was art with a capital A. The public would love it or hate it, but at least it would provoke a reaction. And so it did. More than 55,000 visitors crowded through the doors of the Summer Exhibition that year. When they reached *The Nightmare*, people stopped and stared and gasped and gulped. Some found it thrilling. Some found it chilling. Some had no idea what it possibly meant.

Critics ever since have tried to decode Fuseli's painting. The eighteenth-century essayist William Hazlitt was only half-joking when he said the work was 'a nightmare on the breast of British art'. It was so different from the work people were used to and it provoked some disturbing ideas. The safest interpretations highlighted possible classical motifs. The woman looks like the Sleeping Ariadne statue in the Vatican, some said, while the creature perched on her chest echoes the Hellenistic representations of crookbacked beggars. Others suggested it looked like part of a Bacchanalian tableau. Sleeping women in those sorts of scene were seen as objects of sexual desire and showed that the drunken revellers had enjoyed a night of debauchery. The women were 'maenads', literally 'mad women'. Their behaviour was strange, violent, sexual. They may have experienced hallucinations. Here, Fuseli's maenad may have been hallucinating the imp on her chest and the horse by the curtain.

Other critics turned to Norse fairytales and said Fuseli was having fun – in a rather twisted way – with a pun. The word 'nightmare', they noted, comes from the Old Norse 'mara', a wicked female spirit who trampled on people as they slept, stirring up nightmares. The 'mara' cantered about on a horse. The impact of the clomping hooves on the sleeper left them wrung out and sweaty when they woke. Fuseli represents the 'mara' by including an imp and a horse's head.

If Fuseli was such a fan of wordplay, perhaps he was also toying, some said, with the word 'nightmare' in another way. A nightmare in Fuseli's time was thought to be a case of sleep paralysis. The sleeper would be partially conscious but unable to move and could experience hallucinations. An evil spirit, in the form of an old woman, a black dog or, as with Fuseli, an incubus, was thought to lie upon a sleeper, almost suffocating them. The earliest account of this condition was published in 1664 by the Dutch doctor Isbrand van Diemerbroeck. In one case study, *Of the Night-Mare*, he talked about a woman who 'sometimes believed the Devil lay upon her and held her down'. At other times, she felt a 'great Dog or Thief' was on her chest, making it hard for her to speak or breathe – and yet, she was unable to move to shake it off. A popular reference book, published in 1721 and reprinted until 1802, continued to fuse ideas of nightmares with sleep paralysis and daemons. In *An Universal Etymological English Dictionary*, a nightmare was a 'disease when a man in his sleep supposes he has a great weight laying upon him'. In Fuseli's painting, some say the great weight takes the form of an imp. Samuel Johnson adopted a similar definition of a nightmare in his dictionary, published in 1755, describing it as 'a morbid oppression in the night, resembling the pressure of weight upon the breast'.

Others have proposed that the painting is autobiographical. The woman represents Anna Landoldt, the niece of Fuseli's friend Johann Kaspar Lavater. Fuseli was in love with her and had begun to paint her portrait when he heard that she had married another man. He flipped the canvas over and painted *The Nightmare*. Fuseli dreamed he was in bed with Anna, his 'hot and tight-clasped hands [wound] about her'. He 'fused her body and soul together with [his] own – poured into her [his] spirit, breath and strength'. The painting shows Fuseli's frustrated desires. He had hoped to marry her. Fuseli is the incubus, showing his desire to possess her, even though she was out of bounds. Fuseli was a passionate and dangerous man. He would also have an unusual connection to Mary.

* * *

Henry Fuseli's life started off ordinarily enough in Zurich in 1741. His father, Johann Caspar Füssli, was a painter. As a boy, little Henry enjoyed drawing and colouring in, but his parents had grander ambitions for him. His father wanted him to enter the church. He did as he was told and by the time he was 20 he had been ordained as a Zwinglian minister. It didn't last. He longed to make it as an artist and left Switzerland to travel around the Continent. He stopped off in London, where he met Joshua Reynolds, who encouraged him to pursue painting as a career. Then, in 1770, he moved to Rome. To sound Italian, he changed his name. Fuseli spent months in the Vatican studying Michelangelo's paintings on the ceiling of the Sistine Chapel. He examined them from a bed he brought into the church. The bed allowed him to see the paintings better and have a nap after late nights on the town. Fuseli would return to London eight years later, when he would try to make it as an artist. He had a look of distinction about him. He was short and dapper with perfectly powdered white hair. He was charismatic, too, and quickly developed a wild reputation. It was said he consumed large amounts of opium as well as raw pork chops to fuel his fantastical imagination (opium alone might have done it).

Fuseli didn't just become a successful artist. He helped transform art in Britain. The public were used to static scenes depicting a sitter or a pleasant view. They were not used to paintings like the ones Fuseli had been studying in Italy: ones that told a story. Narrative religious art was rare. Many Protestant leaders during the Reformation had clamped down on biblical scenes, banning them in churches. They distracted people from prayer, they said. Some were even labelled idolatrous. It had taken the odd artist with a sense of audacity to break the mould. The turning point came with the foundation of Royal Academy of Arts in 1768. Artists gathered to talk about the art world and direct its future. As the academy's first president, Reynolds gave talks encouraging students to follow artists like Michelangelo and Raphael and create work with a narrative. Fuseli was on board from the start. But he didn't think contemporary updates of Renaissance classics would really set the world on fire. Artists, he thought, needed to make work that would cause a sensation. He was the man for the job. Not only would his work tell a story; it would also leave an impression. His work was a reaction against the rationalism of the Enlightenment, fitting more comfortably within the Romantic tradition, capitalizing on the value of emotions and imagination, and the Gothic movement, stirring up feelings of fear and foreboding. You could group his work with novels by Ann Radcliffe, Matthew Lewis and Mary Shelley.

Mary Shelley probably heard about Fuseli from her father. He was a friend and visited their house. The friendship might have been a little odd, some might say, because Fuseli had also been a crush – if not an obsession – of her mother's. Mary Wollstonecraft had met Fuseli in 1788 through her publisher Joseph Johnson. Wollstonecraft was trying to make it as a writer and told a friend that she enjoyed 'the rich torrent of [Fuseli's] conversation'. Fuseli had already made it as an artist and described Wollstonecraft as 'a philosophical sloven, with lank hair'. Somehow, he put up with her and, by 1792, Wollstonecraft had become completely taken with this obnoxious man. She wanted to live with him. It was unfortunate that he was married, but it didn't mean she couldn't try. Wollstonecraft suggested to Fuseli's wife, Sophia, that they form a *menage a trois*. Mrs Fuseli was having none of it and the couple cut her off. 'I hate clever women,' Fuseli muttered later, thinking of Wollstonecraft. 'They are only troublesome.' The story of Wollstonecraft's love for Fuseli, as told by Godwin in the memoir of his late wife, would stain her reputation. Not that Godwin held it against him.

Nor did Mary – at least not enough to avoid taking inspiration from his most famous work when she was writing *Frankenstein*. In her 1831 preface, Mary tells us that her story was inspired by a nightmare. At the Villa Diodati in Switzerland, she had a 'waking dream' of a 'pale student of the unhallowed arts' creating a 'hideous phantasm of a man'. 'Horror-stricken', the 'artist' hopes that the creature will disappear, only to wake to find it beside his bed, 'opening his curtains, and looking on him with yellow, watery… eyes'. Her vision describes Victor bringing the creature to life and reacting with 'breathless horror and disgust', before fleeing the scene. When he tries to rest, he has a frightening dream. He imagines seeing Elizabeth, his fiancée, in Ingolstadt. He hugs her, but when he kisses her, her lips 'became livid with the hue of death' and she turns into his dead mother. In one way, Victor appears to kill Elizabeth. Perhaps Mary is saying that he is responsible for the creature's actions. His neglect causes the creature to behave as he does.

Victor's nightmare foreshadows Elizabeth's murder in a scene that echoes *The Nightmare*. Like the woman in the painting, Elizabeth is 'thrown across the bed, her head hanging down'. The woman in the painting is sleeping rather than dead, but both look 'lifeless', and are 'pale' and helpless. Both are oppressed: the woman by an incubus, Elizabeth by the creature. In this reading, the incubus is the creature. An incubus is, after all, a daemon, an insult Victor often throws at his creation. The parallel is even more stark if we allow the possibility that the creature raped Elizabeth. Rape is not explicit in *Frankenstein*, but the creature does threaten to 'ravish' Victor's happiness. The creature's murderous actions come about, some say, not just because he feels isolated but because, without a female mate, he feels sexually frustrated. This reading also works alongside the painting's autobiographical interpretation. If the incubus represents Fuseli, the scene shows how he wishes he could stop Anna's relationship with someone else. This aligns with *Frankenstein*, where the creature really does end a relationship, stopping Elizabeth's life with Victor by killing her. After Victor discovers Elizabeth's lifeless body, he sees the creature at the window, grinning a little like an incubus. In Fuseli's painting, the head of a horse is in a similar place. In the Norse reading of *The Nightmare*, the horse also represents an evil spirit as part of the idea of the 'mara'. Mary, some say, has replaced the spirit in Fuseli's work with the creature in her own.

The Nightmare was so popular that Fuseli painted at least three versions of it. It was also widely copied and satirized, propelling Fuseli to fame. Even if Fuseli's connection with her parents had passed her by, Mary would have known about the work because it was part of contemporary culture. His other work shared similar themes. One series depicted Shakespearean scenes. Sometimes he played up the supernatural elements. In *Queen Katherine's Dream* from *Henry VIII*, he showed the dying monarch being visited by 'spirits of peace'. At other times, he explored the role of women. In *Titania and Bottom with the Ass's Head* from *Midsummer Night's Dream*, he painted Titania as a naked enchantress, a twist on the play where Oberon is the one to cast the spell. Fuseli, some say, saw women's sexuality and independence as a threat. As a man, Fuseli wanted to dominate woman; an idea that makes it hard to imagine what the proto-feminist Wollstonecraft ever saw in him. Perhaps she liked the rebellious type. Fuseli's approach to women and the supernatural also comes through in *The Weird Sisters* from *Macbeth*, where he illustrates the witches. Women are not to be trusted, he suggests. Fuseli's *Macbeth* paintings were, as Samuel Taylor Coleridge said, 'like reading Shakespeare by lightning'.

Ten years after painting *The Nightmare*, a Church of England minister would denounce Fuseli as a 'libertine of painting'. Fuseli was right, it seems, to have escaped the priesthood when he did. His exploration of sexual fantasies and horror in his work doesn't seem quite appropriate for a man in a cassock. And yet, he was embraced by the art world. Fuseli influenced William Blake, who painted and made prints when he wasn't writing poetry. He also taught Theodore von Holst, who would go on to create the frontispiece for the 1831 edition of *Frankenstein*, showing the creature coming alive and Victor fleeing out the door. Six years after the Summer Exhibition, in 1788, Fuseli would be elected to the Royal Academy as an associate, before becoming a full Academician. He would teach there, too, and be Keeper of the Schools from 1804 until he died in 1825. We don't know whether he ever read *Frankenstein* and can only guess what he might have thought of it as work by the daughter of a 'philosophical sloven'. But we do know that the public made a connection. When Richard Brinsley Peake adapted *Frankenstein* for the stage in 1823 as *Presumption! Or, The Fate of Frankenstein*, one reviewer made an interesting observation about the actor playing the creature: 'he powerfully embodied the horrible, bordering on the sublime and the awful,' he wrote, 'with the art of a Fuseli.'

Revolution at Home and Abroad

In 1789, France was on the brink of bankruptcy. It had been expensive to supply revolutionaries in America with gunpowder, loans and troops, and King Louis XVI, who held absolute power, was not about to economize on his household expenses to fund the cause. He had a lifestyle to maintain. It wasn't cheap to run Versailles or keep Marie Antoinette in gowns or gâteaux. That May, the king summoned the Estates General, about 1,200 people from across the country representing the clergy, the nobility and the commoners, to brainstorm solutions to the nation's financial problems. They had the power to decide new taxes and new policies. The Minister of Finances, Jacques Necker, outlined the state of the country's bank balance and proposed the deficit be plugged with levies on the commoners. The commoners were not impressed. They were furious that royalty and the nobility led such extravagant lifestyles while they toiled away. In July, hundreds of them stormed the Bastille, a symbol of royal authority. It generated powerful publicity. The king would lose control of his country. The French Revolution had begun.

The commoners made certain demands. They snatched the aristocracy's privileges away, insisted on what they saw as fair taxes and challenged the authority of the Catholic church. They set out their values in *The Declaration of the Rights of Man and of the Citizen* (1789). All men, they insisted, were free. All men had equal rights. By September 1792, the French monarchy was over and the Republic had been established. The king would be executed early the next year. June 1783 marked the start of the Reign of Terror. Thousands of people seen as enemies of the revolution were killed. Even Maximilien de Robespierre, who had campaigned for the rights of all men and was once considered a leader of the revolution, was executed. The death toll rose to 20,000. In 1795, the Directory, a new regime, took power. It didn't last. The political situation was precarious. In November 1799, Napoleon Bonaparte, leader of the French army, staged a coup, appointing himself France's first consul.

Mary Shelley was 2 when Napoleon took power. By the time she started *Frankenstein*, the French Revolution had been over for nearly twenty years. She could view it from a distance. While she recognized that it had involved 'temporary bloodshed and injustice', she concluded that 'it has produced enduring benefits to mankind'. If only she had been able to talk about it with her parents. William Godwin and Mary Wollstonecraft not only lived through the French Revolution; they made their names writing about it. Their breakthrough works were both responses to Edmund Burke's *Reflections on the Revolution in France* (1790). Burke, an Anglo-Irish philosopher, had railed against the revolutionaries in France, insisting that inherited rights and traditions be upheld and warning that the current discord would result in bloodshed, if not catastrophe. 'In the groves of their academy,' he wrote, 'at the end of every vista, you see nothing but the gallows.'

Wollstonecraft would come to have some sympathy with Burke when she went to France towards the end of 1792 and saw the violence that had ensued, but at the time, she was unimpressed. Like the revolutionaries, she opposed hierarchy and arbitrary power. Within six weeks of Burke's *Reflections*, she would bring out *A Vindication of the Rights of Men* (1790), arguing for a reconstruction of society on the principles of reason and liberty. The following year, she would publish a sequel, *A Vindication of the Rights of Woman* (1791), extending her arguments to women. Wollstonecraft now demanded liberty and equality for both genders. Wollstonecraft would go to Paris to witness the Revolution at the end of December 1792, networking with other leading thinkers, such as Thomas Paine, a political philosopher and author of *The Rights of Man* (1791). She would write up her thoughts in *An Historical and Moral View of the Origin and Progress of the French Revolution and the Effect it Has Produced in Europe* (1795).

Like Wollstonecraft, William Godwin had read Burke's *Reflections* – who hadn't? – and felt inspired to write. He wanted to publish his own treatise on political principles and examine the ideas of French thinkers like Montesquieu and Rousseau. Throwing himself into the task, he blocked off mornings for work, visited friends and colleagues in the afternoons and read in the evenings. As the months rolled on, his treatise developed from a response to Burke to a more original work expounding his own ideas. Godwin believed that society would be improved if people were encouraged to think for themselves and act on their own judgments. There was no place, he said, for government, which he called a 'brute engine', laws, organized religion or marriage. He implicitly approved of the uprising in France. He was, some recognized, an anarchist, but not the violent kind. Godwin proposed philosophical anarchism, arguing that the government didn't have any real authority and suggesting people would live harmoniously and productively without it. *An Enquiry Concerning Political Justice* (1793) came out a couple of weeks after the execution of Louis XVI and would sell more than 4,000 copies. Its radical nature might have got Godwin in trouble with the authorities had they realized so many people would read it (it was pricey at a guinea a-piece and hardly light reading). Godwin became a hero of the left and a model of rational thought. Percy Shelley would come across *Political Justice* almost twenty years later and become a huge admirer. Mary would read it, too.

Godwin would go on to put politics at the centre of his novels. His bestseller *Things as They Are, or The Adventures of Caleb Williams* (1794) tells the story of a young man called Caleb who discovers a dark secret about his employer, Mr Falkland, leading to a relentless pursuit as he struggles to clear his name and reveal the truth in a corrupt and oppressive society. It also explores the key threads of the French Revolution by highlighting issues of power, injustice and mistreatment. The novel critiques the abuse of authority and social hierarchies, reflecting the revolutionary spirit aimed at fighting against tyranny and promoting equality. Through the protagonist's struggles against an unjust system, the story shows how people can be crushed by powerful institutions, like the revolutionaries' struggle against the monarchy. When *Caleb Williams* came out, it flew off the shelves. 'No one that ever read it could possibly forget it, or speak of it after any length of time but with an impression as if the events and feelings had been personal to himself,' wrote literary critic and social commentator William Hazlitt a couple of decades later. When Mary was old enough, she would read it, too.

By the time Mary wrote *Frankenstein*, her mother was long dead and her father wasn't speaking to her (they'd fallen out because she had remained with Percy). But just because they were absent doesn't mean Mary wasn't influenced by their work. Perhaps, as we have seen, she wanted to write about some of their ideas as a way of feeling closer to them. Godwin's influence was especially apparent to contemporary reviewers. '[*Frankenstein*] is piously dedicated to Mr Godwin,' read a critique of her novel in *The Quarterly Review* a little disparagingly, 'and is in the spirit of his school.'

Frankenstein can be read as a commentary on the French Revolution. The creature embodies the revolutionaries. They both dream of a just society underpinned by liberty, equality and fraternity. The revolutionaries comprised a hotchpotch of people from lawyers to shopkeepers; the creature comprised a hotchpotch of body parts. The revolutionaries and the creature took similar approaches. Over in France, the more moderate revolutionaries such as the Girondins had campaigned peacefully for the end of the monarchy. Other revolutionaries turned violent when they realized they weren't going to get their way by negotiation. The creature also first tries to get his way and make friends by peaceful means – he tries to talk to the De Laceys. He turns to violence when they shun him and he realizes he will never be treated fairly. 'I reflected that they had spurned and deserted me, [and] anger returned, a rage of anger,' says the creature, before setting their house on fire. The creature's violent acts then escalate to include the deaths of Victor's family and friends, and eventually Victor himself. In France, the king was executed. Anyone considered an enemy of the revolution was then killed, too. No one came out of the revolution unscathed. Burke had used an analogy that Mary might have found especially apt, when he referred to revolution as 'a species of political monster, which has always ended by devouring those who have produced it'. The creature also 'devoured' the man who 'produced' him.

Further links can be drawn between *Frankenstein* and the French Revolution. Victor is a little like a king ruling over his subjects, expecting the creature to obey him, or like a lord presiding over his peasants. Godwin would have understood. Where Burke had likened the revolution to a 'monster', Godwin had substituted feudalism. Feudalism was a 'ferocious monster', he said in *Political Justice*, 'devouring wherever it came all that the friend of humanity regards with attachment and love'. While the creature is the one who does the killing, Victor is the real cause. He is the one who made the creature and then provoked his murderous rampage by turning against him.

Wollstonecraft would have understood her daughter's sympathies with the creature. 'People are rendered ferocious by misery and misanthropy is ever the offspring of discontent,' she had written in *An Historical and Moral View of the Origin and Progress of the French Revolution* (1794). But just as Wollstonecraft would come to feel uncomfortable about the violence in the French Revolution, Mary would feel uncomfortable about the violence enacted by the creature. The ideal society is not one where people kill each other to get revenge, she implies. It is one composed of people like the De Laceys, who love and care for each other. 'Nothing could exceed the love and respect which the younger cottagers exhibited towards their venerable companion,' the creature notes admiringly, watching how they treat the elderly father. 'They performed towards him every little office of affection and duty with gentleness.' The De Laceys are a microcosm of how society should be. This is the sort of family Mary craves herself. But she cannot condone the creature's behaviour when he is excluded. His actions do not result in a happy society; they result in misery for everyone around him.

* * *

The French Revolution encouraged people across Europe to start dreaming about a new world order. Radical thinkers like William Godwin began to believe that society could be reshuffled. In 1791 and 1792, Thomas Paine, the political philosopher, brought out *Rights of Man*, arguing that individuals have inherent, inalienable rights. Paine, an English-born Founding Father, was on the side of revolutionaries in France, positioning himself against Burke's *Reflections on the Revolution in France*. He wanted to see big changes in England, including education for the poor, a fairer income tax and the removal of aristocratic titles. *Rights of Man* was read eagerly by anyone who could lay their hands on it and read aloud in coffeehouses and inns. It sold half a million copies. Across the country, corresponding societies, aiming to drum up public support for universal suffrage and annual parliaments, sprang up. The British government took measures to stave off social unrest. In 1794, they suspended the act of *habeas corpus*; political leaders could now be arrested without trial. The following year, they tightened the law of treason; it was now almost impossible for people to hold meetings that backed reform. It would be 1832 before the Reform Act, increasing the number of men who could vote and creating more seats for MPs. In the intervening years, there was growing unrest, especially among the working class, who felt the electoral system was unfair and that they had to put up with tough working conditions on little pay. Riots broke out several times when Mary was growing up and at least once when she was finishing *Frankenstein*.

The March of the Blanketeers took place in spring 1817, when Mary had just started redrafting *Frankenstein*. The threat that the lowest in society, the oppressed, would rise up and turn against their benefactor, those that ruled over them, hovered above the page. Textile workers in Manchester decided to petition the Prince Regent for political reform. They planned to march to London to present their demands. The journey would take six days. They would sleep on the ground or in churches under a blanket, giving them the name 'the Blanketeers'. About 12,000 supporters turned up at the start of the march. The main leaders, however, were soon arrested and mounted cavalry caused a lot of the other people to scatter. About 500 people marched on to Ashbourne, where troops were waiting for them. Twenty-five people were arrested. A few got to Derby. Just one reached London to offer up the petition.

Peak unrest took place that June, when about fifty protesters set out from the village of Pentrich in Derbyshire on a fourteen-mile march to Nottingham. They were told that other groups were forming in Huddersfield and Sheffield, Wakefield and Leeds, Nottingham and Leicester, Derby and Birmingham. The north of England was taking on the lawmakers of the south. The working people were revolting. The Pentrich rebels believed about 100,000 people would assemble in Nottingham. Together, they would march south. They would seize the arms depot and revenue in the town hall in Newark, before charging to London and setting up a new government that would nationalize property, sweep away the national debt and taxes, and issue new money. Britain would become a republic. The Pentrich rebels tried to take an ironworks at Butterley but were stopped by police. In Nottinghamshire, they clashed with mounted cavalry. Within three weeks, about eighty-five rebels were arrested. Twenty-four of them were tried in Derby. Those convicted were imprisoned or shipped off to Australia. Three ring leaders, including Jeremiah Brandreth, received a worse fate: they were the last men in England to be hung, drawn and quartered.

* * *

Brandreth had been a Luddite. Mary was 13 when the Luddites began protesting. The Luddites were textile workers in Nottingham in the East Midlands. They were worried about the introduction of power looms. Their name came from their leader, Ned Ludd. The story goes that Ned had been forced to work on a machine when he was a boy. He objected and was whipped. Ned smashed the machine with a hammer and escaped to Sherwood Forest. Ned probably didn't exist. But that didn't matter. It was useful for the workers to have a figurehead to unite them. It was good branding. At first, the Luddites approached Parliament with their concerns. They said they just wanted to safeguard their trade so that everyone would benefit. In response, Parliament removed the rules they had been appealing to. Then they tried to negotiate with their bosses. 'King Ned' wrote to factory owners asking them to stop using the new machines. If they didn't, he would send his army to sort them out. And so he did. By March 1811, King Ned's army were taking matters into their own hands.

Luddites raided factories at night and smashed the new machinery. They used a giant hammer they called 'Enoch' after James and Enoch Taylor, the blacksmiths who had made them. The Taylors also made automation machinery. 'Enoch made them, Enoch shall break them,' the Luddites shouted as they went about their raids. In Nottingham, the Luddite raids were often successful. They even conducted them in daylight with crowds cheering them on. Similar attacks broke out over the coming months in Yorkshire and Lancashire, Leicestershire and Derbyshire. Shoemakers and coal workers joined the crusade. At one point, there were raids almost every day. Thousands of machines were damaged.

The Luddites were on the up. One leader, a cloth finisher called George Mellor, decided it was time to stage a bigger attack. In April 1812, about 150 rebels raided Rawfolds Mill, one of the biggest factories in the West Riding of Yorkshire. But the factory was prepared and had built up its defences. The Luddites smashed through the windows with hammers to gain entry. Soldiers inside shot back. At least two Luddites were killed and the rest retreated. It was their first big defeat. Factory owners started defending their property – by force, if necessary. Mellor was particularly upset. One of his friends, John Booth, was killed at Rawfolds. He wanted revenge. With a few friends, he tracked down William Horsfall, another factory owner he claimed threatened them during the riots, and killed him on his way home. It signalled the beginning of the end for the Luddites, who then lost the support of the public. Mellor and his fellow rebels were put on trial and hanged for murder outside York Castle. Days later other machine breakers were tried and sentenced to death. The factory owners had won.

The word 'Luddite' has become a derogatory term for anyone unable or unwilling to use modern technology, but the original Luddites wouldn't have put themselves in that category. The Luddites didn't hate machinery completely; they just thought it should be operated by skilled workers, like themselves, who should be decently paid. Machines should also not be used to churn out cheap copies; they should produce decent goods. The Luddite protests reflected a wider mood of fear and uncertainty over the rise and rise of machines. No one would deny it was an exciting time, but it was also an anxious one. Each invention brought danger in its wake.

* * *

The steam train was among them. On Christmas Eve 1801, Richard Trevithick, a Cornish engineer, took seven friends for a ride on his latest invention, *Puffing Devil.* It was the first steam-powered passenger vehicle. A few days later, it caught fire and was destroyed. Trevithick refused to be defeated. In 1804, he built the first steam train to run on rails. It chugged along at five miles an hour, dragging five cars with ten tons of iron and seventy ironworkers. After three trips, it broke the track and was forced into early retirement. Trevithick returned to the workshop. In 1808, he launched *Catch Me Who Can*, which took passengers around Torrington Square in London. The track snapped there, too. Trevithick, however, had started a trend. In 1814, George Stephenson unveiled a steam engine that hauled eight coal wagons weighing 30 tons at about four miles an hour. Stephenson would go on to design further engines, laying the foundations for the development of the modern railway. The Stockton and Darlington Railway, Britain's first train line, would open in 1825.

The Scottish writer Thomas Carlyle described the era as 'a mechanical age'. In his essay *Signs of the Times* (1829), published in the *Edinburgh Review*, he warned that technology was changing how people thought. 'Men are growing mechanical in head and in heart, as well as in hand,' he wrote. Was Victor Frankenstein a little mechanical in head and in heart? He shows very little kindness towards the creature. First, he refuses to look after him, showing a lack of compassion. Then, he refuses to make him a companion, failing to understand how much it would mean to the being he has already created. Mary was writing at a time of progress, when man was coming up with brilliant ways to advance society. Victor aimed to advance society too by creating 'a new species'. Mary was also writing at a time of disaster, when man, blinded by his arrogance, was destroying society, wrecking people's livelihood and purpose. Victor would come to see his creation as a 'catastrophe'. He wanted Captain Walton to learn 'how dangerous is the acquirement of knowledge'. People would be less troubled, he continues, if they weren't overly ambitious. 'How much happier that man is who believes his native town to be the world,' he says, 'than he who aspires to become greater than his nature will allow.'

Mary Shelley wasn't necessarily against technology or man's experiments in science. She was more of a Luddite in the original sense: man's creations, whether organic like the creature or inorganic like a steam train or a power loom, should be overseen by someone. They shouldn't be left to operate without supervision, when they could run riot. Mary was not a political revolutionary but a reformist. Like her parents, she wanted change, but not at any cost. She feared what might happen if people revolted against the established order like the revolutionaries in France. There would be chaos. Change should come about gradually. Mary may well have agreed with Victor when he said that 'a human being in perfection ought always to preserve a calm and peaceful mind'. Had people shown 'domestic affections' in the past, the world would have been more peaceful. 'Caesar would have spared his country; America would have been discovered more gradually; and the empires of Mexico and Peru had not been destroyed,' continues Victor. Victor might also have not made the creature. If he had, the creature might not have developed a desire to kill.

The End of Slavery

On 16 March 1824, George Canning, the foreign secretary, made a speech in Parliament that showed off his oratory skills and his familiarity with popular culture of the day. His language and beliefs were very much of their time. 'In dealing with the negro, Sir, we must remember that we are dealing with a being possessing the form and strength of a man, but the intellect only of a child,' he said. 'To turn him loose in the manhood of his physical strength, in the maturity of his physical passions, but in the infancy of his uninstructed reason, would be to raise up a creature resembling the splendid fiction of a recent romance.' The recent romance was *Frankenstein*. Canning's image would have terrified the House. The creature was vengeful, murderous and set on wrecking society. No one wanted that. The warning was coming from an abolitionist. Canning was against slavery. He was just concerned about immediate emancipation. He feared what the 'negro' might do.

Mary Shelley was an abolitionist, too – as were her parents. William Godwin had rallied against slavery in *An Enquiry Concerning Political Justice* (1793). Mary Wollstonecraft had also condemned it, comparing the situation of women to that of slaves. 'Slavery will have its constant effect, degrading the master and the abject dependent,' she had written in *A Vindication of the Rights of Woman* (1792). Mary and Percy protested in a practical way, refusing to eat sugar because it came from West Indian plantations. Mary had been born at a time of change. The Haitian revolution, when slaves had successfully revolted against French colonial rule in Saint-Domingue, now Haiti, had taken place from 1791 to 1804. There would be further slave rebellions in the West Indies in the following decades. The Abolition Act of 1807 had banned slave trading in the British Empire, although slaves in the colonies wouldn't be freed until

1838. The treatment of slaves and their emancipation was a hot topic in the press, in parliament and in parlours across the country.

It was also a hot topic for Mary and Percy. In 1814, Percy got riled up about a letter in *The Times* that detailed the conditions of slaves in Africa. 'See where I have marked with ink, and stifle your horror and indignation until we meet,' he wrote to Mary. Towards the end of the year, they read Mungo Park's account of his travels in Africa, which had been published in 1799. Park made some radical observations. 'Whatever difference there is between the Negro and European in the conformation of the nose and the colour of the skin,' he noted, 'there is none in the genuine sympathies and characteristic feelings of our common nature.' It was an idea Mary could get behind. She was less pleased with Park's acceptance of slavery and the slavery trade. 'Read and finish Mungo Park's travels,' she writes. 'They are very interesting & if the man was not so prejudiced they would be a thousand times more so.'

Mary continued to read up about it. In early 1815, she read Bryan Edwards' account of the slave trade. A plantation owner, he believed people who weren't white were inferior. Africans were descended from monkeys because of the way they behaved. The idea was not uncommon at the time. Mary and Percy's doctor, William Lawrence, held a similar view. He believed Africans displayed 'an almost entire want of… elevated sentiments, mainly virtues, and moral feelings'. That summer, Mary moved to Clifton near Bristol. Bristol had got much of its wealth from the slave trade. Mary may well have seen black men working on the docks. She would be reminded of people's extreme views of slaves as she walked around the city.

As we have seen, many of Mary's experiences and attitudes towards current affairs and society have parallels and echoes in her work. There is no obvious master and slave narrative in *Frankenstein*. Victor, who might be expected to take the role of the master, wants nothing to do with the creature, the most obvious contender for a slave. And yet, there is a clear power struggle between them, a key feature of a master-slave relationship. Victor is the one who has given the creature life and later has the power to make him a female companion. The creature feels that his happiness depends on him. Like a slave, he has no money or property. The power shifts when the creature shows his capacity to destroy Victor's happiness, killing those he cares for most. The creature is a little like a slave who has been freed and is now seeking revenge on those who have wronged him.

The creature does not look or sound English. He has thick black hair, yellow skin and bright white teeth. He is strong and muscular. He shares features with caricatures of Africans and West Indians. 'I was more agile than they and could subsist upon coarser diet,' the creature says, comparing himself to Europeans. 'I bore the extremes of heat and cold with less injury to my frame; my stature far exceeded theirs.' Some people in Mary's day saw Africans or people with darker skin not merely as a morally inferior race, but a different species. The idea has gripped the creature. 'I was not even of the same nature as man,' he says mournfully. 'When I looked around I saw and heard of none like me. Was I, then, a monster, a blot upon the earth, from which all men fled and whom all men disowned?' Throughout the novel, the creature is feared and loathed for his appearance. Slaves, Mary might think, have been subject to the same fate. By allowing the creature to narrate the middle section of *Frankenstein*, Mary shifts readers' sympathies from Victor to his creation. We begin to realize the creature's capacity for humanity and understand why he is intent on destroying his creator. It's a brave undertaking. It would be easier for Mary to encourage readers to side with Victor as a man in power, just as people are used to doing in real life. But this would go against what Mary stands for. Through *Frankenstein*, Mary implicitly attacks a society that holds that people who look a certain way lack a moral compass and the ability to feel refined emotions. She is giving them a voice. She might not write diatribes packed with political rhetoric like her parents, but she has a strong social conscience. It comes out in her writing, whether she intends it to or not.

Mary is likely to have objected to George Canning's description of a slave having 'the intellect only of a child'. The creature starts off like a child – he has to learn about the world from his experience and what he reads in books. But he quickly upskills and becomes as intelligent as any adult. Unlike Canning's crass description of the creature, which he may have got from one of the popular stage adaptations, her creature had developed a maturity in his emotions and his intellect. The creature would not have recognized himself in the politician's description of someone with 'uninstructed reason'. But Percy at least might have had some sympathy with Canning's broad argument that sudden emancipation, without guidelines, could spell disaster. Slaves had, after all, lacked the benefit of education. They had also been ill-treated for years. It would be understandable if they were angry and wanted retaliation. 'Can he who the day before was a trampled slave suddenly become liberal-minded, forbearing, and independent?' Percy wrote in the preface to *Laon and Cythna*, an epic poem about a pair of siblings who lead a political uprising, written in 1817 and published the following year.

The Slavery Abolition Act of 1833 would finally put an end to slavery in most British colonies, but the idea that the creature was an African slave was too irresistible for theatre and film directors to ignore. In plays later that century, costume designers put the creature in African dress, while in James Whale's 1931 film *Frankenstein*, the creature is lynched. It is possible that part of the creature could have African heritage – he was made from body parts collected from anywhere and everywhere – although, as we shall see, there are other claims on his heritage, too.

Encountering 'the Other'

The late eighteenth and early nineteenth century were chaotic times. From the French monarchy to the slave trade, the old ways of working were being bashed, slashed and trashed. Even the calmest person would have justification to feel anxious. In chaotic times, people crave order, and it was fortunate that scientists and sociologists were on hand to give the public something neat and tidy to hold onto. They had been categorizing everything they could.

Carl Linnaeus, the Swedish botanist and physician, had sorted the natural world into a hierarchy. His landmark study, *Systema Naturae* (1735), was so popular that it was reprinted twelve times in his lifetime. Linnaeus had arranged all living organisms into kingdom, phylum, class, order, family, genus and species. It was a mammoth task (genus: Mammuthus) and Linnaeus invented a nifty organizing system to help him keep track of his notes: the index card. He gave each species a latinized two-part name. '*Deus creavit, Linnaeus disposuit* (God created, Linnaeus organized)', he quipped. Big thinkers of the day, from Goethe to Rousseau, idolized him.

Linnaeus was the first naturalist to place man in the animal kingdom. Man sat within the quadruped class (which he would later call mammals) and the anthropomorpha order (which he would later call primates), alongside apes and sloths. Some homo (humans) were outraged by Linnaeus' categorization of man. They said it dismissed the importance God had bestowed on him. 'For although Man ranks first among the animals,' cried the Dutch naturalist Gronovius, 'he should in fact be considered to excel all other living beings which were created by God to Man's delight and benefit.' Linnaeus insisted on his ordering. Man and ape, he said, were uncannily similar. The only difference, he later admitted, was that men had the ability to '*nosce te ipsum*'. They could know themselves.

Linnaeus then divided humans into four varieties based largely on their skin colour. His categories – European white, American reddish, Asian tawny and African black – corresponded to the four continents known at the time. In the 1750s, Linnaeus would add physical and moral characteristics to his divisions. Europeans, he said, were not only fair-skinned; they were also civilized and intelligent. Africans not only had black skin; they were lazy, cunning and savage. Linnaeus was just trying to describe groups of people based on what he knew and never used the term 'race'. That hasn't stopped others, though, using his work to justify scientific racism, arguing that certain groups of people are better than others. Even within Linnaeus' time, the idea that certain groups were superior and inferior was useful. Europe depended on African slave labour. If Africans and Europeans were equal in this way, it would have been hard to justify their role as slaves and curb their liberty. If they were inferior, slavery could chug along guilt-free.

Scientists latched onto Linnaeus' system and put their own stamp on it. Johann Friedrich Blumenbach, a German naturalist and physician, examined Linnaeus' groups of humans and proposed some tweaks. In 1775, he suggested that humans could be classified into five rather than four groups based on skin colour, hair colour, skull shape and physical form. Caucasians (a term he coined) had white skin and blond or brown hair; Mongolians had yellow skin and straight thin, black hair; American Indians had reddish skin and thick, black hair; Ethiopians had black skin and black, curly hair; and Malays had tawny skin and soft, thick, curly hair.

Blumenbach's biggest proponent in England was William Lawrence, professor of anatomy and surgery at Barts hospital and personal doctor to Mary and Percy Shelley. In 1807, Lawrence translated and expanded Blumenbach's seminal work, *A Short System of Comparative Anatomy*, which had recently come out in German. He promoted Blumenbach's idea that humans could be classified into different types. He also backed Blumenbach's theory that the shape of people's skulls indicated their intelligence. He would draw on *Comparative Anatomy* when he wrote his lectures at Barts, which he delivered in 1817 and published in a slightly revised form as *Lectures on Physiology, Zoology and the Natural History of Man* a couple of years later.

Just as Blumenbach developed Linnaeus' work, Lawrence developed the work of Blumenbach. Lawrence would expand on the intellectual and emotional qualities of each category. Caucasians, he said, were superior 'in moral feelings and mental endowments'. The other groups had a mix of positive and negative characteristics. Mongolians were 'susceptible of civilization, and of great advancement in the useful and even elegant arts of life'. Just look at the Chinese and Japanese empires, he said. The fact that their institutions have remained 'stationary' for so long, however, wasn't great, he added. It 'marks an inferiority of nature and a limited capacity in comparison to that of the white races'. Lawrence went on to highlight their tendency towards violence: 'Unrelenting slaughter, without distinction of condition, age, or sex, and universal destruction have marked the progress of their conquests,' he wrote. Mongolians are lazy, he suggested, and barbaric. Lawrence may well have chatted about his views when he saw the Shelleys. The line 'Yellow, and black, and pale, and hectic red' in Percy's poem *Ode to the West Wind* (1819) may well be an allusion to four categories of man: Mongoloid, Negroid, Caucasian and American Indian. (Blumenbach, like Linnaeus before him, had started with four groups.)

Blumenbach may well be one of 'the physiological writers of Germany' Percy is referring to in his introduction to the first edition of *Frankenstein*. One of the first things Mary tells us about Victor and the creature is that they are different races, as we might call them today. First impressions count. Mary wants us to know that this fact is significant. Captain Walton's ship, she tells us, is overtaken by a carriage carrying 'a being which had the shape of a man, but apparently of gigantic stature'. Walton and his crew don't know it yet, but they have just seen the creature. The following morning, they rescue Victor. Victor was 'not, as the other traveller seemed to be, a savage inhabitant of some undiscovered island, but a European'.

We have to wait until the creature's birth for a detailed description of 'the other traveller'. Now we learn he has yellow skin, black hair, white teeth, pale eyes and black lips. Victor finds the creature instantly repulsive. He had employed 'infinite pains and care' to create a being with proportionate limbs and 'beautiful' features. Yet he has ended up with a 'catastrophe'. Victor had said he was aiming to create a 'new species'. He had hoped this species would be an improvement. The creature is not. Yellow skin, we might think, suggests he is Mongolian, an idea backed up by the creature's escape towards the end of the novel to the 'wilds of Tartary and Russia', territory that includes Mongolia.

The creature is then met with hostility wherever he goes because people judge him on his appearance. He looks different; he has 'Mongolian' features. When the villagers encounter him, they are terrified: children shriek; a woman faints. Some run away; others pelt him with stones. Later, when he decides to befriend the De Laceys, he remembers how 'the barbarous villagers' had shunned him. Believing his integration into society is hindered by his appearance, he decides to approach the blind father first, requesting 'warmth and rest'. The father, he reasons, won't be prejudiced by the creature's looks. How right he is. 'I am blind and cannot judge of your countenance,' says the man, 'but there is something in your words which persuades me that you are sincere.' Within moments, however, the father and the creature are interrupted by Felix, Safie and Agatha, who do the judging for him. The creature knows that they believe someone's appearance is linked to their inner nature. In fear, Felix throws the creature to the ground and beats him.

Felix might be justified. The creature – a stranger – had 'seized' the old man's hand. But we can't ignore the significance of the way the creature looks. The creature looks different from everyone around him. As an outsider, he is excluded. This sets him up to be lonely. People weren't just wary of the creature. They were terrified. They already think they know what he is like. Within moments of Victor bringing the creature to life, he describes him as a 'wretch' and a 'monster'. As soon as Felix, Safie and Agatha return to their cottage and see the creature, they react with 'horror and consternation'. Agatha faints. Safie flees. Felix wrestles him to the ground. If they knew about Lawrence's interpretation of Blumenbach and had identified the creature as Mongolian, it is little wonder that they were scared. They feared the 'unrelenting slaughter' that typified the race. They expect the creature to be violent. Even the creature feels a sense of fear when he sees himself. He is 'terrified' when he catches his reflection in a pool. The De Laceys had 'perfect forms', he says, complimenting 'their grace, beauty, and delicate complexions'. He believes he has a 'miserable deformity' and feels like a 'monster'. Perhaps he judges his appearance as ugly because it is so different from the people he has seen so far. Or perhaps he has absorbed the idea that he belongs to a race that is thought to be monstrous. What makes the creature think that his hideous appearance might be matched by an equally hideous character?

Mary didn't like pigeonholing people. The Romantics embraced the uniqueness of the individual, an idea she supported. The creature was unique. 'When I looked around,' the creature says, 'I saw and heard of none like me.' Both Victor and the De Laceys (except for the blind father) misunderstand the creature. Mary humanizes him by giving him a voice. We hear the creature tell us about his earliest experiences. The creature is miserable because of the way he has been treated. 'I was benevolent and good,' the creature tells Victor, 'misery made me a fiend. Make me happy, and I shall again be virtuous.' Mary is challenging Blumenbach's and Lawrence's theories. They might say the creature is Mongolian because of his skin colour. Mongolians are inherently violent. Therefore, the creature is inherently violent. Mary disagrees. Mongolians – or people with Mongolian colouring – are not inherently violent. People just expect them to be like that. They then shun them, causing them to become lonely, resentful and angry. It is this that makes them violent. They don't start off that way.

Mary was progressive in her views. She suggests that it is wrong to stereotype people based on their appearance. The creature – like Mongolians – is not innately aggressive. Had he been accepted by his creator and by society, he would have been friendly and peaceful in return. He longs to be part of society. We see him approach the De Lacey family and be rejected. He also desires a female mate. In trying to persuade Victor to make him one, he describes his gentle characteristics. Like Mary and Percy Shelley, he is vegetarian: 'I do not destroy the lamb and the kid to glut my appetite; acorns and berries afford me sufficient nourishment.' He envisages a simple, tranquil life, sleeping on dried leaves and waiting for the sun to ripen its food. 'The picture I present to you is peaceful and human,' he says. Victor is conflicted. The creature's words move him, but he can't shake his belief that the creature's appearance shows he is a monster: 'when I look upon him, when I saw the filthy mass that moved and talked, my heart sickened and my feelings were altered to those of horror and hatred'. Victor will go on to accede to the creature's request and then, after starting to create a female companion, go back on his word and tear up his work. We know by this point that the creature is not quite the peaceful being he makes himself out to be. He has already burned the house of the De Laceys and murdered William, Victor's brother. And yet in both cases, the creature has been provoked. All he wanted was acceptance and companionship.

There is always a chance that the creature wasn't Mongolian. Some might see the situation as worse: the creature could be part-Mongolian, part-European. The Mongol's hair, according to Blumenbach, was 'scanty'. The creature has 'lustrous' locks. Victor also constructed his body from discarded limbs from charnel houses in Germany: he might have had more access to European bodies. A racial hybrid might have scared people even more because of the implications of racial mixing – that an 'inferior' race could pollute the 'superior' white race. Victor articulates a common fear when he says he worries that the female companion he makes 'might turn with disgust from [the creature] to the superior beauty of man'. The thought horrifies Victor, but it might not have horrified Mary. Mary, we might think, wanted equality between people, regardless of their skin colour or background, and had no qualms about them getting together. She wasn't the only British female writer to feel this way. Just before *Frankenstein* came out, Eliza Bland Erskine Norton had published her poem *Alcon Malazore* (1815), celebrating the marriage between a Spanish woman and an African. Felicia Hemans had also brought out her poem *The Siege of Valencia* (1816), affirming the love between European Christians and Muslims.

The characters in *Frankenstein* fear the creature because of the way he looks – possibly Mongolian, possibly part-Mongolian, or at least different. Mary doesn't. She knows that the creature, whatever race he belongs to, is not inherently bad. Had he been accepted by Victor, the De Laceys, the villagers, he might have been gentle rather than violent. He could have been the first of a new generation who advanced rather than destroyed civilization. It wasn't to be. Instead, the rejection he faces shapes his behaviour and influences the course of literary history for good.

Starting with a *Tabula Rasa*

Everyone loves a bit of pop psychology and Mary Shelley was no exception. In the early nineteenth century, people were fascinated by the nature of the mind and how it developed. William Lawrence, Mary and Percy's doctor, shared his views in a lecture at the Royal College of Surgeons in 1817. Lawrence was a materialist. The mind, he said, was purely a product of the brain. 'Where is the mind of the foetus?' he asked his audience. 'Where is that of a child just born? Do we not see it actually build up before our eyes by the actions of the five external senses, and of the gradually developed internal faculties?' Yes, Mary might have said as she slipped inside the mind of the creature; yes, we do. When the creature comes alive, his body is fully formed, but his mind is like that of a newborn. He has no memory, no language, no conscience and no grasp of innate concepts. We then see him learn everything from scratch. In Percy Shelley's preface to the first edition of *Frankenstein* (1818), he had said that the novel was not trying to push 'any philosophical doctrine of whatever kind'. His emphatic tone preempts the claim that a doctrine or two could in fact be detected. One of them concerns the development of the mind.

The big theory of cognitive development at the time was John Locke's *tabula rasa*: the idea that the unformed mind was like a blank slate or sheet of white paper, as he put it. As an empiricist, Locke believed that all knowledge comes from experience. We know things from reflecting on sensory input. In the autumn of 1816, after returning from the Continent where she had come up with the idea for *Frankenstein*, Mary would pick up a copy of Locke's *An Essay Concerning Human Understanding* (1689), where he goes into his theory in detail. She could shape the creature, she thought, on Lockean principles.

Or broadly Lockean principles. The creature's mind develops more along the lines of work by the philosopher David Hartley, who was born in 1705, the year after Locke died. Hartley was influenced by Locke and their ideas overlap. Like Locke, Hartley believed that we are born with a *tabula rasa*, arguing that all knowledge comes from reflections on external sensations. Like Locke, Hartley also believed that we do things to pursue pleasure and avoid pain. He then went on to explore different stages of cognitive development and the implications for morality and behaviour, ideas that might have especially resonated with Mary. Moral principles, argued Hartley, are formed through the associations we make with pleasurable or painful experiences. If we experience pleasure, we will be happy and benevolent. If we experience pain, we will be miserable and malicious. How clearly we might be able to hear the creature jump in as he tells Victor: 'I am malicious because I am miserable.' The creature is miserable because he has endured painful experiences. Hartley would have understood.

We can trace the creature's development along Hartleian principles from the start. The creature is born with the classic *tabula rasa*: his mind is blank. When he enters the world, he feels lost and muddled: 'all the events of [the original era of my being] appear confused and indistinct,' he tells us. He tries to understand the world through his senses. The creature's first memory comprises 'a strange multiplicity of sensations' that 'seized' him. 'I saw, felt, heard, and smelled at the same time,' he tells us. He then distinguishes between sensations, learning about light and dark. Wandering through the forest, he experiences hunger and thirst, exhaustion and sleep, fear and pain. The creature also starts to experience nature. It gives him pleasure. He feels 'wonder' at seeing 'a radiant form rise from among the trees', which he will later learn is the moon, and enjoys the sound of birdsong. Having stumbled across a discarded camp in the woods, he learns about using fire for warmth, light and cooking. Roasted nuts are moreish, he discovers; roasted berries are not. He also learns that fire can cause pleasure when it emits warmth and light, and pain when it burns.

The creature then observes the De Laceys. Locke had suggested that children learn best about morality from example. 'Virtues and vices can by no words be so plainly set before their understandings,' he wrote, 'as the actions of other men will show them.' Watching the family, the creature starts to acquire language and grasps conceptual ideas of family, love, justice and kindness. He learns how Felix helped Safie's father escape wrongful imprisonment and then how the family accepted Safie, an outsider. The De Laceys are an idealized family. They are kind and sympathetic to each other, qualities the creature recognizes as virtues.

The creature has now reached Hartley's next level of cognitive development, the imagination, arising from 'Natural or artificial Beauty or Deformity'. This includes the beauty of nature, music, painting, poetry and the sciences. The creature has already been struck by the beauty of nature. Now, he experiences 'artificial Beauty', when he hears the father in the De Lacey family strum the guitar. The creature will become acutely aware of the contrast between 'beauty' and 'deformity' when he sees his reflection in a pool of water. Hartley talked about beauty and deformity inspiring honor and shame in people. The creature is ashamed of his appearance. He thinks his ugliness suggests he has a monstrous character. 'I was filled with the bitterest sensations of despondence and mortification,' he says when he sees his reflection. The creature fears his appearance will hinder his attempt to befriend the De Laceys and hopes he can win them round by his 'gentle demeanor and conciliating words'. This corresponds to Hartley's next stage: ambition, arising from 'the Opinions of others concerning us'. The creature recognizes what Hartley calls his 'external advantages or disadvantages'. His disadvantages are his looks, but his benevolent character, even if hidden, is a strength.

The creature has now reached the fourth level of Hartley's system: 'self-interest', arising from 'Our Possession or Want of the Means of Happiness, and Security from, or Subjection to, the Hazards of Misery'. Hartley describes how someone tries to maximize their happiness by sensations, imagination and ambition, before trying to attain 'Pleasures of Friendship, Generosity, Devotion and Self-approbation'. Watching the De Laceys has brought the creature a certain amount of pleasure.

He admires their 'virtue and good feelings... [their] gentle manners and amiable qualities' and longs to befriend them. At the moment, he feels the pain of being excluded and alone. 'I was shut out from intercourse with them,' he tells us, 'except through means which I obtained by stealth, when I was unseen and unknown, and which rather increased than satisfied the desire I had of becoming one among my fellows.'

Hartley's big idea, as we have noted, is that pleasurable experiences make people benevolent and painful ones make them malicious. Insofar as watching the De Laceys has been pleasurable, the creature is benevolent towards them – he feels sympathy for their hardship and helps them by gathering firewood. The pain of exclusion, however, will reach a tipping point when the creature tries to befriend them and is rejected. When Felix encounters the creature and beats him with a stick, the creature feels 'overcome by pain and anguish'. He quickly turns angry. 'My feelings were those of rage and revenge,' he says. 'I could with pleasure have destroyed the cottage and its inhabitants and have glutted myself with their shrieks and misery.'

The creature then seems to regress from man to animal. He has progressed as far as he can – and now seems to be going backwards to a primitive state. The creature wanders in the woods, howling. 'I was like a wild beast,' he says, 'destroying the objects that obstructed me and ranging through the wood with a stag-like swiftness.' Once, nature had given him pleasure. Now, 'the cold stars [shine] in mockery'. He longs to 'tear up the trees [and] spread havoc and destruction around me'. He thinks it will make him feel good. The creature lets his passions take over. Hurt and angry, he sets the cottage ablaze. Mary gives the creature one last chance to redeem his character. A spring morning puts the creature in a more tranquil mood and he rescues a drowning girl. He behaves benevolently. Perhaps, Mary suggests, this is how he would behave all the time, if only society would accept him. And yet, we know they won't. The girl's father shoots him. The creature's hopes had been raised and dashed once again.

Under optimal conditions, when people experience pleasure in their early life, Hartley suggested, they would go on to develop 'theopathy', love and respect for their creator, the source of all pleasures in life. Their 'moral sense' would then be fully developed. This, however, is out of reach for the creature. The De Laceys' hostility towards the creature comes on top of Victor's abandonment. The pain is overwhelming. The creature feels an 'eternal hatred and vengeance to all mankind', and a particular loathing of his creator. He vows 'everlasting war against the species', making Victor his target. His isolation from society has consequences. 'If I have no ties and no affections, hatred and vice must be my portion,' he says.

In the creature's plea for a mate, we see Mary grappling with the idea that the creature could be benevolent if only he experienced a bit more pleasure in life. If Victor makes him a companion, he will be happy, he says, and will act well. 'The love of another will destroy the cause of my crimes,' he says. 'My vices are the children of a forced solitude that I abhor; and my virtues will necessarily arise when I live in communion with an equal.' The creature longs to 'feel the affections of a sensitive being' and be connected to the world. It is not to be. Victor refuses his request – or rather agrees and then destroys his work. The creature is now so unhappy that he starts to act out of what Hartley calls 'pure disinterested Cruelty and Malice' – he is determined to seek revenge.

We don't know whether Mary read Hartley's key text, *Observations of Man, His Frame, His Duty, and His Expectations* (1749). She never mentions it in her diary where she records other books she read, although she could have read it in 1816, when part of her diary is missing. We do know, however, that Percy had read Hartley's book and annotated it. Hartleian ideas were also part of the zeitgeist. Hartley's work was so popular that it was reprinted several times. In 1791, Joseph Johnson, William Godwin's publisher, had published the second and third editions. There were more editions in 1801 and 1810. Mary's parents had both explored his theories.

Pleasure and pain are only one way to understand the creature's cognitive development. Godwin and Wollstonecraft had also emphasized the importance of books in shaping young minds. Godwin had made sure his home library was stocked. He even ran a bookshop. In keeping with Mary's upbringing, there is a strong literary component to the creature's education. He is, as we might say today, self-taught. For this, we turn to the micro library the creature comes across wandering in the woods.

An Essential Reading List

There were some big advantages to not having the internet at home in the nineteenth century. One was how many books you could read. From 1814 to 1817, Mary Shelley would tick off more than 300. She chose to give the creature three to read himself, plus one that he will overhear being read. These books help shape the creature's character. They form his essential reading list.

The first book the creature encounters is Volney's *Ruins of Empire* (1791). Felix De Lacey is reading it to Safie. *Ruins* is a radical text. Volney had proposed the abolition of all the reigning powers in the world and an end to colonization. The creature gets an overview of world history and learns about different groups of people from 'the slothful Asiatics' to the 'wonderful virtue of the early Romans'. He quickly absorbs Volney's liberal bent. He too is for freedom and equality and against the idea that one group of people has the right to rule another and take their land. 'I heard of the discovery of the American hemisphere,' he tells us, 'and wept with Safie over the hapless fate of its original inhabitants.' His reaction suggests that he is a fair and liberal being who would want to avoid conflict or violence – at least for now.

Next, the creature comes across a satchel of three books in the woods. He will read these books himself. These produce 'an infinity of new images and feelings' in him: sometimes he feels 'ecstasy'; often, he feels 'dejection'. All will inform his views and shape his character.

The original readers of *Frankenstein* may well have been familiar with the first book, *The Sorrows of Young Werther* by Johann Wolfgang von Goethe. The book had become a cult hit after it was published in 1774. *Werther* was an epistolary novel comprising a set of letters by a sensitive and passionate artist called Werther about his doomed love affair. Charlotte, the subject of his affections, was engaged to someone else. Werther's pain was so unbearable that he kills himself. The tragic story moved readers so much at the time that young men throughout Europe started to dress like the tragic hero. There was even a spate of copycat suicides. *Werther* was one of the major works of the *Sturm und Drang* literary movement that was having a moment in Germany in the late 1700s. These writers valued intense emotion and individualism. Sound familiar? *Sturm und Drang* paved the way for the Romantics.

For Mary, Goethe's novel, which she read in 1815, had a particular pull. Like Werther, Mary's mother had also had a doomed love affair and tried to kill herself (even if she hadn't succeeded). She too had written about her desolation. In *Letters Written During a Short Residence in Sweden, Norway and Denmark* (1796), Wollstonecraft had talked of her unrequited love for the American businessman Gilbert Imlay. When William Godwin was writing his memoir about her, he had even described his late wife as the 'female Werther'. Perhaps he had this episode in her life in mind. They were reading the book aloud together the night before she would go into labour with Mary. Soon after, his wife died. When Mary included *Werther* in *Frankenstein*, she may have been thinking of her mother. Perhaps this was a way to honour her or, as we have seen, to connect with her. Perhaps her mother was just in her thoughts. We know Mary often identified with the creature. When the creature described Werther as 'a more divine being than I had ever beheld or imagined', Mary could have been praising the 'female Werther', her mother.

Not that the creature would have any idea about Mary's mother when he read *Werther*. He was just reading it for the story and something to do in the woods. *Werther* shows the creature the range of human emotions from passion to despair and gives him the words to express them. The creature talks warmly of its descriptions of 'gentle and domestic manners' and 'lofty sentiments and feelings'. Mary wants us to see the creature as someone who might acquire 'domestic manners' and have 'lofty sentiments', too. How much greater he could be than George Canning's idea of a 'negro' as someone who had 'the intellect of a child' or William Lawrence's idea of an African as someone who had 'an almost entire want of… elevated sentiments, manly virtues, and moral feelings'.

Yet reading *Werther* also makes the creature realize how different he is from other people. He looks odd: 'My person was hideous and my stature gigantic.' He also lacks any relatives: 'I was dependent on none and related to none.' Could the creature really fit into the sort of society painted by *Werther*? The creature finds it unlikely. His self-reflection borders on an existential crisis: 'Who was I?' he cries. 'What was I? Whence did I come? What was my destination?'

In contrast, Plutarch's *Lives*, the second book in the satchel, lifts his spirits. Mary had read it in 1815, returning to it later with Percy. *Lives* was written in the early second century. Plutarch, a Greek philosopher and historian, had paired famous Romans with famous Greeks and compared their characters. The creature comes 'to admire and love the heroes of past ages' and learns how virtues can be practised in society. 'I felt the greatest ardor for virtue rise within me,' he says, suggesting his potential for good 'and abhorrence for vice'. The creature is drawn towards the 'peaceable lawgivers' rather than those who lean towards violence, which he puts down to 'the patriarchal lives of my protectors', his early observations of the De Lacey family. Had he encountered more aggressive characters in his early days instead, he might have gravitated towards the more violent figures from history. Early experiences help form our character, suggests Mary.

But it was Milton's *Paradise Lost*, the final book, that had the greatest impact on the creature and *Frankenstein*. Mary and Percy had been reading it the summer she started writing her novel. Milton's epic poem, published in 1667, told the biblical story of the Creation and the Fall: what happened when God created Adam and Eve and they ate the forbidden fruit. The story teaches the creature about good and evil and stirs up feelings of 'wonder and awe'.

At first, the creature identifies with Adam. Like the first man, the creature was unique. Mary had already prepared her readers for similarities between them by quoting *Paradise Lost* on the title page: 'Did I request thee, Maker, from my clay to mould me man? Did I solicit thee from darkness to promote me?' Unfortunately, the creature quickly realizes a key difference in their situations: Adam's creator, God, cared for him; Adam was 'perfect… happy and prosperous'. The creature's maker, Victor, is absent; the creature is 'wretched, helpless, and alone'.

The creature begins to think he resembles not Adam, but Satan. Like Satan, he feels 'envy' at the happiness of those around him. This is just the start. In the Garden of Eden, Satan had taken the form of a serpent. When the creature vows revenge on Victor for destroying his female companion, he uses a similar image: he will 'watch with the wiliness of a snake', he warns, 'that I may sting with its venom'. As the creature's crimes mount up, the creature slides further into Satan's territory. His murderous acts are evil. Victor would agree. He has called the creature 'devil' from the start.

And yet, the creature is complex. Christian thinkers like Augustine had argued that even the devil was good at the beginning. The creature claimed he was good at first, too. The creature becomes 'a fiend', Mary suggests, because he is unhappy. His fall comes about because of the way man treats him. 'The fallen angel becomes a malignant devil,' cries the creature as he sums up his life. But even that is not the end of it. The devil, adds the creature, was better off than he: Satan had 'friends and associates in his desolation. I am quite alone.' Towards the end of the novel, the creature resembles Adam again. In *Paradise Lost*, Adam pleads forgiveness. At the end of *Frankenstein*, the creature is remorseful. He calls his crimes the 'frightful catalogue of my deeds' and says he will feel 'the bitter sting of remorse' until he dies. Can he really be Satan if he feels such pain?

Just as the creature is sometimes like Adam and sometimes like Satan, so Victor is sometimes like God, sometimes like Satan and sometimes like Adam, too. Were Victor writing the script, he might put himself in the top role. Like God, Victor created a being, the first of a 'new species', one he hopes will 'bless me as its creator and source', just as believers worship God. In Christianity, God is often seen as the Father. Victor also sees himself as a father – and a superior one to any others on earth. 'No father could claim the gratitude of his child so completely as I should deserve theirs,' he says with a touch of arrogance.

When the creature reads Victor's diary a little later, he pairs Victor and God as creators, aligning himself with Adam, a little like Plutarch pairing Greek and Roman figures. 'God in pity made man beautiful and alluring, after his own image; but my form is a filthy type of yours, more horrid from its very resemblance,' he cries. Victor might be godlike in some respects, but he lacks key aspects of God. The classic Christian God is not just powerful; he is good. Victor is just playing the role. He might be a brilliant scientist, but he is still just a man. And a flawed one at that. He brings a creature to life, but he does not know how to look after it. Worse, the being he brings into the world will take life away too, including his own. Throughout the novel, Mary gives us hints that Victor resembles not God but Satan. Some hints are subtle. Professor Waldman, for example, tells us that Victor had 'the sweetest [voice] I had ever heard'. How easily he might use that voice to get others on side. The tempter in *Paradise Lost* had a 'Serpent Tongue', one that flattered Eve into eating forbidden fruit, leading to the corruption of mankind. By the time Victor is on his deathbed, the link is more overt. 'Like the archangel who aspired to omnipotence,' Victor says, 'I am chained in eternal hell.'

Unlike the creature, Victor fails to show real remorse at the end of *Frankenstein*. Earlier in the story, he had shown regret. He feels terrible when Justine, a family friend, faces execution for the murder of his brother William. He 'suffered living torture' during her trial. 'The fangs of remorse tore my bosom,' Victor says, realizing her fate, 'and would not forgo their hold.' After Justine's death, he admits he is responsible for the effect it has had on Elizabeth and his father, who were both grieving. 'All was the work of my thrice-accursed hands,' he cries. Yet even when Victor feels 'torn by remorse, horror and despair', he feels sorry for himself. At one point during Justine's trial, he suggests he is worse off than her. 'The tortures of the accused did not equal mine,' he says. 'She was sustained by innocence.' Then, towards the end of the novel on his deathbed, he describes his downfall in passive terms rather than taking responsibility for his actions. 'From my infancy I was imbued with high hopes and a lofty ambition,' he says, 'but how am I sunk!... a high destiny seemed to bear me on, until I fell, never, never again to rise.'

Milton. Plutarch. Goethe. The creature would have a pretty decent literary education, but no amount of books could save him from the real corrupting force in society: man. To learn more, we turn to Jean-Jacques Rousseau.

Beware the Noble Savage

In 1774, a tall man with dark eyes, long dark hair and tattoos arrived in Britain. Mai had been on one of Captain Cook's ships and had sailed all the way from Tahiti. Mai, sometimes called Omai, was the first Pacific Islander Britons had seen. He was charming, dignified and charismatic. Joseph Banks, who had met him in Tahiti when he had joined Cook's expedition in 1769, volunteered to be his chaperone and introduce him to society. Mai was presented to King George III twice, dined ten times as a guest at the Royal Society and had his portrait painted by Sir Joshua Reynolds. Banks had described Tahiti, which had been discovered by Europeans in 1767, as an earthly paradise, 'the truest picture of Arcadia'. Mai, a darling of the intelligentsia, was held up as an example of a noble savage.

The archetype had been around for some time. It had one foot in the Garden of Eden and another in the golden age of classical civilization. But it had been Jean-Jacques Rousseau who had brought it up to date. The Genevan political philosopher had proposed that the noble savage was the natural state of man. Left to himself, man would be peaceful and compassionate. It was organized society with its artificial inequalities and constructs that corrupted him. Civilization, especially in the Western world, fostered competition and social hierarchies. People became greedy and proud. They chased material wealth and social status rather than valuing genuine connections and social bonds. They engaged in conflict rather than living in harmony. Man can reclaim a degree of liberty and equality, Rousseau suggested, only by agreeing to certain laws, but this would be a compromise. He would then be balancing his own freedom with the common good. 'Man is born free, and everywhere he is in chains,' he wrote in *The Social Contract* (1762) of man's predicament in society.

Man could live as a noble savage, or natural man as Rousseau preferred to call him, no more.

Mary knew all about Rousseau. Her father William Godwin had supported Rousseau's idea that society corrupted human nature. Her mother Mary Wollstonecraft had applied Rousseau's views on education in her children's book, *Original Stories from Real Life*. Wollstonecraft supported Rousseau's attacks on modern manners and elitism, although she disputed his views on women (he thought they were weak and should be passive). Percy followed Rousseau closely, too. He agreed with Rousseau's ideas about freedom – that true freedom comes when we live by laws we set ourselves. When Percy and Mary were in Geneva in 1816, Percy had skipped off to the city with Byron to pay homage to where Rousseau grew up.

Mary read *Emile*, *Julie, ou la Nouvelle Héloïse* and *Les Confessions; suivies de Rêveries du promeneur solitaire*, in 1815, and would turn to the *Reveries* again in 1816 and 1817 when she was writing and transcribing *Frankenstein*. Rousseau expounded his noble savage idea in *Discourse on the Origin of Inequality*, also known as the *Second Discourse* (1755). Unfortunately, there is no evidence that Mary read the *Second Discourse*, although she could have read it during the period in 1816 when her diary is missing and she would have known about the ideas from Percy and her father. Rousseau had also touched upon the idea of the noble savage in his other works. In *Emile, or On Education* (1762) he had warned that 'everything is good as it leaves the hands of the Author of things; everything degenerates in the hands of man', suggesting that society was a corrupting force.

The noble savage represented a man free from organized society. He lives in harmony with nature and himself. Captain Walton thinks that the creature is a 'savage' from the start. On the opening pages, he spots him in the distance and calls him 'a savage inhabitant of some undiscovered island'. It sets the creature up to be wild, undomesticated, primitive, uncivilized, uncouth, fierce, ferocious, cruel, harsh or barbarous, definitions thrown up by the *Shorter Oxford English Dictionary* (1993). Perhaps the creature is fierce and cruel, assuming the word's brutal connotations.

Perhaps he is merely untamed, closer to nature and unfettered by the constraints of civilization. Mai might have been described as a 'savage inhabitant' of a newly discovered land, but he wasn't barbarous. Not all savages were a threat.

As the story goes on, we see that the creature also lived like a savage in the literal sense. 'Savage' comes from the Old French '*sauvage*', which comes from the Latin '*salvaticus*', a version of '*silvaticus*', meaning 'of the woods'. The creature grows up in the woods. Like Rousseau's natural man, he is alone. He also responds instinctively to his environment, gradually learning to differentiate between his senses, and has an instinctive drive for self-preservation, satisfying his basic needs by drinking from a stream and seeking food. Like Rousseau's natural man, he is vegetarian, eating berries, nuts, acorns and roots. He is free, unselfconscious and happy insofar as his animal desires are fulfilled. Nature, we learn, is his happy place. The moon is 'a gentle light', 'the trees… shaded me with their foliage', the birdsong is such a 'pleasant sound' that he tries to copy it. His hovel, he tells us, is a 'paradise'.

And yet his state cannot last. According to Rousseau, the primitive man lacked language, reason, companionship and morals. Observing the De Laceys, the creature gains language and reason. Hearing Felix read Volney's *Ruins of Empire* (1791) to Safie, he learns about 'the strange system of human society' with its laws and unequal distribution of power. We can see the creature move away from his noble savage state, just as Rousseau might have predicted, as he longs for companionship and to fit in. He realizes that society values people rich in possessions, but he 'possessed no money, no friends, no kind of property'. How unhappy he is about his lowly status. 'I cannot describe to you the agony that these reflections inflicted upon me,' he cries, wishing he had 'remained in my native wood'. The more the creature learns about the world, the more he wishes he could return to his original state. 'I wished sometimes to shake off all thought and feeling,' he says sorrowfully.

The creature believes he is 'deformed and loathsome'. He looks and sounds different from everyone around him. 'I had never yet seen a being resembling me, or who claimed any intercourse with me,' he says. He feels left out. 'Everywhere I see bliss, from which I alone am irrevocably excluded,' he tells Victor. He is trapped within society but cannot form any of the social ties and receive any domestic affections to make it bearable. 'I longed to join [the De Lacey family]', the creature tells us as he learns more about them, 'but dared not.' The last time he had tried to meet people, the reception from the 'barbarous' villagers had been hostile. The more the creature learns about society and himself, the more he feels like 'a wretched outcast'. And he doesn't even have someone who will listen and sympathize with him: 'no Eve soothed my sorrows, or shared my thoughts; I was alone'. When the creature does approach the De Laceys, he is rejected. He then seems to lose any façade of being civilized. Instead, he feels 'rage and revenge' and expresses his pain in 'fearful howling'. He is 'like a wild beast' destroying anything that gets in his way and 'ranging through the wood with a stag-like swiftness'. The creature is now more like a regular savage than a noble one. This is a hint of what's to come, but Mary doesn't want to condemn the creature just yet. He still has the potential to be peaceful.

The creature tries to persuade Victor to make him a mate by promising they will leave him alone and go far away 'to the vast wilds of South America', 'the most savage of places'. They will sleep on dried leaves, he says, and feast on acorns and berries. They will live in harmony with nature for the creature has no desire – like the men around him – to kill animals for his benefit: 'My food is not that of man; I do not destroy the lamb and the kid to glut my appetite'. Man doesn't just kill sheep and goats; he kills their young. How brutal he is! The creature wishes to be 'peaceful'. He longs to return to the state of the noble savage, when life was less complicated, if not idyllic. By refusing to agree to the creature's request (or by accepting it and then tearing up his work), Victor denies the creature the chance to see whether he could live as a noble savage once more. If we know anything about modern relationships, we can guess that the honeymoon period would wear off. The creature might be happy for a bit, but the damage has been done. He already knows about organized society and the ways of the world.

As well as the simple life, the creature longs for social ties. The De Laceys show that you can lead a simple life with other people and in harmony with nature. But even they aren't happy all the time. They have also been corrupted enough by society to exclude the creature. They judge him on society's values – by the way he looks. They don't value traits that can be seen as strengths – that he is nimble-footed, can stand the extremes of heat and cold or is tall. These traits become a threat, but they didn't have to be seen that way. The creature is forced to see himself as others see him. 'The savage lives within himself,' Rousseau had written in the *Second Discourse*, 'the sociable man, always outside of himself, knows how to live only in the opinion of others; and it is… from their judgment alone that he draws the sentiment of his own existence.' Through *Frankenstein*, Mary suggests that we should be kinder to each other and accept that people are different. Like her father, she was interested in social affairs. Society was corrupt. It needed to change.

Mai's native society was not quite as egalitarian and free as some might imagine. It wasn't a community of noble savages all sleeping on dried leaves or on white sandy shores of the Pacific. Polynesian society was divided into strict social classes. Mai was originally from Raiatea, a nearby island, and was a commoner. He had little power back home. His family had owned land and been respected. But when Mai was about 10, invaders from Bora Bora conquered the island, killed Mai's father and snatched the land. Mai was taken as a slave but escaped to Tahiti, where he lived in poverty. In 1776, Mai left England with Cook and his crew, settling on Huahine, an island near Tahiti. After his stay in London, where he had been the darling of the intelligentsia, he struggled to fit in. He died in 1780 of a virus. The last chapter of his life was rather anticlimactic. Mary idealized the concept of the noble savage but realized, like Rousseau, that it would never last because of the constraints of the world. Among the social evils Rousseau was keen to combat in the *Second Discourse*, was 'insatiable ambition'. This, he said, 'inspired all men with a vile propensity to injure one another'. There was one character in *Frankenstein* who was suffering from a severe bout of that: Victor. It is time to finally address the subtitle of Mary's novel: the modern Prometheus.

A New Creation Myth

Take this as your trigger warning. Should you be hiking one day in the Caucasus mountains at the time of the ancient Greeks, you may well hear a cacophony of howls and wails. Cover your ears. Cover your eyes. The scene around the corner is harrowing. The Greek titan Prometheus has been shackled to a rock by his wrists and his ankles. He is scantily clothed. Prometheus had stolen fire from Hephaestus, the god of artisans, to give to man. Zeus, the head god, had been furious. This is Prometheus' punishment. Zeus has tied him to the mountainside and is sending an eagle with a vulture complex to him every day to peck away at his liver. Gruesome.

Let's be honest. This might not be the real story. This is the version in *Prometheus Bound*, a play written in the fifth century BC and attributed to the Greek tragedian Aeschylus. A bunch of other versions have been doing the rounds. The one popular in ancient Rome hundreds of years later in the eighth century AD crops up in Ovid's poem *Metamorphoses*. Here, Prometheus, still crafty, still daring, creates man out of clay. By the late third century AD, the ideas had merged. Prometheus was now said to have stolen fire, which he used to animate a human figure. In all the accounts, Prometheus is tortured for defying the gods. He is a rebel, the bad boy of the ancient world.

By the time we get to the eighteenth century, Prometheus had become an intellectual pin-up. How pioneering he was! The German philosopher Immanuel Kant had been full of praise when he called Benjamin Franklin, the scientist and Founding Father, 'the Prometheus of modern times'. Prometheus had stolen a spark (fire) from the gods. Franklin had flown a kite during a storm to see whether a key attached to the string would draw an electrical charge, snatching a spark (lightning) from the sky. Franklin had advanced science by proving that lightning was a type of electricity. He was as great as a Greek titan. Enlightenment thinkers in England had been drawn to Prometheus' rebellious streak. William Godwin, who had included the Prometheus myth in *The Pantheon: Or Ancient history of Gods of Greece and Rome* (1806), a classical primer for children, had admired Prometheus for his defiance, as had Mary Wollstonecraft. Prometheus had stood up to authority to benefit mankind. According to Aeschylus, Prometheus had good intentions: he was driven by compassion. He 'rescued men from shattering destruction'.

Byron would adopt a similar view in his poem *Prometheus*, which he would write in July 1816, just weeks after Mary had started *Frankenstein* at his villa. Prometheus wanted to give man fire, he says, because he was 'kind'. He hoped to lessen 'the sum of human wretchedness'. Byron celebrated Prometheus as a hero. Two of the three stanzas of his poem start with the exaltation 'Titan!' When he talks of Prometheus' 'Godlike crime', he is being ironic. It might be a crime in the eyes of Zeus, but for mankind it is an act of greatness. Prometheus' greatness would be taken up again by Percy, who had translated *Prometheus Bound* for Byron, in his lyrical drama, *Prometheus Unbound*. In the preface, he glorifies Prometheus by referring to him as 'the Champion', before going on to gush that he is 'the type of the highest perfection of moral and intellectual nature, impelled by the purest and the truest motives to the best and noblest ends'. Like Godwin, Percy saw Prometheus as someone who fought against tyranny. He used the Prometheus myth to champion individualism and the pursuit of ideals, key Romantic interests. Percy had written *Prometheus Unbound* in response to *Frankenstein*. He was trying to restore Prometheus' reputation. Mary had put it under threat.

Mary gave *Frankenstein* the subtitle 'the modern Prometheus' to set up readers' expectations of her main character. Victor Frankenstein, readers might have thought, was going to be inventive and daring, all for a good cause. Most of all, he would be worthy of bearing an epithet with a hefty legacy. For many of the Romantics, Prometheus was a hero. Victor, from afar, fitted the bill. He dreamed of 'pouring light into a dark world' to find 'the principle of life', showing he was ambitious and creative. He transcended the 'ideal bounds' of 'life and death' against conventional ideas that this might be a divine domain, making him brave and rebellious. He worked 'with unremitting ardor' for almost two years 'for the sole purpose of infusing life into an inanimate body', offering us a textbook example of what it means to be industrious and focused. To cap it all off, he was successful. Victor does bring a body to life.

But for Mary, Victor's traits have a flipside. She frequently undermines Victor's claim to greatness. Dreaming that he could 'renew life' after death, Victor is made to sound arrogant, never questioning whether he has any right to such a bold move. Nor does he have any real ambitions to help humanity; he is more interested in how his work will boost his status and ego. Victor imagines creating a new species who 'would bless [him] as its creator and source'; he sees himself as above others and worthy of their adoration. Victor's intentions to triumph over death should ring alarm bells, Mary might add. His aim is childish. Victor seems unable to accept a basic fact of life: that it ends in death. This is how nature works. He can't interfere with that and not expect consequences. Victor's method is also far from heroic. He admits to Walton that he spent 'days and nights in vaults and charnel-houses' examining 'the natural decay and the corruption of the human body'. He 'dabbled among the unhallowed damps of the grave'. He 'tortured the living animal to animate the lifeless clay'. Victor then locked himself away in his 'workshop of filthy creation' at the top of a house, cut off from all the other rooms, to finish his project. His behaviour is secretive, suggesting he is trying to cover up something he knows he shouldn't be doing. Perhaps he believes deep down that his work is immoral: creating life is something only God should do. Perhaps he is ashamed of his method.

Victor looks less and less like a hero, too. His work drains his health. Instead of two parents like regular children, his progeny will have just one. It will mirror just him. To create such an epic feat, Victor must draw on all his resources. It 'swallowed up every habit of my nature', Victor says. He looks 'pale' and 'emaciated'. He is 'oppressed by a slow fever'. He grows anxious. 'I shunned my fellow creatures as if I had been guilty of a crime,' Victor says. Some might say he was. Victor's single-mindedness comes at a price. He not only deprives himself of 'rest and health'; he forgets his friends and family, too. This includes his father, who had hoped Victor would write to him regularly. Victor has not. At the time, Victor thinks his father will understand that his neglect is not a 'vice of faultiness'. We can judge this for ourselves. We can imagine what Mary might have been thinking. As someone who held domestic affections in high regard, Mary may well judge Victor's behaviour to be unforgiveable. It will be a while before Victor understands that he was 'not… altogether free from blame' from the tragic consequences of his actions and recognizes that he should have stopped his passions from taking over. 'A human being in perfection ought always to preserve a calm and peaceful mind and never to allow passion or a transitory desire to disturb his tranquillity,' he says. How far Victor had strayed from this idea of a perfect human being.

When Mary suggested Victor was like Prometheus, she might also have been thinking about how Victor brought his creation to life. In one reading of the creation scene in *Frankenstein*, Victor uses a 'spark' of electricity. But fire, for Mary, is not just creative. It is dangerous. We see just how directly destructive it is when the creature burns down the De Laceys' cottage. This is just the start. The outcome of Victor's creation project is chaos and carnage: the creature will go on to destroy everyone he loves. Fire is not what it once was in the time of the ancient Greeks.

How far Victor is from any sort of hero, we might add. He might have been brave dabbling among graves and stepping into God's territory to create life, but as soon as the creature comes alive, he flees in 'breathless horror and disgust'. He is cowardly. Victor had wanted to play God but had been unprepared to look after his creation. Mary later gives Victor the chance to redeem himself a little by making the creature a female companion, quelling the creature's loneliness. Perhaps Victor could now show a bit of courage and kindness. 'I compassionated him and sometimes felt a wish to console him,' Victor says, 'but when I looked upon him, when I saw the filthy mass that moved and talked, my heart sickened and my feelings were altered to those of horror and hatred.' Instead of spending energy looking after the creature, Victor spends energy escaping him. It isolates him even further from society – and anyone who could help.

After the creature kills Victor's brother William and Justine is executed for the murder, Victor sinks into despair. Elizabeth tries to comfort him without success. 'Not the tenderness of friendship, nor the beauty of earth, nor of heaven, could redeem my soul from woe,' he cries, 'the very accents of love were ineffectual. I was encompassed by a cloud which no beneficial influence could penetrate.' As the story progresses, Victor withdraws further and further from society. He must live with the secret that he created a monster.

By the end of the novel, Victor is tormented by 'despair'. At the graves of William, Elizabeth and his father, he hallucinates the creature's voice. He becomes consumed by anger and driven on only by 'revenge'. He leaves Geneva and wanders from country to country facing 'hardships'. As Victor tries to track the creature down, he feels cold and hungry and tired. He believes he is 'cursed by some devil'. He carries his 'eternal hell'. He is thoroughly miserable. 'My life, as it passed thus, was indeed hateful to me.' Victor is a pitiable figure. When we think about Victor, the 'modern Prometheus' is less of a compliment and more of an admonishment.

Captain Walton tries to see Victor in a Romantic light, as a hero. As an ambitious explorer, Walton identified with him. He admires Victor's 'unbounded knowledge' of 'general literature', as well as 'his eloquence'. 'What a glorious creature must he have been in the days of his prosperity,' Walton says, 'when he is thus noble and godlike in ruin!' Yet even Walton admits by the end of the novel that Victor isn't perfect. Victor had urged him to learn from his tale. Victor had been overly ambitious. 'Learn from me, if not by my precepts, at least by my example, how dangerous is the acquirement of knowledge,' he tells Captain Walton, 'and how much happier that man is who believes his native town to be the world, than he who aspires to become greater than his nature will allow.' Victor's actions had resulted in people's deaths – and his own suffering. Walton is at risk of being similarly ambitious by pressing on with his Arctic mission, risking the life of his crew. He realizes he cannot continue. 'I cannot lead them unwillingly to danger,' he says of his crew, 'and I must return.' Walton is hardly ecstatic about his decision. He says he will come back 'ignorant and disappointed' and yet, in the end, he won't be another

Prometheus. By the time we get to the end of *Frankenstein*, we might even question who deserves the Prometheus title. Who is more titan-like? Is it Victor? Or is it the creature? The creature has great physical and mental strengths. He moves with 'superhuman speed'. He is 'more agile' than man and can survive on a 'coarser diet'. He is strong enough to gather firewood for the De Laceys. He is articulate: he gives a detailed account about his beginnings, including how his mind developed, and understands exactly how 'misery made [him] a fiend'. Like Prometheus, he too rises up against his creator.

Mary lived during an exciting time. Scientists were putting forward radical theories about the origin of life and the workings of the brain and the body, and people were openly questioning authority – including God. But while some got caught up in the excitement about how much man could find out about the world, Mary threw in a note of caution. It was all very well advancing human knowledge, but what were the implications? Did this mean man was now top of the world order? What would this mean for society? Victor's neglect of the creature – his act of irresponsible creation – meant he could never really be a hero for someone like Mary. She had learned the consequences of absent caregivers the hard way: from experience. She had been abandoned by her mother (even if her mother had intended to stick around), rejected by her father and ignored by her husband. It had made her feel lonely, depressed and misunderstood. But Mary refused to be a victim. Through the creature in *Frankenstein*, she expresses her fears and her frustrations. Abandoned by his sole parent, rejected by society, denied a mate, the creature fights back. 'I will revenge my injuries,' he says; 'if I cannot inspire love, I will cause fear.' The creature kills the people Victor loves most in the world, frames him for murder and tires him out so much that he dies of exhaustion. And then, perhaps because he is good at heart, he feels regret. 'Polluted by my crimes and torn by the bitterest remorse, where can I rest but in death?' he cries just before he sets himself on fire.

The story of Prometheus, which involved an ambitious titan making man out of clay, had been the Romantics' creation myth. The creation story in the Bible, they said, wasn't good enough. According to the standard

Christian view, the biblical story showed that God was omnipotent and omnibenevolent. The Romantics (or at least many of them) didn't agree. They said it showed God's limitations. Percy argued it proved that God was responsible for the unhappiness of mankind by imposing limits on him. Man should, therefore, revolt against God. The Prometheus myth was inspiring: it showed that man could take control. Mary has another idea. What if *Frankenstein* was the new creation myth? It too was about creating man. This time, it wasn't God in the driving seat or even a titan but man, just as the Romantics might have wanted it. Things didn't go well. The Romantics had put a lot of faith in man. Perhaps it was too much. The Romantics – Byron and Percy particularly – went about doing what they wanted. They loved whoever they wanted. They stopped loving whenever they wanted. They travelled wherever they wanted. They worked if they wanted, if poetry was even work. They championed man's creativity and imagination, but these were not neutral forces. Victor has them in spades – he animates old bones, something no one has ever done before – but they are also dangerous. Victor imagined creating a beautiful creature who would be subservient to him. Instead, he creates a monstrosity who rebels, killing everyone he loves and exhausting him to the end. Rather than taking the podium for his success, Victor ends up lying on a ship in the Arctic, a complete wreck. Through *Frankenstein*, Mary shows the flaws in Romantic ideals. She rejects the Promethean idea of the artist as omnipotent, as divine.

Frankenstein is a critique of Romanticism as much as it is part of the movement. Mary questions whether someone who dreams big, who thinks anything is possible, who puts his own interests before others and thinks that everything is for the taking is necessarily a hero. Her own creation story is a cautionary tale. It warns people about the dangers of being overly ambitious and pursuing your own passion project at the expense of domestic ties – family, friends, relationships. No achievements in poetry or science are worth the sacrifice, she suggests. *Frankenstein* tells us what in life really matters.

Bibliography

Books

Gordon, Charlotte, *Romantic Outlaws* (Windmill Books, London, 2016)

Hay, Daisy, *The Making of Mary Shelley's Frankenstein* (Bodleian Library, Oxford, 2019)

Harkup, Kathryn, *Making the Monster: The Science Behind Mary Shelley's Frankenstein* (Bloomsbury Sigma, London, 2018)

Holmes, Richard, *The Age of Wonder: How the Romantic Generation Discovered the Beauty and Terror of Science* (HarperPress, London, 2009)

Levy, Joel, *Gothic Science* (Andre Deutsch, London, 2019)

Mellor, Anne K, *Mary Shelley: Her Life, Her Fiction, Her Monsters* (Routledge, Abingdon, 1990)

Radu, Florescu, *In Search of Frankenstein* (Robson Books, London, 1999)

Sampson, Fiona, *In Search of Mary Shelley: The Girl Who Wrote Frankenstein* (Profile, London, 2018)

Seymour, Miranda, *Mary Shelley* (Faber and Faber, London, 2011)

Articles

Kaplan, Peter W, *The Real Dr Frankenstein: Christian Gottlieb Kratzenstein?* in vol 95, *Journal of the Royal Society of Medicine* (Sage, 2002)

King-Hele, D. G. *Shelley and Science* in *Notes and Records of the Royal Society of London*, vol. 46, No. 2 (Royal Society, 1992)

King, Louise, *Saints and Sinners: John Abernethy* in *The Bulletin of the Royal College of Surgeons of England* (RCS England Publishing, 2015)

Lepore, Jill, *The Strange and Twisted Life of Frankenstein* in *The New Yorker* (Condé Nast, 2018)

Mellor, Anne K. *Mary Wollstonecraft (Godwin) Shelley* in *British Writers*, Supplement 3, edited by George Stade (Charles Scribner's Sons, 1996)

Mulvey-Roberts, Marie (ed), *Women's Writing*, Volume 6, Issue 3 (Routledge, Abingdon, 1999)

O'Rourke, James, *Nothing More Unnatural: Mary Shelley's Revision of Rousseau* in *ELH*, Vol. 56, No. 3, Autumn (Johns Hopkins University Press, 1989)

Powers, Katherine Richardson, *The Influence of William Godwin on the Novels of Mary Shelley*, PhD diss. (University of Tennessee, 1972)

Ward, Maryanne C, *A Painting of the Unspeakable: Henry Fuseli's The Nightmare and the Creation of Mary Shelley's Frankenstein* in *The Journal of the Midwest Modern Language Association*, Vol. 33, No. 1, Winter (Midwest Modern Language Association, 2000)

Websites

Curran, Stuart (ed), *Frankenstein; or, the Modern Prometheus by Mary Wollstonecraft Shelley* (The Pennsylvania Electronic Edition, knarf.english.upenn.edu)

Podcasts

451 Mary Shelley (The History of Literature, 2022)
Frankenpod 200: Celebrating Mary Shelley's Masterpiece (Science Weekly, 2017)
Frankenstein's Creator: Mary Shelley (National Theatre, 2011)
Frankenstein: Our Dark Mirror, Ep. 256 (New York Public Library, 2019)
In Our Time: Frankenstein (BBC, 2019)
In Our Time: Mary Wollstonecraft (BBC, 2009)
Judgment and Justice: The Life and Diary of William Godwin (University of Oxford Podcasts, 2012)
Mary Shelley Brings Frankenstein to Life (History This Week, 2023)
Mary Shelley's Frankenstein and its Legacy (Royal Institution, 2018)
Podcast #16: Mary Shelley (The Dead Ladies Show, 2018)
The Real Alchemist of Castle Frankenstein (Atlas Obscura, 2021)

TV and Films

Decoding the Past: In Search of the Real Frankenstein (History Channel, 2006)
Mary Shelley and the Birth of Frankenstein with Miranda Seymour (London Library, 2018)
The Romantics – Eternity (BBC, 2011)
The Strange Affair of… Frankenstein (BBC, 1986)

Index